# STUDIES IN FUNCTIONAL LOGICAL SEMIOTICS
# OF NATURAL LANGUAGE

# JANUA LINGUARUM

## STUDIA MEMORIAE
## NICOLAI VAN WIJK DEDICATA

*edenda curat*

### C. H. VAN SCHOONEVELD
INDIANA UNIVERSITY

### SERIES MINOR
90

1971
## MOUTON
THE HAGUE • PARIS

# STUDIES IN FUNCTIONAL
# LOGICAL SEMIOTICS
# OF
# NATURAL LANGUAGE

*by*

JERZY PELC

*Translated from the Polish*

1971
## MOUTON
THE HAGUE · PARIS

LIBRARY OF CONGRESS CATALOG CARD NUMBER: 78-134547

Printed in The Netherlands by Mouton & Co., Printers, The Hague.

# ACKNOWLEDGEMENTS

My heartfelt thanks for the initiative to publish the present book are due to Mouton & Co., Publishers, and especially to Mr. Peter de Ridder and to Professor C. H. van Schooneveld, now of Indiana University, as the editor of the Janua Linguarum series.

I am also indebted to Dr. Olgierd A. Wojtasiewicz, of Warsaw University, for the translation of the Polish originals into English, and to the Polish publishers of the original for their permission for an English-language version.

My debts to many researchers, incurred on theoretical issues, are indicated by the notes: every reference to a person or a publication points to the fact that I realize to have borrowed a person's idea or to have depended on it; and very often I must have done so unconsciously.

JERZY PELC

Warsaw, November 1968

# FOREWORD

Let us begin with a truism: language is an object of interest not only
of linguists, but of logicians as well. It is a historical fact that
originally, in antiquity, there was no clear division line between
interests and competences: rhetors and grammarians were also
logicians. It is also a fact that now such a division does exist, and
in extreme and flagrant cases even becomes a chasm that is difficult
to bridge. This is certainly detrimental both to research and
teaching. There is, accordingly, no need for persuasion that
existing situation is undesirable, and even absurd and harmful.
Hence efforts must be united, and experience exchanged, in order
to remove the causes of the situation which mocks common sense.
In my opinion, semiotics, that is the science of signs, can be a good
meeting place for the various researchers concerned with the study
of language, linguists and logicians above all, but not for them only.

I am very much dedicated to the cause of a fruitful co-operation
of the various specialists interested in the study of language. This
is why, within my modest possibilities and on a small scale, I have
tried to promote common discussions first, and common research
next. In my lectures on logic in Warsaw University, intended for
linguists, literary theorists, art historians and others, I have been
giving the pride of place to the issues of the logical theory of
natural language. In doing so, I have tried to discuss those matters
not in a hermetic language of symbols and formulae, which scares
many a person, but in possibly plain and comprehensible terms.
Further, in the same University I have held for several years a
seminar on the logical semiotics of natural language, attended by

logicians, philosophers, linguists and art theorists, both professors
and instructors and senior students. That seminar promotes a
lively exchange of ideas, and its sphere of influence expands: we
have had visitors not only from other Polish universities, but
occasionally from other countries as well. It seems to me that in
that preliminary stage of co-operation the most important thing is
not so much new results of research as a friendly atmosphere
conducive to mutual understanding. We have seen many a time in
our group consisting of widely diverging disciplines that despite
differences in our mental habits we can find a common language
when talking about language. This requires criticism of the
achievements of one's own discipline; the tendency to learn from
a colleague working in another field instead of instructing him;
readiness to abandon one's own minor habits, especially those of
terminology; and toleration of deeply rooted habits prevailing in
other disciplines. These are, of course, only necessary, but not
sufficient, conditions of interdisciplinary co-operation, and they
outline a programme that is neither revealing nor revolutionary: it
is a minimum programme that makes no recourse to any far-
reaching means. But it seems that it is worth while to begin with
things that are small and unimposing.

The present booklet is just intended to be such a small and unim-
posing thing. Its title, *Studies in Functional Logical Semiotics of
Natural Language*, refers to the first of the five papers it includes,
namely "A Functional Approach to the Logical Semiotics of
Natural Language". The remaining four are: "Meaning as an
Instrument"; "Proper Names in Natural Language: Prolegomena
to a Theory"; "Nominal Expressions and Literary Fiction";
"Semiotic Functions as Applied to the Analysis of the Concept of
Metaphor". The appendix, "A Survey of Views and Theories in
the Logical Theory of Language", is contributed by members of the
seminar referred to above, namely Kazimierz Czarnota, Marian
Dobrosielski, Witold Marciszewski, Barbara Stanosz, and the
undersigned, all of them research workers in Warsaw University,
mostly in the Department of Logic, except for M. Dobrosielski,
who is attached to the Department of Philosophy. The first paper,

"A Functional Approach to the Logical Semiotics of Natural Language", was read at the International Conference on Semiotics, held in Poland at Kazimierz-on-the-Vistula in September 1966. The second paper, "Meaning as an Instrument", was read at the International Semiotic Symposium, held in Warsaw in August 1968. The third paper, "Proper Names in Natural Language: Prolegomena to a Theory", was a lecture read in Italy at the University of Urbino in July 1968. The fourth paper, "Nominal Expressions and Literary Fiction", was read at the International Semiotic Seminar, held in Urbino in July 1968. The last, "Semiotic Functions as Applied to the Analysis of the Concept of Metaphor", was read at the International Conference on Poetics, held in Warsaw in August 1960. Their Polish-language versions have been published in books and in periodicals.

Some explanations are due in connection with the appendix, "A Survey of Views and Theories in the Logical Theory of Language". It came into being as a rather mechanical compilation of summaries of papers read at the aforementioned seminar on the logical semiotics of natural language, held by me in Warsaw University. The text resulting from that compilation was distributed to the participants in the International Conference on Semiotics (Poland, September 1966) with a purely practical purpose: it was not intended to be read at the Conference, and has never been published so far; its destination was merely to serve as a kind of memorandum to those participants in the conference who, being neither logicians nor philosophers, were not acquainted with, or did not keep in mind, some outstanding papers, opinions and logical theories on semantics. Since the Mouton and Co. Publishing House has come to the conclusion that this "Survey", pedestrian as it is, may prove useful as a source of information, I take the liberty, with the approval of the co-authors, to include it as an appendix. The Readers, however, are requested to bear in mind that the compilation was made just for information and was not originally intended for publication.

As the author of the first five papers I have to bear full responsibility for them. This is a fairly heavy burden, as I have to confess that in a couple of weeks, or in a couple of months at the latest, I cease to like what I have written. On the other hand, I simply abhor to correct and rewrite my own texts. Considering the fact that the latest of the papers included in the present booklet was written in 1968, three of them in 1966, and the earliest in 1960, it can easily be understood that I am no longer quite satisfied with them and that I would not be astonished if the readers agreed with me on that point. This is why I would rather like them to be treated as a contribution to co-operation between logicians and linguists, since then they will be appraised not only for the results, but also for the intentions of their author and for the fact that he has proved co-operative.

I take the liberty to believe that certain objective properties of my texts qualify them as contributions to an interdisciplinary discussion. Moreover, those properties are common to all the papers and thus link them to form a coherent whole, and not just a sum of unconnected elements. First, all those papers may be included in the sphere of logical semiotics, that is, such a logical theory of language which has as its parts descriptive semantics, syntactics, and pragmatics, and not just only pure semantics and syntactics, as is the case of papers by some logicians who are concerned with artificial symbolic languages. Secondly, all of them deal with natural language, that is the language which is also an object of linguistic research. Thirdly, all of them avoid, as far as possible, formalization, that is, the use of logical symbols and formulae. Fourthly, they strive to emphasize functional analysis: what is being studied is not isolated expressions, dead lexical items, but the uses of expressions as they occur in definite linguistic contexts and definite extralinguistic situations; moreover, attention is being programmatically paid to the semiotic functions of signs. Fifthly, the basic concepts of semiotics are used in them as instruments in an analysis of concepts belonging to other disciplines, such as linguistics, stylistics, poetics, theory of literature; hence the nature of these papers is interdisciplinary, and their approach instrumental. Finally, one more characteristic they have in common is that they have been written by the same author and thus probably bear the common stigma of his errors and shortcomings, and perhaps also — but this I am not competent to judge — the style of his analysis, typical of the Warsaw-Lwów school of logic, to which I belong as a disciple of Professor Tadeusz Kotarbiński.

It is common knowledge that every author somehow imagines his future readers. This is, of course, largely wishful thinking and need not have much connection with reality. I too have succombed to that weakness. Now not because of the solutions suggested and any strong points of those papers, but because of their subject matter and approach, and above all because of my own desire to engage in a discussion with representatives of related disciplines, I imagine that the present booklet may become the reading matter not only for logicians and philosophers, but also for linguists, literary theorists, and art theorists, whether they are researchers, scholars, or students. If they do not agree with the ideas and assertions presented therein, I hope they may at least find in it stimuli to become interested in the problems discussed and to rethink them by themselves.

Department of Logic                                       JERZY PELC
University of Warsaw
Poland

# CONTENTS

16                CONTENTS

# A FUNCTIONAL APPROACH TO THE LOGICAL
# SEMIOTICS OF NATURAL LANGUAGE

## 0. INTRODUCTION

The term 'functional' and the related 'functionalism' have in the last several decades become associated with the history of linguistic research on the natural language. In the course of that time, the meaning of the term has undergone certain changes: from Jean Baudouin de Courtenay who ninety years ago wrote about functional and non-functional elements in language and who constructed functional morphemics, to de Saussure's *Cours de linguistique générale* of half a century ago and to the rise of modern functional linguistics in Roman Jakobson's Prague School (1928-1930). Even today, after a lapse of thirty years, 'functionalism' and 'functional' may have not as yet become fully univocal and strictly distinct terms in linguistics. Lacking, however, the required professional competence, I do not feel qualified to enter the dispute on this subject. Therefore, in order to avoid misunderstandings, I accept the terms suggested by an authority in linguistics.[1] He characterizes modern linguistics as functional if the following properties can be jointly found in it: synchronism in the description of the language, treatment of the language as a system or as a structure in the broad sense of the term (de Saussure), the text as the main object of linguistic study (Bühler) and the resulting anti-

---

[1] *Cf.* Zawadowski, Leon, "Główne cechy językoznawstwa funkcjonalnego" [The Principal Properties of Functional Linguistics]. Introductory article in *Podstawy języka* [Fundamentals of Language] by Roman Jakobson and Morris Halle. Authorized Polish edition, revised and expanded, edited with footnotes and introductory article by Leon Zawadowski (Wrocław, Ossolineum, 1964), pp. 7-31.

psychological attitude (Bloomfield), stress on the conventional nature of the language (de Saussure) and recognition of its representative and communication functions as most important (Bühler) and finally treatment of language as social and not as individual. It may be that after this explanation the terms 'functional' and 'functionalism', though they are not yet entirely precise, may have attained a degree of clarity that will prevent serious misunderstandings in what I shall say below.

The term 'functional', as used in the title of the present paper, is neither synonymous with, nor equivalent to, the term 'functional' as used in linguistics. However, the two denotations overlap and common properties of connotation may be pointed out. These remarks anticipate the reflections which are to follow. I intend to confine myself to examples illustrating the functional approach TO THE ANALYSIS WITHIN THE SCOPE OF THE LOGICAL THEORY OF NATURAL LANGUAGE. I do not intend to give either a univocal or exhaustive characteristic of functionalism in logical semiotics of natural language, or a nominal definition of the corresponding term.

The terms LOGICAL SEMIOTICS and NATURAL LANGUAGE, occurring in the title, refer to descriptive semiotics as employed by logicians or to the LOGICAL THEORY OF NATURAL LANGUAGE. Without going into the question of whether there ought to be one or more kinds of semiotics, the well known fact is asserted here that in past research, semiotic reflections and publications of the following logicians: Mill, Peirce, Frege, Carnap, Ajdukiewicz, Kotarbiński, Tarski, Quine and many others — existed side by side with the reflections and publications of linguists, such as those mentioned at the beginning and of many others. Although somewhat awkward and veiling a number of underlying puzzling problems, the term 'natural language', used currently in this type of research, is employed here as the opposite of the 'hybrid artificial language' of certain specific branches of science, such as psychology or sociology, and also as the opposite of 'symbolic language', e.g. of formal logic and algebra. The terms 'colloquial language', 'ordinary language' and so on are, occasionally, though not in every context, synonyms of 'natural language'.

Both linguists and logicians are concerned with this kind of language. But they are so in different ways, and they often concentrate on different problems. In ancient times, the same scholar appeared in two and even three capacities: as grammarian, logician and philosopher. Later the separate fields became more distinct and as specialization progressed, the history of linguistic studies became to an ever increasing degree a history of anachronisms and delays in benefiting from achievements in related fields. Today it happens quite frequently that when a linguist looks to logicians for help, he goes back to Mill and particularly to Peirce, hence to the classics who, though undeniably valuable, are not quite new. Rarely does he rely on the results of recent research. Similarly, a logician rarely refers to linguistic studies written more recently than fifty years ago, that is the period of de Saussure. Consequently, only exceptionally can we find an author who quotes linguistic works written a 'mere' twenty five years ago, as did Hans Reichenbach in *Elements of Symbolic Logic* (1947) when he referred to Jespersen's *The Philosophy of Grammar* (1924).

The result of this state of affairs is that we do not mutually possess the latest information from the neighboring field. An unnecessary wall is being raised between the specialized groups, and it is becoming increasingly difficult to find a common language in a group of people who ought to work together.

It is not difficult to foresee that under these circumstances a given information or suggestion may be a revealing discovery to one side while to the other it is like forcing an open door. The same applies to the present case. A logician who has never shown an inclination to make diachronic descriptions of language, may shrug his shoulder at the linguist who states that synchronic treatment of subject matter is a revolutionary discovery in the science of language. In studying the language, further, the logician by the nature of his interests has always concentrated on problems of semantics and the representative function of a sign, neglecting the expressive and emotive functions. That is why the appeals to recognize the representative and communicative functions as the main functions of language (Bühler's *Darstellungsfunktion*), appeals which in the inter-war period were so timely as far as linguistics is concerned, could be justifiably treated by logicians as exhortations to rediscover America. A linguist, on the other hand, would accept as a truism the stress on the necessity of giving consideration to linguistic context. Yet in practice it would be worthwhile to remind logicians, and repeatedly at that, of the significance of context as a modifier of the semiotic function of the sign under consideration.

As can be seen from the above, the logical theory of natural language is in certain respects, by the very nature of things, so to speak, functional in its nature in the sense already mentioned here. I have in mind its synchronic approach: concentration on the signs that appear in a text and not, at least for many years, on the mental experiences of the sign-producer and sign-perceiver; further, recognition of the conventional nature of the expressions of a language as distinct from iconic signs; and especially concentration on the representative functions of a sign: designation, denotation and, with some reservations, connotation. In logical semiotics there has been a marked growth of its branch called semantics, which is concerned with certain functions of the sign, specifically its relation to extralinguistic reality; this fact testifies that the logical theory of natural language is — in a sense — functional.

It would be unnecessary to repeat these facts as both logicians and linguists are familiar with them. Besides they are applied in practice — in logic anyway. On the other hand, I shall not try to avoid repetition of matters which, though they are known in logical semiotics, yet have made themselves neither completely nor prevalently at home in this field. If these matters are indeed important because of the actual state of research in studies on the functional logical theory of natural language, then no doubt it is worthwhile to mention or to recall them even if in the eyes of the linguists these matters should seem commonplace. Let us not hesitate to force an open door, nor to rediscover America as long as there still are people to whom this door may be shut and to whom America is not yet discovered.

## 1. USE OF AN EXPRESSION

What is FUNCTIONAL APPROACH TO THE LOGICAL SEMIOTICS OF NATURAL LANGUAGE concerned with? If I were asked to give a most concise reply to the question, confining myself to the enumeration of the most important points, I would say that it is concerned with HOW THE EXPRESSION analysed IS USED.

Thus, such-and-such USE of a given word, phrase, sentence or group of sentences comes to the fore-front. It must be made clear at the very outset that the word 'use' is ambiguous, vague and perhaps obscure even in this context. It would be advisable therefore to pinpoint its meaning if the manner a word is used is to play a central role in the functional concept of language analysis. We shall try to do so. It may, perhaps, suffice to realize the dangerous misunderstandings that lie in wait.[2]

The first is not especially dangerous, particularly in the Polish language. It may loom larger in English where the term 'use' also appears in the meaning of 'usefulness' and 'utility'. I am concerned with such-and-such an employment of a word, phrase or sentence and such-and-such an application or USE, and not with its USEFULNESS, adaptability and advantages.

Another misunderstanding may result from the fact that the phrase "I use such-and-such a thing in such-and-such manner", "I employ such-and-such a thing in such-and-such manner" can describe three different situations: when the thing is an ORGAN; when the thing is an INSTRUMENT; or when the thing used is an INGREDIENT. For example, I write with my hand, but also with a pen; and to prepare a cocktail I use the ingredient vermouth. Expressions of natural language may appear in all three roles. When I refer to a given thing by a word, I use that word as an instrument.

---

[2] *Cf.* Ryle, Gilbert, "Ordinary Language", *The Philosophical Review*, LXII (1953), 167-186; and in the anthology *Philosophy and Ordinary Language*, ed. by Charles E. Caton (Urbana Ill., University of Illinois Press, 1963), pp. 108-127. Only the distinction between 'use' and 'utility' is according to Ryle. In distinguishing the use of a word in the role of an instrument, organ, ingredient and designatum I have gone beyond Ryle. In the distinction 'use' – 'usage' only the point of departure is common. Our views part company after that.

(One could argue whether it is then always an instrument. Perhaps it is such only when I have used it in a manner approximating the general usage in a given discipline, that is when the word is a precise term and when the thing it refers to is univocally determined by the context and extralinguistic situation. In cases of spontaneous usage, when the word is not used with precision and when it is not determined by context and situation, it perhaps functions as an organ.) When I place a given word in a syntactic construction, I use it also as an ingredient. But the situation becomes complicated in this case, too. For example, in a metalinguistic sentence: "*Dog* is a one-syllable word" — 'dog' occurs not only as an instrument and as an ingredient: its part within the sub-quotes occurs as an object, a designatum. Once we are aware of the various possibilities mentioned here, they will perhaps cease to cause trouble. There is no reason to eliminate any of them. For the use of a word as a designated OBJECT is useful in SEMANTIC considerations. The use of a word as an INGREDIENT, in SYNTACTIC considerations. The use of a word as an INSTRUMENT (or organ), in SEMANTIC, SYNTACTIC as well as PRAGMATIC considerations. In my opinion, however, the most important, from the point of view of the functional approach to the logical semiotics of natural language, is the use of the word as an instrument.

The third misunderstanding is the most dangerous. For instance, when speaking of such-and-such a use of a given term, I may bear the following in mind. The term, the word "dog", for instance, has its defined meaning in a given language and in accordance with this meaning I can use the word "dog" in such-and-such a way to refer to, let us say, my dog Trot. This use will be determined, among other things, by context or extralinguistic situation. I may make frequent use of the word "dog" in the same manner. The class of the tokens of the word "dog", each used in reference to Trot, determines this-and-this use of the word.[3] At other times, however,

---

[3]  *Cf.* Strawson, P. F., "On Referring", *Mind*, LIX (1950), 320-344; and in the anthologies: *Essays in Conceptual Analysis*, ed. by Antony Flew (London, 1956), pp. 21-52; and in *Philosophy and Ordinary Language*, pp. 162-193 (see footnote 2).

I may use the word "dog" in such a way that it would stand for Arthur Conan Doyle's *The Hound of the Baskervilles*, and I could do this more than once. Here again context and extralinguistic situation determine the given use of the word. Each of the uses of the word "dog" mentioned here agrees with the PREVAILING USAGE of that word. Thus, as we see, speaking of such-and-such a usage of an expression, I have in mind a LINGUISTIC PRACTICE, an established LINGUISTIC CUSTOM. The nominal analytical definition of the word "dog" refers to this usage. The usage now discussed is a generalization of the uses enumerated before. There are many uses for a given word and comparatively few usages. The word "orchid", for example, is used in one way only, in the sense of the term 'usage'. The English word "bay" has more usages. It means: (a) a laurel, (b) a creek, (c) a part of a bridge, (d) to bark, (e) a reddish-brown color. It is therefore a polysemic word. "Orchid", on the other hand, is a monosemic word. In the case of the word "bay" the context and extralinguistic situation perform a dual role. First, they jointly determine the usage of the word, hence, whether reference is made e.g. to the laurel tree, or to the creek. Then they determine use of the word, that is what laurel tree or what creek is meant here. In the case of the word "orchid" the role of context and extralinguistic situation reduces to the use of the term.

The term USAGE may, therefore, be accepted as a synonym of the term MEANING, in one of its definitions. It is sometimes said that the meaning of an expression is clear to one who knows how to use the expression in a given language, that is, to what objects outside of that language the expression can refer and in what respect and in what grammatical construction it can correctly be used. However, the following danger lies in wait. Owing to a slight shift of meaning, that is instead of treating meaning of an expression as usage, it is asserted that "the meaning of a given expression as understood by a given person is the way, determined in some respects, in which that person UNDERSTANDS the expression".[4] It is considered here that "the PROCESS OF UNDERSTANDING an expression heard by some-

---

[4] Ajdukiewicz, Kazimierz, *Logika pragmatyczna* [Pragmatic Logic]. (Warsaw, Państwowe Wydawnictwo Naukowe, 1965), p. 23. *Cf.* also pp. 19-61.

one depends on what thought there is in the mind of the listener which then becomes merged into one with his hearing of that expression" as well as that "this THOUGHT constitutes ... the PROCESS OF UNDERSTANDING the expression".[5] Consequently, the way of understanding, i.e. the manner of thinking, becomes the meaning of an expression. The meaning of an expression as understood by a person is not identified here with the thought on which the process of understanding is based, but is identified only with some of its properties. However, this too may raise the objection that this is a psychological interpretation.[6] Although the term 'usage' is pragmatic and not psychological in character, yet, owing to its kinship with the term 'way of understanding', it may become a source of certain undesirable consequences.

'Usage' as a synonym of 'meaning' is troublesome for other reasons. At times the word 'to mean' was understood as if it referred to a certain 'relation' between a given expression and an ENTITY which is disparate from it, namely the meaning of the expression, and such that that expression constitutes the name of the entity.[7] Consequently, a meaning is either hypostatized or confused with the designata of the word. The same applies to 'usage'.

Difficulties of a similar nature may arise from the fact that MEANING is frequently identified with CONCEPT. It is asserted that "we call a concept in the logical sense, and especially a concept in the nominal sense, the meaning of a term".[8] At the same time, it is said that "one can speak of DESIGNATA AND THE DENOTATION OF

[5] See footnote 4.
[6] Cf. Ajdukiewicz, Logika, pp. 24-25: "To understand an expression in meaning Z is as much as to understand it by a thought which in respects that are essential to the meaning is equipped with such-and-such properties. Of these properties of the thought we shall say that they are expressed by expression W in meaning Z. In other words: expression W EXPRESSES in meaning Z the property of thought C is as much as: if someone understands in a given moment expression W in meaning Z, then he understands it by a thought equipped with property C (...). The relation of expressing is the relation which occurs (irrespective of time) between expression W, meaning Z and property C — if the necessary condition of the use of expression W in meaning Z is the understanding of that expression by a thought equipped with property C."
[7] See footnote 2.
[8] Ajdukiewicz, Logika, p. 32.

CONCEPT in the same manner as one speaks of designata and of the denotation of a term. Specifically, the designatum of a concept" will then be "the designatum of a term, whose concept is meaning. The denotation of a concept — the denotation of a term whose concept is meaning".[9] Further, the same is said of the content of a concept which is said of the content, or the connotation of terms: "The content of a CONCEPT is the same as that which constitutes the content of a term whose that concept is meaning".[10] Consequently, the concept, defined initially as a meaning of a term, or as certain properties of thought on which this meaning rests, comes to resemble the term itself, since, like the term it has a designatum, denotation and content. And in consequence one is tempted to resort to a hypostasis, for since the terms, or at least the concrete tokens of a given term, are physical individuals, why then should we deny the existence of concepts — so similar to the terms. One step further would lead us to speculate, in the spirit of Plato or Locke, on the subject of status and derivation of concepts, a speculation which is like the metaphysical disputes on the subject of the status and derivation of ideas.[11]

For this reason the term 'usage' may become a source of one trouble or another. I think it is important clearly to distinguish between use and usage. And when I said that the functional approach to analysis in logical semiotics of natural language is concerned with, to put it most concisely, consideration of how an analysed expression is used, I had in mind USE rather than USAGE.

## 2. USE OF AN EXPRESSION AND THE CLASSIFICATION OF TERMS WITH REGARD TO THE NUMBER OF DESIGNATA

From now on whenever we speak of the MANNER IN WHICH AN EXPRESSION IS USED, we shall mean the USE of an expression.

Taking a few examples, I shall try to explain why the study of

[9]   Ajdukiewicz, *Logika*, p. 42.
[10]   Ajdukiewicz, *Logika*, p. 53.
[11]   See footnote 2.

HOW a given expression IS USED plays such an important role in the FUNCTIONAL treatment of the logical analysis of natural language.

The first example will concern problems of classification of appellations, especially of TERMS. The distinctions customarily made in logic are, among others, following: a term may be GENERAL, SINGULAR or EMPTY, depending on whether it has, respectively: two or more DESIGNATA, one designatum only, or no designatum at all. The designatum of a term is the object DESIGNATED by the term, that is each and only that object about which that term CAN BE CORRECTLY PREDICATED when it has such-and-such a meaning. One-word APPELLATIVES as well as ADJECTIVES are accepted as terms, hence "(a) dog", "red"; so are one-word PROPER NAMES, hence "Socrates", "Apollo"; proper names of more words than one, hence "Mont Blanc"; DESCRIPTIONS of more words than one, hence "the largest Polish city", "(a) member of parliament", and so on. There is a tendency to expand and to modify the meaning of 'to designate' in a manner which enables one to say that functors, especially sentence-forming ones, have their designata. Thus, if the sentence-forming functor "runs" applies to John and not to Warsaw, in that case John is one of the designata of that functor, while Warsaw is not.

This concept of designation calls for certain ontological decisions. A diagnosis establishing whether a given term may be truly predicated about a certain object depends, among other things, on its existence. Hence, when I classified the word "Socrates" as a singular term, I had first to accept that the long dead Socrates exists. And when I assert that one of the designata of the term "dog" is Fido which will be born in ten years, I automatically assert that Fido, which is not yet alive, does exist. If, finally, I accept the term "Centaur" as empty, I assert that Centaurs do not exist. This opens a whole field for discussion on existence and on designata.

The MEANING in which a given term appears is essential to the above concept of DESIGNATION. E.g., "Siren" as a name of a mythological character is an empty term, and as a name of instrument which produces sound it is a general term. Thus the USAGE of the word intervenes here.

It may be noted on the margin of the problem of designation that the sentence "two persons understand certain expressions in the same meaning" demands precision. It is said that one of the necessary conditions of this kind of understanding — when it depends on thinking of a certain object — is that the persons in question have the same object in mind.[12] And yet everyone will agree that John and Peter can understand the word "dog" in the same way although each one has a different dog in mind. There is a further problem. The person who classifies the term "siren" as a name of more than one object, does so because he understands it in such-and-such a meaning. But on the other hand, one of necessary conditions of understanding the term in that particular sense is that the thoughts on which that understanding hinges refer to more than one such object. Here again greater precision is necessary, for one may easily be caught in a vicious circle.

But for the time being let us set these problems aside. We are at present interested in the fact that meaning, or usage, plays an essential role in the explanation of designation and of the classification of terms with regard to the number of the designata. I do not deny that meaning is important in consideration of this kind, but I should like to note that as far as analysis of natural language is concerned relativization with regard to meaning is INADEQUATE. For it would then seem that empty terms, and besides that singular, and besides that general terms, appear in language in the same way as people, and besides that dogs, and besides that cars, appear in extralinguistic reality. This classification does not adequately sum up the actual situation in natural language. It classifies terms OUT OF CONTEXT and gives consideration only to the LEXICAL MEANING of each of them, without taking into consideration their FUNCTIONING in a language. As a result, we receive a static and non-functional representation of the state of affairs.

A FUNCTIONAL description ought to take account of the following circumstances, made familiar by experience. The word "dog" may be used in a variety of ways, depending on extralinguistic situation and context. Let us assume that I found my dog Trot sleeping in the wardrobe on top of my suit which he had pulled down from the hanger. Shaking my finger at him, I say, "Bad dog; what has he

---

[12]    Cf. Ajdukiewicz, *Logika*, pp. 19-23.

done? The dog slept in the closet". In this context and situation the word "dog" functions WITH REGARD TO ITS BEING USED — as a singular term. When I inform someone, "Trot is a dog", or when I say, "You should talk to a dog", then the expression "dog" functions with regard to its being used — as a general term.[13] Then again when Arthur Conan Doyle refers to the dog hero of *The Hound of the Baskervilles*, then the term used in this manner functions as an empty term. Finally, all the sentences given above were used by me in the same way in a certain respect, that is they were used as examples. In this situation, in the text of the present article, I did not use a single sentence in order to TALK about a concrete dog, or about every dog, or even about a fictitious dog. The word "dog" did not once REFER to a dog; it could not really be predicated about anything. Therefore, the word functioned WITH REGARD TO THE FACT THAT IT WAS USED as an example, as an expression which is neither empty, nor singular, nor general, because the question simply does not arise.

The term "dog", taken out of context, isolated from the situation in which it is spoken or written, that is devoid of relativization with regard to such-and-such use, is also neither singular, nor general, nor empty, as long as it appears as an item in a dictionary. Or, if one prefers, is at the same time both the first, and the second, and the third. That is, it may be used in such a manner as to form a potential predicate of a true proposition about every dog, or some dogs, or about one given dog; and finally, in such a manner, where

[13]   It might be objected that the example fits well only into those languages which, like Polish, have no articles; while in English and in other languages which make use of articles it is not the word "dog" alone which occurs in sentences given above as instances, but "the dog" or "a dog", and it is the change of an article which accounts for the singular or general character of the use of the expression. I admit that languages without articles provide best examples of the change in use, discussed in this chapter. On the other hand, however, it seems that those examples could be expanded so that they would fit into languages which do have articles, e.g. English. In order to do that it would be necessary to consider articles "the" and "a", which occur in our examples, as parts of the context in which the analysed word "dog" is inbedded. Then it would be one and the same word "dog", and not "the dog" or "a dog", which is used in different ways — as a singular, or general, or empty term, or as none of these.

there would be no object about which that term could be truly predicated.

I would contest the view which holds that since the term "dog", treated as an isolated lexical item, is suitable, owing to its usage, that is owing to its meaning, for the role of a predicate of a true assertion about more than one animal, then this fact determines its general character. I feel that we are dealing here with a mis-understanding similar, though not so glaring, as the one below:

"The word *Pustelnik* is a Polish place name, but it is also an appellative which means 'hermit'. In the second case it may be correctly predicated about many persons. In that case the word will always be a general term, hence also in the first case, when it is a proper name."

An equivocality arises owing to the impermissible change in the meaning of the word "Pustelnik". In our examples, the word "dog" did not change meaning. The very meaning, or usage, identical in all the given examples, hence also when the word was an isolated lexical item, determines its various uses: as a general term, or as a singular term, at that referring at one time to this and at another time to that concrete dog, or finally, as an empty term. The meaning is characteristic of a given WORD-TYPE, or of the class understood in the distributive sense, of all TOKENS OF THE WORD. On the other hand, emptiness, singularity or generality are characteristic correspondingly of this, that or another use of a given word, or of a certain sub-class composed of only some of its tokens. The word "dog" appeared in the examples given above in a different use each time. Because in one of its uses the word "dog" was proved a general term ("You should talk to a dog"), one cannot correctly infer that in every use it will be a general term. Specifically, there-fore, in the example "Bad dog; what has he done? ..." the word "dog" refers to my dog Trot only, and owing to its use it cannot be made a predicate of the sentence "Trot is a dog", without first changing its given use. In the last sentence whose equivalent is "Trot is an element of the class of dogs", the term "dog" was used in a general manner which differs from the first.

It is evident, therefore, that it is not so that there are general terms, and also singular, and also empty terms. But that the same term is once used as a general, once as a singular, once as an empty term, and once in such a way that the question of its generality, singularity or emptiness does not arise at all. The generality, singularity or emptiness is a RELATIVE trait, made relative to a given use of a term. There is a difference between terms classified from this point of view and the classification of things as people, dogs, cars and others. More like the classification of women according to the degree of kinship; we do not distinguish mothers, and besides that sisters, and besides that aunts, since one woman may be a mother, a sister and an aunt at the same time.

### 3. USE OF AN EXPRESSION AND THE CLASSIFICATION OF TERMS ACCORDING TO THEIR SINGULAR OR GENERAL INTENTION

Here is another example testifying to how important it is that the use of an expression be given consideration in a functional approach to the semiotic analysis of natural language.

It is known that substantive or nominal expressions may also be classified according to MEANING INTENTION, as general, singular and at times empty expressions, but in a different sense than previously. It is said that " 'Zeus' is a term with a SINGULAR intention; 'centaur' — a term ... with a GENERAL intention, although from the point of view of denotation both are empty terms." [14] "Denotation" is understood as a class of existent designata of a term, in the meaning defined previously. Thus, the singular or general intention of a term does not depend upon its denotation but on USAGE; it is — so to speak — built into the meaning of the term. Qualifying the term "centaur" as general, we refer to denotation in another meaning,

[14]  Kotarbiński, Tadeusz, "Z zagadnień klasyfikacji nazw" [Selected Problems of the Classification of Terms] (Łódź, 1954), *Rozprawy Komisji Językowej Łódzkiego Towarzystwa Naukowego* [Proceedings of the Language Commission of the Łódź Scientific Society]. Vol. I; reprinted in Kotarbiński, *Elementy teorii poznania, logiki formalnej i metodologii nauk* [Elements of Gnosiology, Formal Logic, and Methodology of Sciences] (Warsaw, Ossolineum, 1961), 461-462.

which Lewis[15] calls "comprehension", or a classification of all consistently thinkable things to which the term would correctly apply. And classifying the term "centaur" as empty, we refer to its denotation. According to the present subdivision, "red object on my desk" will be a general term. "The red object on my desk" will be singular regardless of whether one red object or more than one was, is or will be on my desk or finally whether it never was, it is not and none will ever be.[16] In the present understanding, the "square circle" may be recognized as an empty term, for its meaning determines zero-comprehension, since nothing can be consistently thinkable as a square circle. It will be an empty term in the previous understanding too, since it also has zero-denotation because square circles do not exist.

As can be readily seen, here too the problem is formulated as if generality, singularity or emptiness in the present understanding depend on the meaning of a term, on its usage. This case, however, is analogous with the former. USE is decisive. In the sentence about the Cyclops Polyphemus, "The Cyclops was blinded by Odysseus", the word "Cyclops" is used with singular intention, while in the sentence, "Polyphemus was a Cyclops", the intention of the word is general. The expression "my brother", analysed as an isolated lexical item, has general intention. But context or situation, hence such-and-such use, may make it singular as in the sentence, "My brother gave me this book."

Thus, *mutatis mutandis*, in this case too considerations of the USE of a given expression blazes the path for FUNCTIONAL analysis of natural language. As long as the classification of terms as discussed here is based on the meaning of expressions, on usage, the expressions are shown to us as dead, static and isolated lexical items. Application of analysis with regard to use — not only assures that the general or singular character of expressions is a relative property, but, and this is more important, puts them into

---

[15]  *Cf.* Lewis, C.I., "The Modes of Meaning", *Philosophy and Phenomenological Research*, IV, No. 2 (Buffalo, New York, 1943), 236-249.
[16]  See footnote 15.

a CONTEXT and a situation which accompanies the expression, and demonstrates how that expression actually FUNCTIONS.

## 4. USE OF AN EXPRESSION AND CLASSIFICATIONS OF TERMS ACCORDING TO THEIR SUBJECTIVE OR PREDICATIVE CHARACTER

Since the days of Aristotle a distinction was made between INDIVIDUAL and GENERAL terms in still another, fairly puzzling, sense. The former can be used only as SUBJECTS OF ELEMENTARY INDIVIDUAL PROPOSITIONS, that is propositions that speak of individuals; the latter can be used as PREDICATES.[17] A number of interpretations is possible. The word 'term' may be taken as an equivalent of the phrase "an expression which appears in an atomic categorical sentence as a subject or a predicate", or as referring to extralinguistic entities, namely — those elements of a proposition, and not of a sentence in the grammatical sense, which correspond to a subjective or predicative expression. In this connection the words 'subject' and 'predicate' must be understood, respectively, either as a GRAMMATICAL SUBJECT and a GRAMMATICAL PREDICATE or as a LOGICAL SUBJECT and a LOGICAL PREDICATE. Moreover, as each of these is ambiguous and vague, other doubts arise regarding interpretation. This is neither the time nor place for seeking a solution or even discussing this problem at length. It will suffice to assert that according to the fairly prevalent exemplification of the above distinction, an example of the individual term is the so called pure proper name, "Socrates", and of the general term — the predicates: "man", or "an immortal creature", or "the longest river in Poland", or "the youngest Olympic god". The latter category covers, according to the first classification, both the names as well as the descriptions, both the general and the singular as well as empty terms, and, according to the second classification mentioned here, terms distinguished by SINGULAR INTENTION and by GENERAL INTENTION. The matter is posed as if the classes of

---

[17] See footnote 14.

individual terms and general terms were MUTUALLY EXCLUSIVE, as if, therefore, individual terms did exist and besides them also general terms.

This opinion could be formed owing to a failure to give consideration to the use of these expressions, not to speak of the fact that the relativization of these terms to an elementary individual sentence, or a sentence which speaks of a certain individual, must evoke protest. In Chapter VII I shall try to explain that such sentences do not exist, for talking about something is not a property of a sentence but of such-and-such a use of a sentence. It may be sufficient to call to mind at present the examples given by Quine[18]:

    (1)  *Lamb* is scarce,
    (2)  Agnes is a *lamb*,
    (3)  The brown part is *lamb*,

where the word "lamb", a general term in each of the understandings discussed so far, changes its role depending on its use. First, it appears as a CUMULATIVE, or COLLECTIVE term, used as an INDIVIDUAL TERM; secondly, as a GENERAL term which refers to every individual of the *Ovis aries* species; thirdly, as a CUMULATIVE term used in a GENERAL way so that it refers to every serving of lamb.

Incidentally, it becomes clear that the distinction between cumulative and non-cumulative is, if the analysis takes account of use, relative. The same expression may be used in a collective or non-collective manner.

As regards distinguishing INDIVIDUAL (that is SUBJECTIVE) and GENERAL terms (that is PREDICATIVE), the above examples would indicate that the above traits are connected with use of expressions. The same word may be used in each of these roles. One or another potential syntactic character — suitability for the role of a subject, suitability for the role of a predicate — is not here a characteristic trait of usage, or of the meaning of a word, but, simply, of its use. Whenever a given word is analysed as an isolated and static lexical item, account been taken of usage only, it always appears to be

---

[18]  *Cf.* Quine, Willard van Orman, *Word and Object* (New York, The Technology Press of M.I.T. and John Willey, 1960), pp. 90-185.

ambivalent in character from the point of view of the analysis: if it is suitable for the role of a subject, it is also suitable for the role of the predicate of a sentence, and *vice versa*. Only a study of use, hence functional analysis of a word in a certain type of context and a certain type of situation, discloses whether the word appears as an individual or as a general term in the meaning discussed at present.

### 5.  USE OF AN EXPRESSION AND THE DISTINCTION: PROPER NAME — NAME — DESCRIPTION

Since the origin of Russell's[19] theory of descriptions and even earlier, beginning with Frege's "Über Sinn und Bedeutung",[20] a distinction has been made, especially in Anglo-Saxon logic, between PROPER NAMES, NAMES, DEFINITE DESCRIPTIONS and INDEFINITE DESCRIPTIONS. This distinction is not popular among Polish logicians; it has been used neither by Ajdukiewicz nor by Kotarbiński.

I cannot at present devote myself to the defects of this classification or to the differences of standpoint represented by various authors. But it may suffice if I explain my position. I shall take examples from the English language which has definite and indefinite articles and is therefore more suitable for this purpose than a language that has no articles.

A 'pure' PROPER NAME is usually considered a one-word name of a real individual, e.g. the word "Socrates"; however, there is a difference of opinion as to whether a one-word name of a fictitious individual, or a name, consisting of two or more words, of a concrete or fictitious individual is a proper name. A DEFINITE DESCRIPTION is a substantival phrase having "the so-and-so" form, where "so-and-so" appears in the grammatical singular and where the

---

[19]    *Cf.* Russell, Bertrand, *Introduction to Mathematical Philosophy* (London, Allen and Unwin, 1919), Chapter XVI "Descriptions"; and "On Denoting" by the same author, *Mind*, XIV (1905).
[20]    *Cf.* Frege, Gottlob, "Über Sinn und Bedeutung", *Zeitschrift für Philosophie und Philosophische Kritik*, 100 (1892).

whole is singular in character in the first or in the second of the
two meanings of the adjective "singular" discussed above, there
being no full agreement as to in which of the two. Nor is there
full agreement with regard to the following matters: (1) Is "the
river" as well as "he", "she", "it" a definite description, as Quine
would have it,[21] or must it be a phrase composed of independent
parts, as "the king of England", as Russell would have it.[22] (2) Can
singular phrases beginning with demonstrative pronouns "this",
"that", e.g. "this queen of England", or relative phrases composed
of a predicate and a proper name, e.g. "Napoleon's mother", also
be definite descriptions, as Reichenbach proposes,[23] or not, as
Quine says? Russell is prepared to accept as an INDEFINITE
DESCRIPTION a phrase which has "a so-and-so" form where this
"so-and-so" must be composed of independent symbols. Reichenbach, however, also accepts as an indefinite description an expression in which the article "a" is followed by one-word predicate,
i.e. "a man". Both agree that a definite description must be
strengthened by the requirement of singularity which does not
apply to indefinite descriptions. They also note that indefinite
descriptions are connected with pure assertions concerning
existence. The stand on NAMES depends on what is considered a
proper name, a definite description and an indefinite description.
Most often the following are accepted as such: "the lion", "a lion",
"man", "water", and, with reservations about its syncategorematic
character, "red". It is a matter for discussion whether the pronouns
"this", "that", "he", "she", "it" and others should be included
among the names. The popular distinction "names and descriptions"[24] usually pertains, on the one hand, to 'pure' proper names

[21] See footnote 18.
[22] See footnote 19.
[23] *Cf.* Reichenbach, Hans, *Elements of Symbolic Logic* (New York, The
Macmillan Company, 1948), pp. 256ff.
[24] *Cf.* Ayer, Alfred J., "Imiona własne a deskrypcje" [Proper Names and
Descriptions], *Studia Filozoficzne* [Philosophical Studies], 5(20) (Warszawa,
1960), 135-155; and "Names and Descriptions" by the same author, in the
collection: *Thinking and Meaning: Entretiens d'Oxford 1962 Organisés par
l'Institut International de Philosophie*, 5,20 (Paris, Ed. Neuvelaerts, 1963),
pp. 199-202.

("Socrates"), and on the other hand, to definite descriptions of the Russell type ("the author of *Waverley*").

The differences enumerated here are a result not only of the subjective divergencies of opinion but also of the fact that the distinction is not satisfactory. One of the reasons for this is the notorious failure to give consideration to the use of the expressions here discussed.

Yet the singular character of proper names and definite descriptions, each of which is understood to possess one designatum only or to have singular intention, is bound with the use of a given word. Hence, from that point of view, one cannot correctly distinguish a class of proper names or a class of definite descriptions, but only at best a class of expressions USED AS PROPER NAMES WITH REGARD TO SINGULAR INTENTION, or as a class of expressions USED — OWING TO THEIR SINGULAR CHARACTER — AS DEFINITE DESCRIPTIONS. Further, singularity cannot be used to distinguish definite descriptions from indefinite descriptions or names, for expressions are not singular once and for all. They can only be USED IN THE SINGULAR MANNER. This refers, e.g., to the definite description "the king of England". I can use it in a way in which it would not mention any individual. For instance, when the description occurs in the sentence given as an example. Then again, I may employ an indefinite description or a name as singular, as in the sentence, "I met a man", where "a man" refers to some person. Definite and indefinite descriptions as well as names, construed with regard to the manner in which they are used as singular in character, do not constitute mutually excluding classes. It would be correct to state the following: a given expression, owing to its singular character, is used here as a definite description, or as an indefinite description, or as a name.

It may be that a certain kind of expression which, owing solely to its use, appears in a given case in the role of a definite description, may not, from another point of view, be qualified as an expression used in a descriptive sense. Here is another example:

(1)  The author of *The Tempest* was a glove-makers son.

(2)  The author of *The Tempest* is also the author of *Romeo and Juliet*.

In each of the above sentences "The author of *The Tempest*" was used as a singular expression, for it refers to Shakespeare and to him only. But in the first case I used the periphrase solely for the purpose of IDENTIFYING a given person and to avoid monotony I tried not to repeat the proper name "Shakespeare" — for instance, in a long article. In the second sentence, taking the content of the whole sentence into consideration, I am interested not only in pointing to the person of Shakespeare, but also in INFORMING that he wrote *The Tempest*. In the first case, I could have equally well written "Shakespeare" or "the author of *Hamlet*" instead of "the author of *The Tempest*". I could not do this in the second case because I was interested in giving the following information about the same person: that he wrote *The Tempest* and that he wrote *Romeo and Juliet*. Hence, in the first sentence, I employed the phrase "The author of *The Tempest*" as a PROPER NAME. In the second instance, however, I used it to a greater extent DESCRIPTIVELY. In turn, in the second sentence the predicative expression "the author of *Romeo and Juliet*" was used more descriptively than the subject "the author of *The Tempest*". For the subject also performs a DEMONSTRATIVE function, that is it performs the role of an indicative gesture, it performs a REFERENTIAL, IDENTIFYING function, and that is considered characteristic of proper names and not of descriptions. The phrase "the author of *The Tempest*" was used in a mixed manner: AS A PROPER NAME AND AS A DESCRIPTION. And the predicative expression "the author of *Romeo and Juliet*" is used exclusively in an ASCRIPTIVE role; it does not serve to indicate the person of Shakespeare because that has already been done by the subject. It may at best be correctly or wrongly predicated, and that depends on the empirical state of affairs. All these properties are ascribed to descriptions. We have here then a purely descriptive use.

It appears again that consideration of use of an expression, hence of its context and situation, leads to a break with absolute distinctions, in this case with the antithesis: proper names versus descriptions. Instead one ought to speak of the use of an expression as a proper name or of its use as a description. Moreover, one may here indicate the gradations, whereby a given phrase may to a greater or smaller degree appear in the role of a definite description or in the role of a proper name.

Descriptions are at times distinguished from names on the ground that the first are made up of two or more words while names should be made up of one word. According to this view, the expression "therapy by injecting the patient's own blood" would be an indefinite description, while the word "autohaemotherapy" would be a name (of an abstract entity). We shall analyse the example taking into account the use of the second expression. We compare the following two sentences:

(1) A doctor in a clinic explains to the students: "Autohaemotherapy is effective in cases of *furunculosis* (furuncles or boils)."

(2) Another doctor corrects a student by saying: "This is not an ordinary blood transfusion; it is autohaemotherapy."

In the second sentence, although the word "autohaemotherapy" is a single word, it is used as a description. This fact is indicated by the situation, context and the syntactic position of the word. In order to grasp the contradistinction which the doctor wishes to make it is necessary to go into the etymological structure of the word "autohaemotherapy" and to know the meaning of its separate parts, that is, the word must be treated as a three-word description or at any rate more closely analysed than in the first example where it performed a referential function, characteristic of demonstratives.

The same applies to proper names. They are used at times as descriptions. This pertains to what are called *nomina-omina*, that is proper names that have a meaning, as for example the names of comedy characters ("Mrs Malaprop" from "*mal à propos*"), and to predicates in sentences, like "this man is Socrates", "This city is Warsaw".

As can readily be seen, the same expression may be used as a proper name, as a description or as a name. Thus, there is no situation in natural language in which there are proper names, and besides that names (terms), and besides that definite descriptions, and besides that indefinite descriptions. These are not MUTUALLY EXCLUSIVE classes of expressions, but VARIOUS USES. Moreover, there is a GRADATION within the area of each of these uses, that is a greater or lesser intensity of descriptiveness, nominal character or proper-nominal character. Beyond the 'pure' uses there are also 'mixed' uses, with some descriptiveness and some proper-nominal character. It is necessary to state each time in what respect a given expression was used in a given manner. From the point of view of FUNCTIONAL treatment of the logical semiotics of natural language, it is necessary to put an end to the rigid division that has so far prevailed in the subject under discussion and instead to classify the given expression AS USED IN A GIVEN RESPECT, IN SUCH-AND-SUCH A MANNER AND IN SUCH-AND-SUCH A DEGREE.

## 6.  USE OF AN EXPRESSION AND THE SENTENCE

Before I discuss the USE OF SENTENCES, I should like to emphasize that something which I shall call DENOMINALIZATION — is an essential point of the program which sets out to FUNCTIONALIZE semiotic analysis of natural language.  Logical tradition in this type of study, deriving from Mill, Frege and young Russell, treats language as if it were composed exclusively of TERMS, or principally of terms, or at least as if the terms constituted the "salt of the earth".  Natural language repudiates this experience.  One of its basic functions, the COMMUNICATIVE function, is realized primarily by means of SENTENCES. The same applies to EXPRESSIVE and EMO-TIVE functions. Traditional logical theory of language, focused on certain REPRESENTATIVE functions — DESIGNATING, DENOTING, CON-NOTING — and absorbed in the contemplation of IDEAS, CONCEPTS and MEANINGS, noticed this empirical fact in too small a degree. Analysis concerned with the usage of terms, and consequently concentrated on isolated expressions and static lexical items, overestimated the role of terms in language. Although the disproportion was less harmful in the study of artificial languages within the area of pure semantics, it was nevertheless painfully noticeable in logical descriptive semiotics of natural language.

I claim that by taking account of the use of an expression in semiotic analysis, and in this connection by fully appreciating the importance of context and extralinguistic situation, a contribution may be made toward the denominalization of semiotics: will ascribe to sentences the place they deserve in language and thus also will restore the upset balance.

The time has come to give some examples. Analysed from the point of view of use, the distinction between SENTENCES and NON-SENTENCES loses its absolute character. Ajdukiewicz has remarked that "noun-expressions, hence terms, are used at times to express certain assertions; for example the noun 'fire' is used in the same meaning as the sentence 'Something is burning'. From our point of view these expressions are declarative sentences for in that meaning they assert a certain fact." [25] I would like to modify this remark and replace the relativization with regard to meaning by a relativization with regard to use. This follows from our earlier considerations. Therefore I would say that in certain circumstances (context and situation) I use the word "fire" so that it functions as a proposition. Similarly, when a teacher calls, "Silence!" in a class, he uses the term as an imperative sentence, hence, as a sentence in the grammatical sense, which, however, is not a proposition.

The opposite of this is possible. In the sentence, "Caesar said: 'Alea iacta est'", the expression "alea iacta est", being a DECLARATIVE SENTENCE from the grammatical point of view, is used as a NAME, namely as a name of what Caesar said.

There are instances where a grammatical interrogative sentence, a rhetorical question, occurs as a declarative sentence and at the same time as a proposition, owing to such-and-such a use, and

[25]   Ajdukiewicz, *Logika*, p. 27.

where a grammatical declarative sentence, e.g. "All the children will write", is used as an imperative sentence.

I shall now dwell for a moment on the subject of the distinctions between DECLARATIVE SENTENCES and PROPOSITIONS, and on the subject of the TRUTH-VALUE of the latter. It is usually asserted that a proposition is a TRUE OR FALSE statement, and an equation mark is placed between grammatical declarative sentences and sentences understood as propositions.[26] It is added that a non-declarative sentence, for example an interrogative and imperative sentence, is not a proposition. In a word, the class of propositions is treated as a sub-class of the class of grammatical sentences.

It was evident from the foregoing remarks on the subject of declarative sentences used imperatively or in the role of a name, that the identification of the declarative sentence with the sentence in the logical sense cannot be sustained. This fact is borne out by further observations in which the use of a sentence is taken into account.[27]

For example, "In 1966 Warsaw is the capital of Poland", can be used so as to say something about Warsaw; the expression will then be used to make a true assertion. I may, however, use the same sentence only as an example, as I did a moment ago. In that case, the sentence is not used to speak about Warsaw or about any other thing. Nor am I making a true or false assertion. Consequently, it is not the sentence that has a truth-value, that is, it is either true or false (from the point of view of the classical two-valued logic), but only the sentence used in such-and-such a manner.

More controversial is the case of the sentence "The emperor is naked". In Andersen's tale it is used as an expression which speaks about a ficticious character, or, in other words, speaks about no one; for if the model of language is modified, the meaning of the word "about" undergoes an essential change. Consequently, used in the above manner, the sentence does not make an assertion, whether a true or a false one. When, however, the sentence is used, and not in the metaphorical sense, to say something about Franz

[26]   See footnote 4.
[27]   See footnote 3.

Josef, the emperor of Austria, as he reviewed the military parade, then the above expression is used to make a false assertion.

And when a person uses it to speak about the present emperor of Ethiopia as he is in his bath, then the sentence is used to make a true assertion.

Finally, in all these cases, I employed the sentence exclusively as an example: with its aid I did not speak about anyone, nor did I make an assertion. Consequently, it is not the sentence that has such-and-such truth-value, but the sentence used in such-and-such a manner.

It is not hard to predict what the objections to the above analysis will be. First, it is possible to point out that we are dealing here with the error of an incomplete proposition. Removing this error, we have the following sentences: "Franz Josef is naked at $t_1$ time", "Haile Selassie is naked at $t_2$ time", and so on, and these, as it is asserted, simply ARE true or false and are not USED as true or false. This, however, does not refute the argument that each of the sentences, even when they are completed and are precise, may be used not for the purpose of speaking about Franz Josef at $t_1$ or about Haile Selassie at $t_2$, but as examples. Then the sentences will be neither true nor false. Moreover, the interpretation whereby a sentence such as "The emperor is naked" is considered incorrect because it is incomplete, seems to ignore the general linguistic practice which would then be consistently commiting such errors, hence also logical errors in expressing thoughts. Closer to the needs and to the spirit of natural language is an analysis in the style of Strawson[28] or Bar-Hillel,[29] presented here by me; according to that analysis, there is no need to disqualify the majority of natural language sentences as erroneous.

A second kind of argument against the stand represented here by me would be that the word "emperor" in the sentence "The emperor is naked" — is an OCCASIONAL term. It would be claimed that in that case we have sentences which, though homomorphous, are not

[28]   See footnote 3.
[29]   Cf. Bar-Hillel, Yehoshua, "Indexical Expressions", Mind, LXIII, No. 251 (1954), 359-379.

synonymous, a fact which may lead into the error of equivocality. When completed, they become heteromorphous, as they were formerly. In reply to this argument, I should like to state that I have no objections to the view that the word "emperor" is occasional. However, I do object to the opinion that the above sentence was polysemic. I shall endeavor to enlarge upon this remark.

I assume that OCCASIONALITY IS A PROPERTY OF A VAST MAJORITY OF EXPRESSIONS OF NATURAL LANGUAGE. Together with ELLIPTICITY of expressions it constitutes its characteristic property. Contrary to accepted opinion, not only words like "I", "here", "now", are occasional, allegedly in contrast to other non-occasional words. Also occasional are words, like "table" or the phrase "elligible for voting" and what is called a 'pure' proper name "John", as well as the verb "stand" and others. One may at best note the difference in the DEGREE OF OCCASIONALITY and the difference in the degree of the dependence of referential function upon context and situation. Being a general property of expressions of natural language, occasionality should not be classified as a defect in the communicative function of the language. From a certain point of view, it is even an asset, for it enables one to employ a given expression in a wide range of circumstances. Occasionality is not a property of word meaning, it is not governed by changes in the usage of the term, by changes which depend upon new circumstances. It does, however, concern USE and depends upon changes which occur within the REFERENTIAL FUNCTION. Thus, the word "I" may refer to different persons, according to its use, whereas its meaning, that is its usage, is — within certain limits of time and space — constant in a given language. The rule by which the word ordinarily refers to the person who employs it, applies to various uses.

The same applies to the sentence "The emperor is naked". The sentence is occasional because it can speak about different persons, and at times it speaks about no one. The word "emperor", within the sentence, may refer to various persons, it may mention, point out, identify them or it may indicate and mention no one. But the meaning of the sentence "The emperor is naked", or the meaning of the word "emperor", the usage of the expressions, remains unaltered under the changing circumstances of their use. Hence, truth-value is not connected with a given sentence solely because of such-and-such meaning, such-and-such usage of the sentence, but is connected with a given sentence also because of such-and-such use. The declarative sentence must not be identified with the proposition. When the statement "The emperor is naked" is used so that it speaks about no one and does not make an assertion, it does not, nevertheless, cease being a declarative sentence. It is not, however, a proposition, for truth-value does not apply to it. With this relativization, we need not, however, renounce the LAW OF EXCLUDED MIDDLE. True, in a given meaning a sentence may be true or false or it may be neither the one nor the other; but with an additional relativization with regard to a given use, it turns out to be either only true or only false, which fact depends on the actual state of affairs, or else the question of its truth-value does not arise.

Thus, analysis of the use of expressions leads to the following conclusions. It should not be said that a given expression is, e.g. a sentence, or even that it is a sentence in a given language and in a given meaning, or usage. This kind of relativization is not adequate. It must be added that it is so because of a given use. Briefly: expressions ARE NOT sentences, but are sometimes used as sentences. The same applies to the classifications of types of sentences. The same expression may be used as a declarative sentence, or, e.g., as an imperative sentence; also, at one time as a term and at other times as a sentence. Declarative sentences must not be identified with propositions: I can employ a declarative sentence as a proposition, but I do not have to. In the same manner, I can at times employ a term or an interrogative sentence. And finally comes the truth-value problem. It applies to an expression with regard to its use, such use namely which in the given case turns a sentence into an assertion.

### 7.    USE OF EXPRESSIONS AND FUNCTIONAL LOGICAL SEMIOTICS OF NATURAL LANGUAGE

By means of examples I tried to demonstrate wherein lies the essential aspect of a FUNCTIONAL approach to analysis within the scope of logical semiotics of natural language. The examples pertained only to some problems, that is to selected questions in term classification, further they concerned the problem of distinguishing the latter from proper names on the one hand and from descriptions on the other and, finally, of distinguishing expressions which are not sentences from sentences, and the classification of the latter, especially with regard to purported identification of declarative sentences with propositions. In each of these instances it was shown that absolute division or distinction ought to give way to relative distinction. For the characteristic situation of natural language is that a given expression may appear in various roles, depending on its use. Language is not, therefore, composed of mutually exclusive classes of expressions, such as terms and sentences, and among terms — empty, singular and general terms, or proper names and descriptions, and among sentences — declarative, interrogative and imperative sentences. A given expression is not so much such-and-such, for example, definite description, as in certain cases it had been used as such-and-such in such-and-such respect and in such-and-such degree. It seems that this phenomenon is more general in character. It may be extended beyond the scope of the examples analysed here. Hence, it may be discovered in the distinction between genuine NAMES and ONOMATOIDS, i.e. names of abstract entities, in the distinction among grammatical PARTS OF SPEECH and among PARTS OF SENTENCES, hence within the scope of SYNTACTIC relations, etc. (Such relations are also noted within the structure of a single word as occurring between its etymological members.)

In the analysis made here, I devoted my attention chiefly to the USE OF AN EXPRESSION. I think that it is the most essential, if not the central, aspect of the FUNCTIONAL approach to the LOGICAL THEORY OF NATURAL LANGUAGE. This by no means indicates a retreat from the meaning of expressions, from usage. On the contrary, it must be borne in mind that there are certain essential relations between use and usage. For when I encounter the Polish expression "*dwukilowy jacht*", I can decide only by analysing its use, whether it means "a yacht with two keels" or "a model (of a yacht) weighing two kilograms" (the confusion arises only in Polish where the adjective "*dwukilowy*" can equally well mean one and the other). Thus, USE serves to establish USAGE. It must also be borne in mind that relativization with regard to use is complementary in relation to relativization with regard to the meaning of the word; it occurs within the scope of the second. That is, a given expression may be used in such-and-such a use, only when it appears in such-and-such a meaning (usage). Thus, there is no underestimation of meaning. The point I wish to make is that relativization only with regard to meaning, which may be sometimes adequate in pure semantics and also in descriptive semiotics of artificial language, gives a static image when we confine ourselves to it in the analysis of natural language: it discloses the expressions of that language as isolated lexical items and fails to disclose the actual functioning of words, phrases and sentences in language context and in extralinguistic situation.

Consideration of the use of expressions does not shift the direction of language analysis but is a step forward in enriching it. Consequently, I would not wish to have the things I said understood in the following manner: "The classification of terms into empty, singular and general ones is a mistake; distinction between proper names and descriptions is a mistake; distinction between sentences and non-sentences is a mistake." I do not assert this. However, I do think that the classifications or distinctions mentioned here are, as far as natural language is concerned, more superficial because they are less functional; the characteristics pointed out in the examples probe deeper into the nature of that language since they are more functional. The traditional ones have a reason for existence because they construct certain ideal types of kinds of expressions. This idealization is useful not only for didactic reasons, since it makes typology possible, typology understood as an arrangement of concrete acts of speech with regard to the degree of intensity of properties occurring in it. In this sense, the traditional classifications and characteristics were the point of reference of our analysis, a sort of springboard. For example, since Russell has established the meaning of the term "definite description", I was able to say that a given expression may be used as more or less descriptive in character. Hence, in studies on natural language one cannot do without those traditional principles. But I think they are not sufficient. On the other hand, in the construction of artificial languages they are not only necessary but sometimes sufficient.

Logical semiotics of natural language makes other demands on the researcher than does logical semiotics of artificial language. In the former, as I have tried to make clear so many times, it is necessary to take the use of expressions into consideration. The importance of that requirement is closely related to a certain characteristic property of natural language, to which I drew attention in passing: that by the very nature of things this language is occasional. That explains why in semiotic analysis relativization is becoming so important with regard to language context of the expression analysed and to extralinguistic situation in which it was used, hence relativization with regard to use. Without it we would have to classify the majority of the expressions of that language as incomplete and hence faulty in the logical sense. That verdict will be passed by those analysts who rest satisfied with relating an expression to its meaning. I am afraid that such a verdict would be unjust. It would be based on the failure to understand the manner in which a natural language functions. Its expressions are not supposed to play their representative, communicative, expressive and emotive role alone. They can do so only in a group, together with their linguistic environment, and together with extralinguistic situation. That is the normal state of affairs. A normal state of affairs should not be treated as a fault. It would be wiser to accept the fact that it is so and to draw appropriate conclusions.

I think that the acceptance of the use of expressions, which constitutes the foundation of the functional analysis of natural language, is precisely this kind of conclusion, and a very important one. The examples I have discussed here do not exhaust all the possibilities of the functional approach to the logical theory of that class of languages. They do not even exhaust the possibilities which are connected with the analysis of use; and, after all, functional analysis does not stop at the study of use. Thus, for instance, I had no time to mention the fact that the consideration of the use of an expression leads to further promising distinctions and character-istics. One may distinguish, among others, such aspects of the expression as the primary and secondary conceptual content symbolized, i.e. presented and evoked; the propositional attitudes (with regard to these), expressed and evoked; emotions and conative attitudes expressed and evoked; the emotional tone; the emotions and attitudes revealed; other kinds of effects; the purpose. One may further distinguish the cognitive and non-cognitive elements, etc.[30] I shall only make here the general remark that the study of the use of expressions may help fill the gap which is evident in analysis in the field of the logical theory of natural language as usually limited to the study of its representative functions. It may enrich them by giving proper consideration to EXPRESSIVE, EMOTIVE, PERFORMATIVE and OTHER FUNCTIONS.[31] Based on the consideration of the use of an expression, functional logical analysis of natural language is, by its nature, a SEMIOTIC analysis and not only a SEMANTIC analysis, while the traditional logical theory of language was confined mainly to semantics.

This is a separate and important problem which ought to be developed. Although this cannot be done here, it can neither be completely ignored. When I analysed the semantic function of an expression with regard to its use, then by the same I introduced pragmatic problems into those considerations. The same occurs within the scope of the study of syntactic relations. I think that the ADDITION OF THE PRAGMATIC FACTOR IS A NECESSARY CONDITION OF A FUNCTIONAL ANALYSIS OF NATURAL LANGUAGE. Logical theories of artificial languages may at times do without pragmatic

[30]   Cf. Frankena, William K., "Some Aspects of Language"; and: "Cognitive and Noncognitive", in the volume *Language, Thought and Culture*, ed. by Paul Henle (Ann Arbor, The University of Michigan Press, 1958), Chapter V and VI, pp. 121-172.
[31]   Cf. Austin, L.J., "Performative — Constative", in the volume *Philosophy and Ordinary Language* (see footnote 2), pp. 22-54.

relations. On the other hand, a logical theory of natural language would be crippled without pragmatics. Metaphors and personifications of the kind: "the term designates something", "the sentence speaks about something", which are so common in the description of natural language, always imply the man who employs that term or sentence. Thus, if an analysis concerned with the use of expressions helps to decode that metaphor or personification, if the true relation between semantics or syntax and pragmatics is discovered, and if a way is paved for reducing semantic or syntactic problems to pragmatics, then this fact is worthy of emphasis and of a penetrating study. I think that this is the field where a solution is to be sought to the problem of the specific character of natural language and accordingly to the specific traits of its semiotics.

It now remains to me to apologize to the logicians who "hope to replace philosophizing by reckoning",[32] for not having fulfilled

[32] Ryle, "Ordinary Language", p. 125: "The appeal to what we do and do not say, or can and cannot say, is often stoutly resisted by the protagonists of one special doctrine, and stoutly pressed by its antagonists. This doctrine is the doctrine that philosophical disputes can and should be settled by formalizing the warring theses. A theory is formalized when it is translated out of the natural language (untechnical, technical or semi-technical), in which it was originally excogitated, into a deliberately constructed notation, the notation, perhaps of *Principia Mathematica*. The logic of a theoretical position can, it is claimed, be regularized by stretching its non-formal concepts between the topic-neutral logical constants whose conduct in inferences is regulated by set drills. Formalization will replace logical perplexities by logical problems amenable to known and teachable procedures of calculation (...). Of those to whom this, the formalizer's dream, appears a mere dream [I am one of them], some maintain that the logic of the statements of scientists, lawyers, historians and bridge-players cannot in principle be adequately represented by the formulae of formal logic. The so-called logical constants do indeed have, partly by deliberate prescription, their scheduled logical powers; but the non-formal expressions both of everyday discourse and of technical discourse have their own unscheduled logical powers, and these are not reducible without remainder to those of the carefully wired marionettes of formal logic. The title of a novel by A.E.W. Mason *They Wouldn't be Chessmen* applies well to both the technical and the untechnical expressions of professional and daily life. This is not to say that the examination of the logical behaviour of the terms of non-notational discourse is not assisted by studies in formal logic. Of course it is. So may chess-playing assist generals, though waging campaigns cannot be replaced by playing games of chess. I do not want here to thrash out this important issue. I want only to show that resistance to one sort of appeal to ordinary language

in these remarks what Gilbert Ryle called "the formalizer's dream",[33] a thing Ajdukiewicz cautioned against when he prophesied, and was partly right, that after he is dead, participants in logical conferences, instead of talking like normal people, would cover blackboards with formulae and symbols. This was not necessary here. Besides I incline toward the opinion that the logic of a natural language, and even the logic of the statements of scientists, cannot be adequately represented by means of formal logic.[34] It does not mean, however, that I think that reflections in the style of Church,[35] who tries to make an artificial language a model for natural languages, are fruitless. But studies within the scope of functional logical semiotics of natural languages neither start nor end here.

In conclusion, to banish the spectre of banality which, it may be, haunts my reasonings, I shall repeat that we should not fear to force open doors or to rediscover America as long as there is someone to whom the door is tightly shut and to whom America is not yet discovered.

Warsaw, June 1966.


## SUMMARY

0. *Introduction.* — The term 'functional', which occurs in the title of this paper, is neither synonymous nor equivalent with the same term as used by linguists. But the extensions of these two terms overlap.

---

ought to involve championing the programme of formalization. 'Back to ordinary language' can be (but often is not) the slogan of those who have awoken from the formalizer's dream. This slogan, so used, should be repudiated only by those who hope to replace philosophizing by reckoning."

[33]  See footnote 32.
[34]  See footnote 32.
[35]  *Cf.* Church, Alonzo, "The Need for Abstract Entities in Semantic Analysis", *Proceedings of the American Academy of Arts and Sciences*, No. 1 (1951). Also *cf.* Copi, Irwing M., "Artificial Languages", in the anthology *Language, Thought and Culture* (see footnote 30), pp. 96-120.

1. *Use of an Expression.* — What is the functional approach to the logical semiotics of natural language concerned with? It is concerned with how a given expression is used. I mean thereby a certain use of an expression, and not its usefulness. Moreover, we are mainly concerned with the use of an expression as an instrument, but we shall also consider its use as an organ, ingredient, or designated object. The distinction between use and usage is important. When I speak of use I mean the following situation. A given expression, be it 'dog', has its established meaning in a given language, and in accordance with that meaning I may use that word so that it should refer to my dog Trot. Such a use is determined by a context and by an extralinguistic situation. I may, of course, use the word 'dog' many a time. Now the class of the tokens of the expression 'dog', each used with reference to Trot, determines a certain use of that expression. Such a use of this word is in agreement with its usage, with the use of that word common in a given language, with the linguistic practice established for the word 'dog'. The term 'usage' may be considered a synonym of the term 'meaning' in one of the senses of the latter. When saying that the functional approach to the logical semiotics of natural language is concerned with how a given expression is used I mean above all the use of such an expression.

2. *Use of an Expression and the Classification of Terms with regard to the Number of Designata.* — Names may be general, singular, and empty, according to the number of designata they have. But this classification does not adequately reflect the state of things in natural language. The names thus classified are separated from their context, and it is only their dictionary meaning that is taken into account, whereas a functional analysis ought to take into account the fact that the same word may be used in different ways, according to the extralinguistic situation and the context. The word 'dog' is being used sometimes as a general, sometimes as a singular, and sometimes as an empty name, and sometimes so that the problem of its generality, singularity, and emptiness does not arise at all. The general, singular, and empty nature of a name is a relative property, connected with a given use of a given word.

3. *Use of an Expression and the Classification of Terms According to their Singular or General Intention.* — Nominal expressions are also classified according to their meaning intention by making a distinction between those to which we ascribe a singular intention ('Zeus'), those to which we ascribe a general intention ('centaur'), and those to which we ascribe an empty intention. But here too the use, which depends on the context and the extralinguistic situation, imparts to the same expression different intentions on different occasions. For instance, 'my brother' is an expression with a general intention, when examined in isolation as a dictionary item, but in the sentence "This book was given to me by my brother" the expression acquires a singular intention.

4. *Use of an Expression and Classifications of Terms According to their Subjective or Predicative Character.* — Since Aristotle a distinction has been made between individual and general names. The former (e.g., 'Socrates') may occur only as the subject of an elementary singular proposition, while the latter (e.g., 'philosopher') may occur as predicate. But the functional analysis of words occurring in definite contexts and definite extralinguistic situations reveals that these properties are associated with the use of expressions and that the same word may be used in either of these two functions.

5. *Use of an Expression and the Distinction: Proper Name — Name — Description.* — Since Frege and Russell a distinction has been made between proper names, names, definite descriptions, and indefinite descriptions. But from the point of view of the functional analysis of words we do not have here to do with mutually exclusive classes of expressions, but with different uses of expressions. Moreover, each of these uses is subject to gradation, so that a given expression can be used to a greater or a lesser extent as a description, a name, or a proper name, and also in a mixed function. This is why a given expression ought to be classified as used in a given respect in a given way and in a given degree.

6. *Use of an Expression and the Sentence.* — The logical tradition dating back to Mill, Frege, and Russell treats language so as if it consisted solely or mainly of names. This is contrary to facts as far as natural language is concerned, since the basic functions of that language are performed by sentences. This is why something I would term 'denominalization' is an essential item in the programme to make the semiotic analysis of natural language more functional. The distinctions into sentences and non-sentences, and also that into declarative, interrogative, and imperative sentences, lose their absolute character when examined from the point of view of the use of expression (i.e., in conformity with that programme). Declarative sentences ought not to be identified with propositions: I may use a declarative sentence to express a proposition, but I need not do so. When I use such a sentence so that it does not refer to anyone and does not serve to construct an assertion, it does not cease to be declarative sentence, but is not a proposition and the problem whether it is true or false does not arise at all.

7. *Use of Expressions and Functional Logical Semiotics of Natural Language.* — A given expression, when examined from the functional point of view, is not such-and-such, but happens to be used so-and-so in such-and-such respect, and in such-and-such degree. This is more general and can cover other examples than those discussed in the present paper. Relativization to use is something complementary to relativization to meaning, that is, to usage. Hence any disparagement of meaning is here quite out of question. The requirement that use be taken into consideration is closely associated with this that natural language by its very nature is occasional. This is why the relativization of the expressions examined to their linguistic context and the extralinguistic situation in which they occur is so important in semiotic analysis. Otherwise we would have to consider most expressions belonging to natural language as logically defective. Such a verdict would do injustice to natural language.

# MEANING AS AN INSTRUMENT

"Suppose that I ask 'What is the point of doing so-and-so?' For example, I ask Old Father William 'What is the point of standing on one's head?' He replies in the way we know. Then I follow this up with 'What is the point of balancing an eel on the end of one's nose?' And he explains. Now suppose I ask my third question, 'What is the point of doing ANYTHING — not anything in PARTICULAR, but just ANYTHING?' Old Father William would no doubt kick me downstairs without the option. But lesser men, raising this same question and finding no answer, would very likely commit suicide or join the Church. (Luckily, in the case of 'What is the meaning of a word?' the effects are less serious, amounting only to the writing of books)".

(J. L. Austin, "The Meaning of a Word").[1]

## 0. INTRODUCTION

The last sentence in the passage quoted from Austin might suggest that my intention is to write a book on the meaning of words. But the reader should not grow alarmed: it will be only a paper of moderate length. Neither do I intend to suggest in it one more theory of meaning. True, the title "Meaning as an Instrument" could imply that, since it refers to such concepts of meaning as those to be found in Wittgenstein's *Philosophical Investigations*,[2] somewhat

[1]  J. L. Austin, "The Meaning of a Word", in Charles E. Caton (ed.), *Philosophy and Ordinary Language* (Urbana, University of Illinois Press, 1963), 5.
[2]  L. J. Wittgenstein, *Philosophical Investigations* (Oxford, 1953).

earlier in Dewey's *Experience and Nature*,[3] Mauthner's *Beiträge zu einer Kritik der Sprache*,[4] in Peirce's pragmaticism,[5] and in James's pragmatism,[6] and much earlier, in the 13th century, in the writings of William of Sherwood, Peter of Spain, and Lambert of Auxerre, which speak of suppositions of various kinds, of copulation and appellation as dependent on use, in the 4th century in St. Augustine's *Principia Dialecticae*,[7] namely in his concept of force (*vis*), and finally in antiquity in the instrumental variations of the *lekton*[8] of the Stoics. Such semiotic concepts as the functional approach to language analysis and the approach to speech as an instrument of action, concepts which seem to be most modern, are to be found in all those works. This is true, but in all the authors quoted above it is LANGUAGE which occurs as an instrument, whereas I, as the title of this paper indicates, want to analyse the instrumental nature of MEANING.

In this connection certain explanations must be made at the very beginning. First, I am concerned with the meaning of expressions in natural language, although I am convinced that my analysis can be extended so as to cover other languages as well. Secondly, I am concerned with expressions interpreted broadly, in some cases as words and/or phrases, and in some cases as sentences and/or groups of sentences. Thirdly, which will appear later, I am not concerned with meaning in a single selected sense of the term, but with interpretations of that term which may vary from case to case. A special mention is due to the term 'instrument', which also occurs in the title. It is used, of course, metaphorically, and not as a scholarly term. My point was to avoid a long title, and to have a title that would appeal to the reader. I do not know how far I have succeeded

[3] J. Dewey, *Experience and Nature* (Open Court Publishing Co., 1925).
[4] F. Mauthner, *Beiträge zu einer Kritik der Sprache* (Leipzig, 1923).
[5] Ch. S. Peirce, *Collected Papers*, Vols. 1-8 (Cambridge, Mass., 1958-60); see also, by the same author, "What Pragmatism Is" (1905) in *Values in a Universe of Change: Selected Writings of Ch. S. Peirce* (Stanford, Cal., 1958).
[6] W. James, *Collected Papers and Reviews*, ed. R. B. Perry.
[7] St. Augustine, *Principia Dialecticae* (384) in *Basic Writings of St. Augustine*, Whitney J. Oates (ed.) (New York, Random House Inc.).
[8] Diogenes Laertius 7, 55-57; also Sextus Empiricus, *Adversus Mathematicos*, 8, 11-12; Plutarch, *On the Contradictions of the Stoics*, 1037 d.

in that, but I realize what is the price I have to pay for that figure of speech. This is why I now have to explain at length what I mean (actually it is something which is quite trivial and well-known). Now the concept of meaning, or, should anyone prefer to have it that way, the term MEANING, is used in many various semiotic analyses intended to answer various questions concerned with the theory of language. In this sense meaning is used as an instrument. It is known otherwise that the success of a job done by means of instruments largely depends on how well a given instrument is adapted to a given task. Some operations can best be performed with a hammer, some with an axe, and some with a saw. When I alternately use a hammer, an axe, and a saw, no one objects that I am inconsistent if I do not use the hammer in all the cases. This has led to the temptation to look at the instruments of semiotic analysis, in our case at meaning, from an analogous point of view. Perhaps I am naive and carefree, since I expose myself to the objection of eclecticism. But nevertheless I shall make a step in that direction, my consolation being that to be accused of eclecticism is better than to be accused of absurdity. In Austin's paper quoted above it is said at the very outset that questions about what is the meaning of a word or a sentence in general — are examples of absurdity. Unfortunately, I have to ask myself such questions in the analysis that follows. Such being the case, I am not inclined to be bothered much with the issue of eclecticism. This, as can be seen, is a negative consolation, but it is better than none.

## 1. THEORIES OF MEANING

My recent, though scanty and superficial, reading in the history of semiotics has left me with the impression that — at least in the European tradition — the last 25 centuries of semiotic studies have been dominated by the tendency to reject earlier theories whenever they were found unsatisfactory, rather than to improve them whenever they were found to contain a grain of truth. This is, of course, just a vague impression, and exceptions would be easy to quote. But I still claim that generally criticism prevailed over good will that would consist in bringing out the strong point of earlier theories. And yet it is a striking fact that those earlier theories abound in excellent ideas and positive results. (Parenthetically speaking, it would be worth while to study the Middle Ages, little investigated so far, which would require assistance on the part of classical philologists, experts in Low Latin and trained in philosophy and logic.)

This has given birth to the intention to run against the trend and to look at the earlier theories, whether fairly recent, or old, or quite ancient, with a more favourable eye and to find out whether that great treasury of wisdom does not hold, in addition to gems that are now purely historical in value, things that would still be useful.

In his "Notes on the Theory of Reference"[9] Quine says that what is vaguely termed SEMANTICS actually covers two different fields, namely the THEORY OF MEANING and the THEORY OF REFERENCE. He would even be inclined to restrict the term SEMANTICS to the former theory, which is concerned with meaning itself, synonymy (*i.e.*, the identity of meanings), signification (*i.e.*, having a meaning), analyticity (*i.e.*, truth based on meaning alone), and — indirectly — entailment (*i.e.*, the analyticity of implication). The theory of meaning gives rise to more troubles than does the theory of reference, and Quine is not the only person (*cf.* his "Two Dogmas of Empiricism"[10] and "The Problem of Meaning in Linguistics"[11]) to complain of the sad state of that field of semiotics, yet it cannot be denied that the problems of meaning have formed the core of the science of signs since the 5th century B.C. It must also be added that Quine's interpretation of the theory of meaning is rather narrow and logically oriented. Should we take into consideration the semiotic interests of philosophers, linguists, art historians, and representatives of other disciplines which are directly or indirectly connected with semiotics, we would see that the theory of meaning

---

[9]  W.v.O. Quine, *From a Logical Point of View: Nine Logico-philosophical Essays*, 2nd ed. (New York, 1963), p. 130.
[10]  *Ibid.*, p. 20.
[11]  *Ibid.*, p. 47.

expands signally by absorbing many a problem of the theory of reference, for instance naming, designating, denoting, extension, truth, *etc.* It is in its expanded form that the theory of meaning, and in fact the theory of both meaning and reference, occurs in the history of semiotics. And when I shall hereafter refer to the theories of meaning I shall refer to them in that broad sense, lacking precision, but many a time documented in the history of philosophy. Obviously, this is not to be construed against the differentiation made by Quine: it is an indisputable fact that meaning is not the same as reference, and hence, with a more rigorous and precise use of terms, the theory of meaning and the theory of reference are two different things.

The ideas developed since the Sophists about the broadly interpreted meaning of expressions amount to hundreds of different theories. They could be classified in various ways, but in most cases such classifications would be neither disjunct nor exhaustive. But this is not important at the moment.

First, a distinction can be made between the THEORIES OF THE MEANING OF A *de facto* SINGLE WORD and the THEORIES OF THE MEANING OF A *de facto* SENTENCE. The qualification '*de facto*' is due to this that the authors of both groups of theories were convinced that they were explaining in general what every expression of a language, *i.e.*, both a word and a sentence, means. Thus the ancient, except perhaps for the Stoics, probably all mediaeval philosophers, all the 16th and 17th century authors, and later Johnson and Mill, and still later Frege and also partly Husserl, Meinong, Russell in his early period of work, and Wittgenstein, but only as the author of *Tractatus Logico-Philosophicus* — all of them *de facto* constructed theories of the meaning of proper names and/or names, and tried, with varying success, to extend them to all linguistic expressions, above all to sentences. In doing so they were motivated by the belief that the meaning of a sentence, as a whole constructed from individual words, is a function of the meanings of its components.

The second trend has, in my opinion, its forerunner in Berkeley as the author of certain formulations, which, though scanty and scattered over various places in *The Principles of Human Know-ledge*,[12] nevertheless have the value of precedents. Contrary to his earlier book, *Philosophical Commentaries*,[13] in which he assumed after Locke[14] that words mean only because in the mind of the speaker they replace ideas, a couple of years later Berkeley started formulating loose remarks that were critical of his earlier opinions, and also of those of Locke. He claimed that words can have meaning even if they do not occur in lieu of ideas; this applies, for instance, to the *syncategoremata*, but not to them alone. Their signification is due to the fact that they replace SPIRITS or ACTIVITIES. For instance, a particle replaces an operation of the mind. And when I say *Melampus is an animal*, I have to do with one idea, and not with two. But if a person says to me *Aristotle asserted the same*, the signification of that sentence is not any idea; its meaning is to develop in me respect for, and approval of, the opinions expressed. This shows that Berkeley after a very long interval referred to the tendency represented by the Stoics and revised the then current opinion that the problems of meanings of expressions can be confined to the relation between the name and the *nominatum*. He also attacked Locke's concept of private language, which was also later done with passion by Wittgenstein in *Philosophical Investiga-tions*.[15] This path was followed by Bentham, Humboldt, Peirce, James, Dewey, Mauthner, Wittgenstein (as the author of *Philo-sophical Investigations*, to be contrasted with his *Tractatus*), and representatives of logical empiricism, that is, the Vienna Circle with Carnap. As they developed the new approach and made it more radical, they came to construct theories of the meaning of the sentence as a whole, and tried to cover with them all expressions of a language, and hence the individual names as well. In so doing they started from the belief that the meaning of a single word is a function of the meaning of the sentence in which that word occurs. On the whole, these endeavours to extend the theory of meanings

[12]   G. Berkeley, *The Principles of Human Knowledge* (1710).
[13]   G. Berkeley, *Philosophical Commentaries* (1707-8).
[14]   J. Locke, *Essay Concerning Human Understanding*, Book III (1690).
[15]   *Cf.* N. Kretzmann, "History of Semantics", in *The Encyclopedia of Philo-sophy*, Vol. 7 (New York, The Macmillan Co. and The Free Press, 1967), 382-4.

of statements to all expressions, not fully satisfactory as they are, yield better results than the endeavours in the opposite direction, that is those which extend the concept of the meanings of names to sentences.

This classification of the theories of meaning coincides in part with the non-disjunct classification in which distinction is made between the REFERENTIAL concepts of meaning on the one hand, and the CONTEXTUAL, or OPERATIONAL, concepts of meaning on the other.[16] The former partly correspond to the theories of the meaning of names, and the latter to those of the meaning of sentences. In the former, the meaning of an expression is seen to be either in an extralinguistic referent of that expression, that is in the *designatum, denotatum, descriptum, nominatum,* or *denominatum,* or in the relation between the expression and its referent. In the latter, meaning is identified with the use or the usage of an expression, especially of a sentence analysed in its linguistic and situational context; in this connection language is treated as an instrument, and speech, as a kind of operation performed by means of linguistic instruments, that is as a language game. Both groups of these theories, but especially the first, are strongly differentiated, which is proved by the classification to be discussed next.[17]

According to this classification, which again is neither disjunct nor exhaustive, there are three types of theories of meaning: REFERENTIAL theories, IDEATIONAL theories, and STIMULUS-RESPONSE theories, on the one hand, and the above-mentioned OPERATIONAL theories, on the other. The former group is classed as traditional, the latter, as modern.

The REFERENTIAL theories are in principle patterned on the relation between a proper name and that person or object which bears that name. According to those theories, AN EXPRESSION HAS A MEANING amounts to AN EXPRESSION REFERS TO A CERTAIN THING, and its meaning is interpreted either as that thing, or as that relation,

---

[16]   *Cf.* S. Ullmann, *Semantics, An Introduction to the Science of Meaning* (Oxford, 1967), 55-67.
[17]   *Cf.* W. P. Alston, "Meaning", in *The Encyclopedia of Philosophy*, Vol. 5, (New York, The Macmillan Co. and the Free Press 1967), 233-41.

generally termed reference. Not to speak of very many ancient (Epicureans) and mediaeval philosophers, also Meinong (to some extent) and Russell in his early works held that rather naive opinion that, generally speaking, what is termed referent is the meaning of an expression. Mill's distinction between connotation and denotation, developed by Frege, resulted in a modification of that view: meaning came to be interpreted as connotation, that is the set of the properties which is characteristic of all the *designata* of a given name and "expressed" by that name (as Frege put it at first) or "connoted" by it (as was the later formulation). This conception gave rise to certain difficulties: it departed from its own starting point, since it denied connotation to genuine proper names; further, it required the assumption that every word has its referent, which is particularly troublesome in the case of syncategorematic expressions; and, finally, it required specific acrobatics if it was to cover sentences.

The IDEATIONAL theories, most common in antiquity and in the Middle Ages, in modern times found their typical representative in John Locke, who wrote: "The use [...] of words is to be sensible marks of ideas; and the ideas they stand for are their proper and immediate signification."[18] The origin of these ideas goes far back. Aristotle[19] said that words are natural signs (*semeia*) of mental modifications and can refer not only to things (a 'something'), but also to 'qualifications', 'substance of a qualification', and 'quality' or *modus*. The Stoics asserted that a sign (*to semainon*) has its counterpart not only in a physical entity (*to tynchanon*), but also in a non-physical *lekton*, which in turn corresponds to a logical idea (*logiken thantasan*). They identified those *lekta* with potential thoughts or intentions of the speakers, and the intentions were associated by them with the tasks and actions performed by means of speech.[20] Epicurus thought our impressions, ideas and emotions connected with sensory objects to be the final counterparts of expressions (*hypotetagmena*), and his followers pointed to *typos*, *i.e.*, the general idea of an object, associated with a given word in

[18]   *Cf.* footnote 14.
[19]   Aristotle, *Categories*, Chap. 5; *Sophistical Refutations*, Chap. 22.
[20]   *Cf.* Sextus Empiricus, *Adversus Mathematicos*, 8, 11-12.

the act of *prolepsis*,[21] as such a direct counterpart (*to protos hypotetagmenon*). In the Middle Ages, St.Augustine adopted the analogues of the Stoic *lekton* in the form of *dicibile*, *i.e.*, that which is perceived in the word by the mind, and not by the ear, and *dictio*, *i.e.*, the result of a word in our mind.[22] Likewise, Abélard[23] said that meaning consists in constituting a concept. In modern times, similar opinions were represented by Bacon[24] and Hobbes[25] even before Locke. The former said that words are images of thoughts, the latter, that words are names not only and not always of things, but always of some mental entities. The same idea is repeated in Arnauld's *Port Royal Logic*[26] with the modification that among the counterparts of words he distinguished individual ideas in the case of proper names and/or individual names, and general ideas in the case of general names. He also mentioned that words can signify not only ideas, but also things and the modes and objects of our thoughts. Thus he either accepted the referential theory, at least in part, or believed ideas to be direct counterparts of expressions, and things to be their indirect counterparts. More important still, he introduced the distinction between comprehension and extension, which in Hamilton recur as intension and extension, and in Mill and Frege as connotation and denotation. Those ideational conceptions sometimes have a more objective tinge, when the idea comes close to a general entity, an *universale*, and sometimes a more subjective tinge, when a certain state of mind is concerned. In this connection, in some cases the approach is less psychological, when it is claimed that expressions have counterparts in types of thoughts, or in potential thoughts, or in intentional objects[27] (then the

[21]   *Cf.* Diogenes Laertius, 10, 33.
[22]   *Cf.* footnote 7.
[23]   P.Abélard, *Logica "Ingredientibus"*, ed. B.Geyer.
[24]   F.Bacon, *Novum Organum*.
[25]   T.Hobbes, *Human Nature* (1650) and *Elementa Philosophiae, sectio prima "De Corpore"* (1655).
[26]   A.Arnauld, *Port Royal Logic* (1662).
[27]   For instance E.Husserl, *Logische Untersuchungen* (1900), and in particular his essay *Expression and Meaning*. In Poland, Roman Ingarden. Husserl was criticized by A.Meinong, *Über Annahmen* (1902), and *Über Gegenstandstheorie* (1904).

conception becomes programmatically anti-psychological), and in some cases it is clearly psychological, when actual mental experiences of the speaker are meant.[28] In the latter case, since the ideas of which a thought is formed are directly accessible to the experiencing person only, the language expressing those ideas becomes a private language (Locke). In the case of psychologically oriented ideational theories we have to do with a form of the view termed associationism, which when applied to the theory of meaning was brilliantly criticized by Ajdukiewicz.[29] On the other hand, the non-psychological and objective variations, together with the phenomenological conceptions of meaning, are near the border-line between the ideational and the referential theories, since they include elements of both categories. The phenomenological theories might even form a separate class. As mentioned above, the classifications discussed here are neither disjunct nor exhaustive. There is nothing strange in this fact: the terms REFERENTIAL THEORY and IDEATIONAL THEORY are rather vague, and the conceptions subject to classifications are neither pure nor homogeneous.

The third group of views on the meaning of expressions is formed of the STIMULUS-RESPONSE theories. They are behaviouristic in nature. In their more primitive variation they state that the meaning of an expression is that situation in which that expression has been uttered, and the listener's response to that utterance as a stimulus.[30] In their more refined form (Ch. Osgood, Ch. Morris) the theory emphasizes the response to the stimulus, while the stimulus situation is disregarded. The starting point here was an analysis of indexical signs, or natural signs, as opposed to conventional symbols. The modification consists in that a definite response to an utterance ceases to be considered the meaning of that utterance; it

---

[28]   *E.g.*, J. Bentham.
[29]   K. Ajdukiewicz, "O znaczeniu wyrażeń" [On the Meaning of Expressions], in *Język i poznanie, wybór pism* [Language and Cognition, Selected Writings], Vol, I (Warsaw, 1960), 102-36.
[30]   L. Bloomfield, *Language* (New York, 1933). These views were developed and corrected by Ch. Osgood, *Method and Theory in Experimental Psychology* (New York, 1953), and Ch. Morris, *Signs, Language, and Behavior* (Englewood Cliffs, 1946).

is replaced in that rôle by the type of response, *i.e.*, a regular and potential response. This theory is, as it were, a behaviourist, external aspect of associationism: the association of thoughts and/or ideas is replaced by a relationship between acts or types of behaviour. In both cases, however, the underlying idea is that of certain psychological and physiological regularities, with the proviso that the latter prevail in the case of the stimulus-response theory. The latter makes a bridge to the operational theory, which also is based on certain (active) forms of human behaviour.

The OPERATIONAL theories, the pedigree of which has been outlined in the Introduction, on the whole do not hypostatize meaning and do not turn it into a separate fictive and abstract entity, whether ideal or real. This fact distinguishes them from the theories discussed before, since the latter might suggest that when we have to do with language we come to face two, three, or even more, separate entities: one of these might be the word *dog*, the second, a definite dog, *e.g.*, Trot, and the third, the meaning of the word *dog*. Wittgenstein's recommendations in his *Philosophical Investigations* were: "Don't look for the meaning, look for the use." "Look at the sentence as an instrument, and at its sense as its employment."[31] What he was concerned with was the use of words, or rather sentences, not only for the purpose of information, but for the purpose of action through language, such action being conceived in its broadest sense. The agent is the speaker, and it is on him that attention is focussed. Austin[32] added to this theory by making a distinction between three types of acts of linguistic behaviour: locutionary, illocutionary, perlocutionary. The first is the act of uttering expressions. The third consists in the consequences of an utterance, for instance, the fact that the hearer calmed down, grew alarmed, or started some action. The second is implicitly inherent in the utterance itself and constitutes its meaning, determined by the notoriously repeated use of a given expression, or the performance (regular in this sense) of the locutionary act always in specified circumstances. It is a debatable point in this new theory whether

[31] *Cf.* footnote 2 (I, 241).
[32] J. L. Austin, *How to Do Things with Words* (Oxford, 1962).

the illocutionary act is connected with a given locutionary act, *i.e.*, a given type of utterance, on the strength of actual regularities, or on the strength of potential unwritten rules — by analogy to the rules laid down and explicitly formulated for artificial languages. As is the case of most key concepts in the theories of meaning, that illocutionary act remains something mysterious. Intuitive interpretations tend to link it with the use of a sentence rather than a single word in the rôle of an instrument that serves to perform actions in a given sphere of activity or language game. Hence that potential illocutionary act is linked with the set of the conditions imposed by the context; that act is never performed in isolation, in a dictionary. (A similar idea was advanced in the Middle Ages in connection with the concept of supposition of an expression. The representatives of *logica moderna* — its modernity being not very new, as it dates from the 13th century — considered the problem whether the words occurring in sentences in a closed book have any supposition. Common sense suggested the answer in the negative, but some philosophers would not accept such a decision, because that would deny the truth of such a statement as *God exists*.[33]) Concerning the concept of potential illocutionary act it may be said that while that concept cannot easily be used to explain the concept of meaning of expressions, it can more easily be used to explain the concept of synonymy, especially of sentences;[34] in the latter case analysis is based on interchangeability *salva veritate*. This procedure, however, involves certain difficulties, first indicated by Frege,[35] and recently, very suggestively, by Quine.[36]

At any rate the operational theories made a step forward by linking the problem of the meaning of expressions with the conditions imposed by the context. This has been hailed by the linguists, who used to accuse logicians and philosophers of too isolationist tendencies in the analysis of language. Moreover, the

[33] *Cf.* footnote 15; p. 373.
[34] *Cf.* Alston, *op. cit.*, p. 239.
[35] G. Frege, *Über Sinn und Bedeutung* (for the English-language version see *Philosophical Writings of G. Frege*, ed. P. Geach and M. Black, Oxford, 1962)
[36] *Cf.* footnote 9; "Two Dogmas of Empiricism" and "The Problem of Meaning in Linguistics".

field of analysis has been broadened by the inclusion of the wide range of EMOTIVE MEANINGS, which has proved particularly fruitful in the field of ethics, aesthetics, literary theory, and art theory. These problems brought to the field of the theory of meaning, still more than previously, the issues of pragmatics, the third section of semiotics (after semantics and syntax). These issues could clearly be seen in Peirce and his predecessors and successors, and also in Wittgenstein and Morris.[37] They became obscured in the verifiability theories of meaning, e.g., in Carnap's works,[38] and in the falsifiability theories of meaning, e.g., in Popper's works,[39] since logical empiricists were mainly concerned with cognitive meaning, to analyse which they resorted to such semantic criteria as verifiability, confirmability, and testability. But discussions concerned with the emotive meaning of words and sentences, connected with expressing and evoking emotions and attitudes, revived the problem of the speaker and the listener. Since the time when Ogden and Richards took up again the old issues of the emotive and expressive force of language in their book *The Meaning of Meaning*,[40] and Moore[41] analysed the difference between what a sentence expresses, implies, and asserts, while Stevenson[42] analysed the nature of ethical judgments and terms and the difference between descriptive and emotive meaning, the pragmatic approach to semiotics has become usual in the logic and philosophy of natural language and has continued to manifest itself in the writings of the members of the Oxford group: e.g., Ryle,[43] Austin,[44] Strawson,[45] and also in

[37]    Ch. Morris, *Signs, Language, and Behavior* (New York, 1946).
[38]    R. Carnap, "Testability and Meaning" in *Philosophy of Science*, Vol. 3 (1936), No. 4; Vol. 4 (1937), No. 1. Idem, *Introduction to Semantics* (Cambridge, Mass., 1942). Idem, *Meaning and Necessity* (Chicago, 1947).
[39]    K. Popper, *Logik der Forschung* (1935).
[40]    C. K. Ogden and I. A. Richards, *The Meaning of Meaning* (London, 1923).
[41]    G. E. Moore, *Ethics* (1912); see also *The Philosophy of G. E. Moore*, ed. P. A. Schilpp (1942).
[42]    C. L. Stevenson, *Ethics and Language* (1944), and *Facts and Values* (1963).
[43]    G. Ryle, "Ordinary Language" and "The Theory of Meaning", both in *Philosophy and Ordinary Language*, ed. Ch. E. Caton (Urbana, 1963).
[44]    J. L. Austin, *cf.* footnote 32, see also "Performative-Constative", in Caton's anthology (*cf.* footnote 43).
[45]    P. F. Strawson, "On Referring", in Caton's anthology (*cf.* footnote 43).

the American school, as represented by Black,[46] Frankena,[47] and many others.[48]

This lengthy and boring, but still incomplete and superficial, review of the theories of meaning was needed by myself more than by the reader, and its objective was not so much to order the issues, which I have not achieved, but to confirm the following conclusion. Many of the striking differences between the views enumerated above are in fact less essential than it would seem at the first glance: frequently they are due rather to differences in formulations than in *de facto* differences of standpoints. Each group of these theories includes pertinent observations, based on self-evident empirical facts. Thus, it is true that we use language to speak about the external world. It is true that we use language to express our thoughts and other experiences. It is true that we learn language by training, with repeated responses to stimuli and unconditional and conditional reflexes. It is true that changes in meanings and evolutions of meanings are linked with associations of ideas. It is true also that language becomes speech in the course of human activities, and that language itself is a kind of activity and an instrument in the communication process. Many other examples of such correct observations could be added to this list. What then are the defects of those theories? They consist largely in simplifications, exaggerations, absolutizations, lack of toleration toward other views, and ambitions to arrive at too broad generalizations. Thus, for instance, although it is true that some expressions have their referents, which in some cases are real objects existing in extra-linguistic reality, it is not true that every expression has a referent and that it would lose meaning if it did not have one. In a word, the fact that a given theory explains well a certain group of phenomena does not imply that that theory can successfully explain every

[46] M. Black, "Saying and Disbelieving", in *Analysis*, Vol. 13, No. 2 (1952). *Idem*, "Some Questions About Emotive Meaning", in *Language and Philosophy* (Ithaca, N.Y., 1949).
[47] W. Frankena, "Cognitive and Noncognitive", in *Language, Thought, and Culture*, ed. P. Henle (Ann Arbor, Mich., 1958).
[48] *Cf.* W. P. Alston, "Emotive Meaning", in *The Encyclopedia of Philosophy*, Vol. 2 (New York, The Macmillan Co. and the Free Press, 1957), 486-93.

linguistic phenomenon, nor does it imply that a different theory is entirely false.

The case of Wittgenstein *qua* the author of *Tractatus Logico-Philosophicus*[49] and *qua* the author of *Philosophical Investigations* seems particularly instructive in that respect. He stated in his *Tractatus* that a sentence is a picture of reality such as we conceive it; it is a model of that reality. A newly encountered sentence is comprehended without explanations if it consists of known words. A sentence shows its sense. It must contain as many elements as there are in the state of things it portrays. This concept of sentence is based on a name, that is a simple sign, consiting of one word, employed in a sentence and standing for a simple object. That very simple object is the meaning of that name. But the name does not portray that object, since the function of portraying is an attribute of a combination of names only, that is of a sentence, which mirrors a configuration of objects. The conviction that simple unchanging objects exist is *a priori* in nature: it is a logical necessity resulting from the fact that sentences have definite meanings. A given way in which names are combined into a sentence tells us that analogous relations hold between simple objects in the world. Only tautologies and contradictions are not pictures of the world, but neither are they genuine sentences. Every sentence assumes the whole of a given language: to comprehend it one has to know not only all the objects connected with it, but also all the possible objects and all the possible states of things. In *Philosophical Investigations* Wittgenstein attacked himself and rejected all that he had published in *Tractatus*, including those things which were correct. He states that a sentence assumes a language game, which, however, is only a small fragment of language as a whole. The game consists in linking expressions with actions. When a bricklayer calls out *Bricks!* his assistant passes them on to him. The word in question, together with the situation in question, forms the said language game. But different language games have no traits in common, as is also the case of other games in general. That which links them together, which makes all of them games, is not any common characteristic, but at the most something like a family

[49]   L. J. Wittgenstein, *Tractatus Logico-Philosophicus* (London, 1922), p. 78.

resemblance, a large number of overlapping relationships. This is as among relatives: A and B have similar eyes, B and C have the same complexion, C and D have the same colour of the hair and the same outline of the chin, *etc.* When making a thread we twist the various fibers together, but none of them goes the full length of the thread. The same applies to language. The former postulate of the existence of simple and unchanging objects is rejected in *Philosophical Investigations* as a philosophical illusion. The assumption of the ideal of complete exactitude under the surface of our speech also is such an illusion. A sentence is not a picture. Its meaning consists in its use, employment, and application. A picture must be used. If I am shown a drawing of a cube and am told to bring something like that it may happen that acting in good faith I bring a prism. Likewise, if a picture shows an old man leaning on his stick and climbing a steep slope, it may happen that I interpret, that is use, that picture so that the old man is sliding down the slope. Only the way an image is used determines that of which it is an image. It is not true that we always understand a grammatically correct sentence whenever we understand the words that are its components. A sentence is an instrument by means of which we perform a certain task. Language does not consist of names, and naming is not primary with respect to the meaning of a sentence. The meaning of a word never is the thing — if such exists — to which that word refers. Before we learn which thing a given name stands for, we have to master the language game in which that name participates. Before a word becomes a name, we have to become acquainted with the kind of use which that word will have, and the circumstances in which it will be applied. The fact whether a sentence has an application is one of the criteria of the meaningfulness of the combination of its elements. The order in which things happen is not that we first grasp the meanings of expressions and then know how to apply them, so that meaning as it were comes before use. It is exactly *vice versa*. It does not follow that we have to reject rules, language rules in particular. Yes, we observe them, but it is exactly the way we apply a rule in given cases which determines its meaning. There is a striking agreement between what we say and what we do. The content of the rules increases as our activity increases. It is not so that the rules of logic and mathematics captivate mankind, but human practice lays down the rules. The meaning of an expression is its use, that is, the language game in which that expression participates, that is a homogeneous, regular relation between that expression and certain circumstances.[50]

It seems to me that this example of two diametrally different theories of meaning, or even philosophical systems, is particularly striking, because it is contained within one and the same fascinating personality of their author. There is some dramatic in the lack of theoretical toleration for one's own earlier opinions. This is not a modification of, and improvement upon, one's rejected views, but a self-annihilation. I perceive in it certain characteristics typical of the general historical development of the theories of meaning: the various concepts used to arise not through an expansion and reconstruction of earlier ones, but as it were on their ruins.

I ask myself the question whether the theory of meaning is something like a religion. Does a person who accepts fragments of several different semiotic conceptions become thereby an apostate? Must the opinions on the nature of meaning resemble the possession of more than one wife — or, rather, more than one marriage certificate — in a monogamous legal system? Common sense and observation of the state of things in the field of the theories of meaning suggest a quite different solution. Now most theories have sinned with excessive ambitions. They failed when they wanted to solve all problems in the theory of language, or even sign systems, whereas they were able to offer a good explanation of a certain fragment only. In doing so they were not inclined to accept other people's successful partial solutions. Why should we not put an end to this undesirable state of affairs?

Accordingly, here is the principal proposal included in the present paper: instead of penalizing the practice of freely selecting the achievements of the various theories of meaning, let us sanction such a behaviour as rational.

[50] *Cf.* N. Malcolm, "Ludwig J. Wittgenstein", in *The Encyclopedia of Philosophy*, Vol. 8 (New York, The Macmillan Co. and The Free Press, 1967), 327-40.

This leads to the following minimalist programme: I shall not strive for a universal theory of meaning that would cover all kinds of linguistic expressions, *i.e.*, sentences, names, syncategorematic words, quantifying words, *etc.*, not to speak of artifical languages and all kinds of signs. It seems that the construction of such a universal theory that would prove satisfactory cannot be achieved. I prefer instead to select concepts of meaning according to the theoretical task I may be facing in a given case. I must only see to it that my choice has praxiological values, *i.e.*, that the conception of meaning used in a given case be operative in a given situation; that it well, conveniently and effectively serve its purpose of answering a given question. Hence the meaning of MEANING will be related to a given question, and I refuse to be bothered by the fact that when analysing another issue I use another concept of meaning; I find this procedure much more convenient. The important point is that I realize those differences and accept them deliberately, since then I am not threatened with contradictions. This is an INSTRU-MENTAL approach to the problems of the meanings of expressions. This is why the present paper bears the title "meaning as an INSTRUMENT".

A number of examples is now to be given by way of conclusion.

## 2. MEANING AS AN INSTRUMENT

Frege's concept of CONNOTATION[51] is a convenient instrument of analysing descriptions, in particular of finding semantic differences between equivalent descriptions. The well known example of *the Morning Star* and *the Evening Star* as two non-synonymical names, or, more strictly, descriptions of the planet Venus, can easily be explained by means of the distinction between connotation and denotation. Both expressions denote, or, as we would say today, designate one and the same concrete object, but the former connotes the property of being a star (in the colloquial, and not in the astronomical, sense of the term) and the property of being visible

[51] *Cf.* footnote 35.

in the morning, whereas the latter connotes the property of being a star and the property of being visible in the evening. The difference in meanings becomes evident at once.

The grasping of that difference by means of a more primitive concept of meaning, also referential and stating that the meaning of an expression is its extra-linguistic referent, would be much more difficult, if at all possible. We would have to assume that the expressions *the Morning Star* and *the Evening Star* have two different referents. They would be two different objects, determined respectively by each of these two expressions, in a mysterious sense of the word *to determine*. They might be two ideal objects, or two spatio-temporal phases of the concrete planet Venus, and hence certain abstractions. It would then be a matter of empirical facts, in a sense 'accidental' and lying outside the sphere of language analysis, that the Evening Star (not *the Evening Star*) and the Morning Star (not *the Morning Star*) are one and the same real object. On the other hand, should we assume that these two expressions have one common referent, which is their meaning, it would follow that these expressions are synonymous. It is common knowledge how embarrassing are the consequences of such a solution in the case of intensional contexts. Should we, in the presumably true sentence *Handbooks on astronomy state that the Morning Star is the same planet as the Evening Star*, replace *the Evening Star* by its alleged synonym *the Morning Star*, we would thus obtain the probably false sentence *Handbooks on astronomy state that the Morning Star is the same planet as the Morning Star*. And thus we find ourselves in the mess of problems with which Bertrand Russell had to cope in the case of his *Walter Scott* [52] in the field of the theory of descriptions.

Likewise, should we in the analysis of this simple case wish to use one of the ideational concepts of meaning, in Locke's sense, we could easily imagine the emerging difficulties. What is the difference between the idea connected with the expression *the Morning Star* and that connected with the expression *the Evening Star*, if both are names of one and the same object? It is only in certain external

[52]   *Cf.* B. Russell, "On Denoting", in *Mind*, XIV (1905).

situations, for instance, when the uttering of the words *the Evening Star* is accompanied by the actual perceiving of that planet after the sunset, that the 'state of mind' of the speaker is determined by the circumstances. But if a person is making a list of planets, with *the Evening Star* as one of the items, is the idea associated with that expression different from the idea that would develop in his mind if instead of these words he wrote *the Morning Star*?

*Mutatis mutandis*, these remarks could be repeated with reference to the endeavours to analyse the difference in question by the concept of use, in accordance with Wittgenstein's *Philosophical Investigations*, or Austin's concept of illocutionary act, or similar tools worked out by Peirce, James, and Morris. Apart from the theoretical difficulties resembling those specified above, we would have to cope with a practical problem: we do not have, and probably shall never have, at our disposal a complete comparative repertory of the linguistic and situational contexts of the uses of the expressions *the Morning Star* and *the Evening Star*. Hence the difficulties both in grasping the actual regularities, and the potential rules, that determine the meanings of these descriptions.

In a word, it seems that in the case under consideration, and also in similar cases, the instrument in the form of meaning in the sense of Frege's connotation proves convenient and operative. The same applies to such tasks as determining the meanings of expressions which are explicitly conjunctions of two names, such as *beautiful and good*, and those which are such conjunctions implicitly, for instance, conventional abbreviations of the type *square*.[53] (Let me note parenthetically that the related word *squareness* does not lend itself to an analysis that resorts to the concepts of connotation and denotation, as constructed by Mill. He claimed that the word *squareness* does not have any connotation at all, as is also the case of the proper names, but merely denotes a single attribute.)

But to revert to Frege, the same instruments — connotation and denotation — prove much less efficient if, for instance, we want to establish the connotation of the simple name *dog*, and quite useless

[53]   *Cf.* K. Ajdukiewicz, "Proposition as the Connotation of Sentence", in *Studia Logica*, Vol. XX (1967), 87-98.

in the case of a genuine simple proper name, such as *George*. Hence, in carrying out such tasks as establishing the meaning of a simple name, a proper name, a connective, *etc.*, there is no reason to stick to the use of the concept of connotation as an instrument of analysis. This is why Ajdukiewicz's wish, expressed in his paper published posthumously,[54] to generalize the relations of connoting and denoting so that we might speak of connotation and denotation also with reference to expressions other than names, seems to be ambitious and theoretically interesting, but of little practical value. This opinion of mine does not, however, apply, in its second part, to his idea of constructing the concept of the connotation of proposition.

Let me take this opportunity to recall the old troubles connected with the distinction between the analogues of the connotation and those of the denotation of a name. St. Anselm (1033-1109) in his dialogue *De Grammatico*, Chap. XII, analysed paronyms, *i.e.*, denominatives, such as *illiterate*, and pondered on the problem whether they signify a quality or a substance. At first he thought that they signify sometimes one and sometimes the other, but later, when analysing the sentence *illiteracy is illiterate*, he came to the conclusion that it would be risky to assume that the word *illiterate* sometimes signifies a quality only, since he reserved the latter as the referent of the word *illiteracy*. His solution was similar to Frege's: the word *illiterate* signifies neither an illiterate person as an individual, nor illiteracy as an individual object, but it signifies illiteracy *per se* (directly), and the person *per aliud* (indirectly). For should it be assumed simply that such a paronym signifies *per se* a THING THAT HAS A CERTAIN PROPERTY, and not THE POSSESSION OF THAT PROPERTY, the following problem would arise: suppose that *white* always signifies something white; it is known that the signification of a word is that which is presented by its definition, and that which is presented by the definition may be replaced by the word being defined; hence instead of the sentence *Socrates is white* we may by replacement obtain the sentence *Socrates is something white*, and then in turn *Socrates is something, something white, etc.*,

[54]   *Cf.* footnote 53.

*ad infinitum.*[55] This concept of signification also was an instrument of semiotic analysis, and quite precise at that. But we probably shall not use it.

But to come back to the modern times, suppose that we have to demonstrate the semantic difference between the COMPLEX NAMES *good and cheap* and *good or cheap.* Frege's concept of connotation will not prove a good instrument here, since in both cases it will merely point to the sets of properties corresponding to the component names: goodness plus cheapness, but will not grasp the syntactic difference. This is an example of the phenomenon mentioned previously: a good partial theory loses its value when extended so as to cover those cases which it cannot explain. The same applies to the attempts to grasp the MEANING and the DENOTATION OF SENTENCES by means of the traditional instruments of connotation theory. In Frege's opinion the denotation of a sentence is the ideal entity Truth (with the capital T) or Falsehood (with the capital F), and the meaning (or connotation) of a sentence is a proposition. He decided to adopt this view as he wanted to save the homogeneity of his theory. For that purpose he decided to treat sentences as names, or rather, in his terminology, as the proper names of those entities. He also wanted his theory to be general. That was why he extended upon sentences that which naturally held for expressions of the type *the Evening Star,* thus destroying that naturalness. The conception that the expression *the Evening Star* denotes a definite planet and at the same time through its connotation informs about the properties of that object to which it draws attention, is intuitive and natural. The view that the sentence *the Evening Star is brighter than the Polar Star* denotes an ideal object named Truth, and that the same object named Truth is also denoted, for instance, by the sentence *London is the capital of the United Kingdom,* is much less natural. We now have three ways out: either to reject that theory *in toto* because of its defects, or to accept it and to tolerate those defects because of the doubtless partial advantages of the theory, or to take from that theory only that which is useful as an instrument for the performance of definite

[55] *Cf.* footnote 15; p. 368.

tasks, and when facing other tasks, to look for a better instrument.

I declare myself for the third solution, which I believe to be the most rational of all. In the case under consideration I would suggest, for instance, as an instrument Ajdukiewicz's concept of SYNTACTIC PLACE. That interesting idea, developed in his papers "Proposition as the Connotation of Sentence"[56] and "Intensional Expressions",[57] and outlined in "A Method of Eliminating Intensional Sentences and Sentential Formulae" (in Polish),[58] resembles Carnap's idea of INTENSIONAL ISOMORPHISM[59] and is a continuation of Wittgenstein's opinion, as expressed in *Tractatus*, that the number and the combination of the names which form a sentence POR-TRAY the number and the configuration of simple objects in extra-linguistic reality. Ajdukiewicz constructs the new concept of connotation so that its components are counterparts of all component parts of a phrase or sentence, and not of the component names only. For that purpose he defines the connotation of a complex expression so that it reflects not only the words included in that expression, but also their syntactic places within that expression. The preparatory step consists in expanding all the conventional abbreviations included in a given expression as its components. When this is done, the expression in question includes only simple elements, whose syntactic places are definitely established within that expression. The grammatical markers of those syntactic places may take on the form of the position of a given word within a syntactic group, inflexional form, and some other syntactic means, which depend on the type of the natural language in question. As suggested by Ajdukiewicz, in the phrase *round or red*, where components are simple elements that occupy ultimate syntactic places, we single out the basic operator *or* and mark its place by the number (1,0),

[56]   *Cf.* footnote 53.

[57]   K. Ajdukiewicz, "Intensional Expressions" in *Studia Logica*, Vol. XX (1967), 63-86.

[58]   K. Ajdukiewicz, "Pewna metoda eliminacji intensjonalnych zdań i formuł zdaniowych" [A Method of Eliminating Intensional Sentences and Sentential Formulae] in *Język i poznanie: Wybór pism* [Language and Cognition: Selected Writings], Vol. II (Warsaw, 1965), 365-70.

[59]   R. Carnap, *Meaning and Necessity: A Study in Semantics and Modal Logic*, Sec. 14 and 15 (Chicago, 1947).

and its two arguments: *round*, at the syntactic place (1,1), and *red*, at the syntactic place (1,2). The entire phrase is assigned the number (1) as the symbol of its syntactic place. In the expression now under consideration we have to do with one basic operator and its arguments, that is, with elements of the first order. The same applies to the sentence:

$$\begin{array}{ccc} Socrates & likes & Alcibiades \\ (1,1) & (1,0) & (1,2) \end{array} \qquad (1)$$

On the contrary, in the case of the compound sentence:

$$\begin{array}{ccccccc} (1,1,1) & (1,1,0) & (1,1,2) & & (1,2,1) & (1,2,0) & (1,2,2) \\ Plato & est & philosophus & et & Socrates & est & philosophus \end{array} \quad (1)$$
$$\begin{array}{ccc} (1,1) & (1,0) & (1,2) \end{array}$$

we have to do with elements of an order higher than one. As can be seen, Ajdukiewicz obtained a one-one correspondence between simple components of a given expression and their ultimate syntactic places. The function determined for those places, which establishes that correspondence, is characteristic of that expression. The next step was to assume that there is also a one-one correspondence between the component words that occupy the ultimate syntactic places within a given expression, and the denotation of those words. Then for every expression there exists a function which establishes that correspondence between the syntactic places and the denotations of the words which occupy those places. This function is the connotation of the expression under consideration, *i.e.*, in a given case, of a sentence. Thus, the symbol of the connotation of the phrase *round or red* will be:

$$((1,1) — round; (1,0) — or; (1,2) — red),$$

and the symbol of its denotation will be:

$$\begin{array}{ccc} round & or & red \\ (1,1) & (1,0) & (1,2) \end{array}$$

Constructed in this way, connotation univocally determines

denotation. Moreover, that connotation depends on the objective equivalents of all the components of a given compound expression, not only on the equivalents of names and not only on the equivalents of those words which explicitly occur in a given expression. Finally, connotation interpreted in this way takes into account the syntactic place of each component expression.

Following Frege, Ajdukiewicz assumes that PROPOSITION is the CONNOTATION OF A SENTENCE, but, having constructed a new concept of connotation he has creatively developed and improved that view, which in Frege is rather vague. The concept of proposition, as that which constitutes the connotation of a sentence, has thus acquired an explanation: a proposition is a LOGICAL FUNCTION THAT ESTABLISHES A ONE-ONE CORRESPONDENCE BETWEEN THE SYNTACTIC PLACES OF THE WORDS IN A SENTENCE AND THE DENOTATIONS OF THOSE WORDS.

If I now have to analyse the connotation of a sentence or of an expression of the type *round or red* and I can choose between the instrument in the form of connotation as constructed by Frege, and the instrument in the form of connotation as constructed by Ajdukiewicz, I am sure to resort to the latter, because I consider it to be better. I will do the same in the case of INTENSIONAL SENTENCES. To analyse them I will resort to Ajdukiewicz's method of eliminating intensionality, and not to the less convenient and less intuitive procedure suggested by Frege, which consists in assuming that a proposition, that is, that which would be the connotation of an equiform independent sentence, is the denotation of a dependent sentence. On the other hand, when analysing the difference in meaning between the expressions *the Morning Star* and *the Evening Star*, I will rest satisfied with the instrument suggested by Frege. Thus I neither have to renounce Frege's idea *in toto* nor to accept Ajdukiewicz's conception unreservedly. In the latter, for instance, I do not like this that the relation of stating of the proposition by the sentence is treated as semantic, and not as pragmatic, and I accordingly do not approve that view. Neither do I like Ajdukiewicz's opinion that the TRUTH-VALUE OF A SENTENCE is its DENOTATION, which leads to the conclusion that all true sentences have the same denotation.[60] But this does not force me in the least to reject Ajdukiewicz's conception of the CONNOTATION of a sentence. I can confine myself to not using such a concept of the DENOTATION of a sentence as an instrument of research. (Let it be added parenthetically that in the last case Ajdukiewicz followed Frege's idea in the latter's paper *Über Sinn und Bedeutung*. Yet it seems that Frege did not always hold the view that a sentence has as its *denotatum* Truth or Falsehood. For instance, his *Funktion und Begriff*[61] seems to suggest that he wanted to deny the status of a proper name, and hence probably also the possession of ideal *denotata*, to those sentences which are actually used in the construction of statements, as distinct from those used by way of examples.)

As can be seen, I stand here for practical solutions and for flexibility in theoretical issues. In the extreme cases one should not, I think, hesitate to extract a useful detail even from a theory which is opposed in principle. I can imagine that we can encounter in semiotics such problems in the handling of which Meinong's concept of pure idea (*Vorstellung*) or his concept of *obiectiva* corresponding to negative or false sentences, based in turn on the idea of *Sosein*,[62] may prove useful. For there probably are some cases in which a golden mountain is really golden, and a circular square is both circular and square; semiotic analysis covers all the uses and applications of language, and language also happens to be a language of fictions and phantasms.

I hope that the foregoing historical remarks and examples, even if they failed to convince the reader, have at least persuaded him not to reject what I would term the INSTRUMENTAL approach to semiotic issues. And since I am inclined to treat as an instrument not only the concept of meaning, but also other concepts used in that discipline, I think that my analysis may have wider applications. That is why, as on another occasion when I tried to win readers to

---

[60]  *Cf.* footnote 57; p. 64.
[61]  G. Frege, *Funktion und Begriff* (1891).
[62]  A. Meinong, *cf.* footnote 27.

the FUNCTIONAL point of view,[63] now I take the liberty to encourage them to take an instrumental look at the analysis of natural language.

SUMMARY

0. *Introduction.* — The present paper is concerned with an instrumental approach to the problem of meaning, in the broad sense of the latter term. It is concerned with the meaning of expressions in natural language, although it can be expected that the results will find application in the analysis of artificial languages and of signs other than expressions. The analysis covers in turn the meaning of a single word, a phrase, a sentence, a group of sentences, according to a given task of semiotic analysis. No single theory of meaning is adopted as the foundation, nor is a new theory suggested. In each case the choice from among the known conceptions of meaning is guided by a given semiotic issue. It is in this sense that the concept of meaning becomes an INSTRUMENT in semiotic analysis.

1. *Theories of meaning.* — The problem of meaning has been studied for the last 2500 years. The studies have been dominated by the tendency to reject previous theories whenever found unsatisfactory rather than to accept and to improve that which was found good in them.

Semiotics covers the theory of meaning and the theory of reference. The former is concerned with the problems of meaning itself and those of synonymy, signification, analyticity, and — to some extent — entailment. The latter, with the problems of naming, designating, denoting, extension, and — to some extent — truth. But in the past the theory of meaning used also to be conceived so broadly that it covered both those fields. In this paper,

[63] J. Pelc, "Funkcjonalne podejście do semiotyki logicznej języka naturalnego" [A Functional Approach to the Logical Semiotics of Natural Language], in *Studia Filozoficzne*, No. 2 (49) (1967), 109-34.

too, that broad interpretation of the theory of meaning is used.

The theories of meaning can be CLASSIFIED in different ways. In most cases such classifications are neither disjoint nor adequate.

First, a distinction is made between the THEORIES OF MEANING of a single WORD and those of the meaning of a complete SENTENCE. Theories of the former kind were constructed by philosophers from antiquity on up to the 18th century, and later by Mill, Frege, Husserl, Meinong, Russell in the early period of his activity, and Wittgenstein as the author of *Tractatus Logico-Philosophicus*. They, however, tried to cover the sentence too, since they thought that the meaning of a sentence is a function of the meanings of the words which occur in that sentence. Theories of the latter kind were due to the Stoics (partly), and in the modern times to Berkeley, Bentham, Humboldt, Peirce, James, Dewey, Mauthner, Wittgenstein as the author of *Philosophical Investigations*, and members of the Vienna Circle. They covered the single word, too, as they thought that the meaning of a word is a function of the meaning of the sentence in which that word occurs.

Secondly, a distinction is made between REFERENTIAL and OPERATIONAL, or CONTEXTUAL, theories of meaning. This classification partly coincides with the former. The referential theories state that the meaning of an expression is either its referent, i.e., an extra-linguistic, real or unreal, object to which that expression refers, or the relation that holds between a given expression and its referent. The operational theories state that the meaning of an expression, usually a sentence, always taken in its linguistic context, is its use under given extralinguistic circumstances, or its usage.

Thirdly, a distinction is made between the traditional theories of meaning, i.e., the REFERENTIAL theories, the IDEATIONAL theories, and the STIMULUS RESPONSE theories, on the one hand, and the OPERATIONAL theories, on the other. The referential theories were represented for instance by Mill and Frege. The ideational theories state that the meaning of a word is the idea in the mind of the speaker, associated with that word. What is meant is either the actual state of mind, or the type of thought, or — as in the case of the phenomenologists, e.g., Husserl, an intentional object, or, strictly, the act of constituting it. The ideational theories were represented by Aristotle, the Stoics, Epicurus, Abélard, Locke, partly Berkeley, Bacon, Hobbes, Arnauld. In the case of Locke, one of their typical representatives, they were connected with the concept of PRIVATE LANGUAGE. The stimulus-response theories assume that the meaning of an expression consists in the whole made of the situation in which that expression is uttered (stimulus) and the response of the listener (cf. Bloomfield). According to another variation (cf. Osgood, Morris) its is only the response, actual or potential, i.e., conceived as a type, which is the meaning. The operational theories neither hypostatize meaning, nor treat it as a separate entity. They have representatives in the pragmatists (e.g., Peirce, James, Morris), partly Quine, Wittgenstein as the author of *Philosophical Investigations*, in the Oxford circle, with Austin, who introduced his concepts of locutionary, illocutionary and perlocutionary act, and in the Vienna Circle, whose members thought that the cognitive meaning of a proposition is the method of its verifying, confirming or testing. A different opinion was held by Popper, who saw the meaning of a sentence in the method of its falsifying. The adherents of the operational theories also gave rise to the concept of EMOTIVE MEANING (Ogden and Richards), fertile with contributions to ethics (Moore, Stevenson, Black) and aesthetics (Richards). Wittgenstein switched from the referential theory, based on the meanings of names, as formulated in his *Tractatus*, to the operational theory, based on the use of sentences, in his *Philosophical Investigations*.

On the whole, each of the theories specified above contributes correct observations, but each also has certain defects, due to simplifications, absolutizations, and the striving to cover all semiotic phenomena with partial theories of meaning that are good in explaining some phenomena only. This is why I renounce the idea of selecting or constructing an universal theory of meaning, applicable to all signs and languages. I suggest instead an INSTRU-MENTAL approach to the problem, that is, treating meaning as an instrument, as mentioned in the "Introduction".

2. *Meaning as an instrument.* — This suggestion is both illustrated and verified by examples. I use them to show that the distinction between CONNOTATION and DENOTATION, worked out by Frege after Mill, is a good instrument of analysing EQUIVALENT but NON-SYNONYMOUS DESCRIPTIONS, the meanings of CONJUNCTIVELY COMPOUND NAMES and their CONVENTIONAL ABBREVIATIONS. In those cases other conceptions of meaning, e.g., ideational and operational, prove less effective as instruments. On the other hand, Frege's theory turns out to be not fully satisfactory as an instrument of analysis when it comes to the meaning of simple predicates, and fails in the case of genuine simple proper names. Also the study of the meaning of NON-CONJUNCTIVELY COMPOUND NAMES, and SENTENCES, and the analysis of the PARADOX OF INTENSIONALITY seem not very convenient and not very intuitive when performed by means of Frege's concepts of connotation and denotation. For those purposes I suggest as instruments of research the more suitable concept of SYNTACTIC PLACE and the concept of connotation, or rather CODENOTATION OF A SENTENCE, both worked out by Ajdukiewicz (the latter being modified in the light of the former). These examples are intended to support the general hypothesis that in every case of semiotic analysis we have so to select theories or concepts as to have in them instruments most operative from the point of view of a given research problem.

# PROPER NAMES IN NATURAL LANGUAGE:
## PROLEGOMENA TO A THEORY

### 1. LINGUISTIC CHARACTERISTICS OF PROPER NAMES

John and Fido, a man and a dog, respectively, have held patronage over proper names in logic for several decades. And yet the category of what in natural language is called proper names is rich, differentiated, and has not been strictly defined so far. In any case, it certainly goes beyond the set of expressions determined by the above two examples which have by now become proverbial. There is no doubt that in striving to solve those problems which have been historically connected with proper names, for instance, the singularity, the subjective function, and the meaning of such names, we have first to define what it is for an expression of natural language to be a proper name.

We have, accordingly, to ask linguists for assistance. They[1] tell us that proper names include the following subclasses.

(a) PERSONAL PROPER NAMES: "John", "Smith"; if John Smith is called "John Smith", or "John", or "Smith", then, the linguist[2] claims, "John" is synonymous with "Smith", and the latter in turn with "John Smith", where "John" and "Smith" are abbreviations of the expression "John Smith".

(b) TOPOGRAPHICAL PROPER NAMES:

(b1) Names of rivers: "the Thames", where, as the expert says, "the" is neither an article, nor a generic determinative, but simply a syllable. On the contrary, in the expression "the river Thames"

[1] H.S. Sørensen, *Word Classes in Modern English, with Special Reference to Proper Names:—With an Introductory Theory of Grammar, Meaning, and Reference* (Copenhagen, G.E.C. Gad Publisher, 1958), p. 189 (IX, §§ 79-87).

[2] Sørensen, *Word Classes in Modern English.*

"Thames" is not a proper name and not even a sign.[3] The entire expression is a construction that introduces a name, in analogy to "the boy Peter". In that construction, "Thames" is a designator: "the river that is called Thames", i.e., "the river that is denoted by a sign the designator of which is 'temz'". "Newcastle-on-Tyne" is a single proper name, an abbreviation of which is "Newcastle". "Paris on the Seine" includes two proper names.

(b2) Names of oceans and seas: "the Atlantic", where "the" is not a determinative, since one may not ask: "what Atlantic Ocean?".

(b3) Names of straits and channels: "the Golden Gate", for it is not possible to ask "what golden gate?" and to answer "the golden gate that connects San Francisco Bay with the Pacific Ocean"; hence "the Golden Gate" is not in a determinative contrast position with "a golden gate". On the other hand, "the Channel" is not a proper name, but an appellative, because, as the linguist claims, it is possible to ask "which channel?" and to reply "that which separates Britain from the Continent".

(b4) Names of countries: "the United States" is an appellative construction, that is a common name, in which "the" occurs as a definite article. On the other hand, "the Sudan" is a pure proper name, in which "the" occurs just as the syllable "ðə" and is not a determinative. Such names as "France" also are proper names.

(b5) Names of islands: "Greenland", "the Hebrides" are proper names; in the latter case, "the" is not a determinative, but a syllable.

(b6) Names of lakes: both "Windermere" and "Lake Michigan" are pure proper names.

(b7) Names of mountains and mountain ranges are proper names, too. This applies both to names consisting of a single word, such as "Scawfell", and to compound names ("Mount Everest") and names beginning with "the", which is then treated as a syllable, and not as a determinative ("the Pyrenees", "the Andes"). On the

---

[3] Sørensen (cf. 1, § 7) gives the following definition of sign: a sign is the field of the relation 'is designated by' ('is denoted by') no element of which is a field of relation between those elements between which the relation 'is designated by' ('is denoted by') holds.

other hand, "the Alps" is a common name, because it is possible to ask "what A(a)lps?" and to answer "the A(a)lps in Central Europe (in Switzerland)".

(b8) Names of cities and towns also are examples of proper name: "London" or "the Hague", where "the" is not a determinative, but a syllable.

(b9) Names of parks. "Hyde Park" and "Central Park" are proper names; so is "the Green Park", because, the linguist says, it is not possible to ask "what green park?" and to answer "I mean the G(g)reen P(p)ark in London". Hence "the" is not a determinative, and the variant form "Green Park" is possible, whereas it is not possible to add the ending s to form a plural.

(b10) Names of streets and roads. "Oxford Street", "Park Lane", "Camden Road" are proper names. But what about "the Edgware Road" or "the Vauxhall Bridge Road"? It rarely happens that "the X Road" = "the road to X", although it is correct to say that the X Road almost always leads to X, although, conversely, the road to X is not always called the X Road. "The X Road" and "X Road" also are proper names, for they are not abbreviations of the formulation "the X Road that I am thinking of", and are not parallel to the expression "the X train", used as a common name. Moreover, such expressions as "the Edgware train" can sometimes occur as proper names. Likewise, "the High Street" is a proper name, being an expression which is not in opposition, as to definiteness, to "a high street".

(c) NAMES OF BUILDINGS AND SHIPS:

(c1) Names of buildings. Not only are "Windsor Castle", "Westminster Abbey", "Eton College" and "Buckingham Palace" proper names, but so are "the Dorchester (Hotel)", "the Carlton (Club)", and "the Trocadero (Restaurant)", being analogical to "the Atlantic (Ocean)". Further, "the Hotel Cecil" is analogical to "the river Thames", and "the Vatican", to "the Sudan". The names like "St. Paul's" also are proper names. When taken in its full form, the expression "St. Paul's Cathedral" proves in fact not to consist of any component parts: it is a linguistic fossil, in which "St. Paul's" does not occur as a genitive.

(c2) Names of ships. "Kent" is synonymous with "the Kent", and both are to be treated as proper names; the same applies to "the cruiser Kent", which is an analogue of the expression "the river Thames".

(d) TITLES OF BOOKS AND PERIODICALS. Regardless of their form, that is, regardless of whether they are singular nouns, phrases, or sentences, they are to be considered proper names, because they are used as such, and not as abbreviations or summings-up of the contents of a given book or paper. This can be shown by the example: the sentence "do you like *The Dream and the Business*?" is not an abbreviation of the sentence: "do you like the dream and the business you have learnt about after reading this book?".

(e) COMPOUND PROPER NAMES. From the grammatical point of view it is not possible, as the expert claims, to single out grammatical components in what is termed 'compound proper names'. For instance, "Eton College" may not be split into two signs, "Eton" and "College", the latter of which would be an appellative. "College" here is just two of the syllables which belong to a single designator "Eton College". At the most, "Eton College" may be treated as a compound in the sense that the entities of which it allegedly consists form parts of its definienses; or else, it may be treated as genetically compound, because the words "Eton" and "College" are signs when they occur separately elsewhere. Titles in the expressions of the type "the Emperor Alexander" are to be analysed by analogy to "the river Thames". Poetic personifications, such as "Time", are proper names.

(f) QUASI-PROPER NAMES:

(f1) "God", "Christ", "Satan", "H(h)eaven", "H(h)ell" are examples of proper names.

(f2) "The sun", "the world", "the moon" are common names, for we may ask "what sun?" and answer "the sun that the earth goes round". On the other hand, "the earth" is a proper name, because that expression is not in a determinative opposition to 'an earth' or 'some earth'.

(f3) "Monday", "June", "Christmas", "summer" are doubtlessly examples of proper names.

(f4) "Father", "mother", "nurse", "cook" also are, in the opinion of the linguist quoted, proper names, which is indicated by the lack of an article.

(g) "Man" and "woman", contrary to appearances, are not generic names of uncountable entities, but prove to be proper names. Obviously, this applies to the words "man" and "woman", as distinct from both "the man" and "the woman", and "a man" and "a woman".

The above classification of proper names, illustrated by the examples quoted, is based on a linguistic syntactical and semantic analysis which results in the following definition of a proper name.

"A proper name" $=_{df}$ "a four-dimensional primary A-nominal junctional which is not compatible with an a-relative clause, but which is compatible with a b-relative clause and which is in all constructions compatible with a verb which contains a perfect tense flexive, and which contains neither a number flexive nor a determinative flexive."[4]

Let us try to explain roughly what is the basic idea of this definition. A proper name is described as an expression which from the grammatical point of view represents the class of names (*nomina*), which includes, for instance, nouns and adjectives. It is pointed out that a proper name does not take on any plural ending (for instance, in English *s*) or an article. Further, it is treated as an element of a syntactical structure compatible in all constructions with a verb that contains an inflexional element of the grammatical tense present perfect, preteritte perfect, or future perfect. It is also pointed out that a proper name is in a syntactical agreement with those relative clauses which do not occur as elements of nominal phrases. On the other hand, it is not in a syntactical agreement with those relative clauses which may occur as elements of nominal phrases. Finally, a proper name is itself a nominal sign, since it can be singled out in a non-minimal sentential on the basis of removability-irremovability. The primary character of a proper name consists, to put it briefly, in its nominal nature, as distinguished from non-primary: adjectival or adverbial. The four-

[4]  Sørensen, *Word Classes*, § 74.

dimensional nature of a proper name consists in its indispensable occurrence in syntactical structures: if a proper name occurs in a nominal structure, it may not be deleted from it, in contradistinction from the adjectives, numerals, and adverbs that modify the proper name.

It seems that, in accordance with the definition quoted above, other subclasses of proper names might be added to the preceding list. Thus, under (b) I would add NAMES OF PARTS OF THE WORLD (b11) and NAMES OF HEAVENLY BODIES (b12); the latter would even better be treated as a separate subclass (h), or as an addition to (f2). Under (f3) I would mention NAMES OF HISTORICAL PERIODS AND CULTURAL MOVEMENTS, and under (a) and (b), PROPER NAMES OF FICTIONAL PERSONS AND PLACES, to be found in literary works. Much more important, I would form an additional and numerous subclass (i) consisting of PROPRIETARY TERMS, THAT IS, PROPER NAMES OF MANUFACTURED GOODS, FOODSTUFFS, COSMETIC, PHARMACEUTICAL, ETC., PRODUCTS.

Various comments might be made on the classification outlined above, and also on the various points of interpretation, which raise doubts to a varying extent. But the point here is not to criticize any selected linguistic theory of proper names. I have referred to this one just because it is the latest and the most exhaustive study of the problem, and not because I fully agree with it, or because among the linguists there is a *consensus omnium* concerning the solutions it suggests. One point is certain: it offers a comprehensive list of examples of proper names. Those examples are in English, that is, a language which uses the articles "the" and "a", that have more than two semantic and pragmatic functions. Thus English offers more opportunity for an analysis of certain semiotic problems than does, for instance, Polish, in which no articles occur. Now those examples, by being diversified, suggest that those expressions which are commonly, and even in the light of a linguistic theory, considered to be proper names do not always behave as "John" and "Fido" do. In analysing the meanings of proper names is it possible to disregard differences between such expressions as "John", "the Atlantic", "the river Thames", "Sorcerer's Disciple", "Curzon

Street", etc.? In considering the singular character of proper names is it possible to disregard the fact that, for instance, "Wednesday", "Mont Blanc", and "Robin Hood" differ from one another in that respect? To put it briefly, John and Fido do not suffice to solve, and even correctly to formulate, many issues in the logical semiotics of proper names. Hence THE FIRST REQUIREMENT: ONE HAS TO BEGIN WITH A POSSIBLY COMPREHENSIVE LIST OF EXAMPLES OF PROPER NAMES.

## 2. LOGICAL CHARACTERISTICS OF PROPER NAMES

The requirement is quite to the point, because it has not been observed in practice.

Mill[5] was to some extent responsible for the fact that his followers equated proper names with all names, and then in turn nearly all linguistic expressions with names. It was so because he used to define names in two ways: in one case, as words or phrases that can function as subject or predicate in a sentence, and in the other case as words or phrases that can function only as subject, and thus as proper names in one of the current interpretations of that term.

Frege[6] states explicitly: "... by a sign or a name I mean any expression which functions as a proper name and whose designatum is therefore a definite object." Further in the text he several times uses alternately the terms 'name', 'sign', and 'proper name', also in such contexts where he certainly means common names. He says, for instance, "A proper name (word, sign, group of signs, expression) expresses its sense, and designates, or denotes, its designatum." And it is only in a footnote that he makes a distinction by mentioning "genuine proper names, such as 'Aristotle'."

This initial period in the history of modern logic, in which we may still include the young Russell, is followed by a gradual abandoning

[5] *Cf.* G. Ryle, "The Theory of Meaning", *British Philosophy in the Mid-Century*, ed. by C. A. Mace (London, 1957), pp. 239-64.
[6] G. Frege, "Über Sinn und Bedeutung", *Zeitschrift für Philosophie und Philosophische Kritik*, 100 (1892).

of the idea that consisted in excessively expanding the extension of 'proper name'. Extreme reaction is represented by Russell's later opinion.[7] He thought that some proper names, typical in the current interpretation of the term, for instance such as "Scott", are very often veiled descriptions, and hence are apparent proper names only. To ward off the danger of such appearances Russell suggested his idea of logical proper names, which would guarantee by their sense that there is one and only one extralinguistic referent of each of them. In his opinion, the word 'this' also pretended to that rôle for some time; its counterpart would consist in sensory data.

The requirement of singularity with respect to denoting has since never abandoned the concept of proper names.

For instance, for Reichenbach[8] "a proper name is a symbol coordinated by definition to an individual thing." If a term is to be called a proper name, then, he claims, it is necessary that there is a corresponding thing. Finally, he concludes, "mythical names, like 'Zeus', are therefore not proper names, but only NAMES, that is words used like proper names, namely as arguments of functions."

The tendency to restrict the extension of the concept of proper name, and to belittle its rôle in language, originated by Russell's theory of descriptions and his concept of names which are proper in the logical sense, has found followers in recent times. Many of the authors who have recently dedicated special monographs to the problem of proper names, declare themselves in favour of their at least partial elimination.

Ayer[9] suggests that ordinary proper names be replaced by de-

---

[7]  B. Russell, "On Denoting", *Mind*, XIV (1905); and "Descriptions" (Chap. XVI in *Introduction to Mathematical Philosophy* (London, Allen and Unwin, 1919).

[8]  H. Reichenbach, *Elements of Symbolic Logic* (New York, The Macmillan Company, 1948), pp. 255-6.

[9]  A. J. Ayer, "Imiona własne a deskrypcje" [Proper Names Versus Descriptions], *Studia Filozoficzne*, 5(20), (Warszawa, 1960), 135-55; and "Names and Descriptions" in *Thinking and Meaning*, Entretiens d'Oxford 1962 organisés par l'Institut International de Philosophie. *Extrait de Logique et Analyse*, Nouvelles Série, 5e Année, No. 20 (Louvain, Editions Nauvelaerts; Paris, Béatrice-Nauvelaerts, 1963), 199-202.

scriptions and that in this way the purely ostensive expressions, words-gestures, be eliminated. In a language so designed it would suffice to adopt only one proper name, which might even be empty, referring, as if a sign post, to some object and some event. In this way that language would acquire determination in space and time, something like the zero point in a system of co-ordinates. And though that object and event (possibly fictitious) could be described, the corresponding descriptions would be different from the said proper name that could be understood without any reference to them.

Xenakis[10] restricts the set of proper names to those nouns which are proper names of persons, places, and animals, such as "Fido", "Rilke", "John", "Robinson Crusoe", "Olympus". He deliberately disregards such expressions as "Mount Olympus", because that, as he puts it, "is something more than a proper name in my sense", and also such as "the Sun", "the Pyramids", "the University of Massachusetts", because these, in his opinion, are not proper names but merely words and/or phrases that have adopted capital letters. Yet he thinks that he contributes to the theory of proper names, and calls his paper "The Logic of Proper Names."

Searle[11] goes still farther in restricting the scope of his analysis: in his paper on "Proper Names" he is solely concerned with one-word names and/or surnames of persons. In his opinion, they are the classical proper names; such terms as "The Bank of England" he calls degenerate proper names.

Quine[12] apparently seems the most radical as, influenced by Russell, he suggests that all singular terms, including such as "Socrates" and "Pegasus", be reduced to general terms, and strictly speaking to the category of predicates, for it is so that he interprets generality. Thus all proper names would vanish in Quine's lan-

---

[10] J.Xenakis, "The Logic of Proper Names", *Methodos: Language and Cybernetics*, VII, 25-26 (Milano, Editrice Fiaccola, 1955), 13-24.

[11] J.R.Searle, "Proper Names", *Mind*, LXVII (1958), 166-73.

[12] W.v.O.Quine, *Word and Object* (The Technology Press of The Massachusetts Institute of Technology and John Wiley and Sons). *Studies in Communication* (New York – London, 1960), §§ 19-27 and 37-8.

guage. But that is only a proposal. The actual starting point is quite different: in received natural language Quine interprets proper names very broadly. He says that for him the term 'name' is very close to the grammatical 'proper name'. A 'name' is any singular term, different from a variable, and simple. Singularity here is to be understood not as the property of having a single designatum, but as a complex of grammatical, semantic, and syntactical properties: the term in question does not occur in the plural, pretends — because of the meaning of a given expression — to denote one object only, and syntactically does not occur as a predicate. Its simplicity means that it does not possess any inner structure we would like to preserve. Recognizing whether a given term is singular and simple does not depend on the way we have first learnt to use it, nor on whether it consists of one word or many words; it depends on the current needs of our reasoning and/or research. This shows that the category of names, that is, the category of something like proper names, is very comprehensive in this interpretation.

It can easily be seen that logical studies in the last decades have offered examples of widely divergent interpretations of proper names: from too broad to excessively ascetic ones. I think that even this cursory review results in THE SECOND REQUIREMENT: WHEN PROCEEDING TO CONSTRUCT A THEORY OF PROPER NAMES ONE HAS FIRST TO DECIDE WITH WHAT THAT THEORY IS TO BE CONCERNED. Is it to be a theory of proper names in natural language, as they are interpreted in current intuition, or is it to be a theory of proper names in the grammatical sense of the term, close to current intuition, or is it to be a theory of a group of expressions, singled out from natural language by a certain principle and with a certain goal in view, and termed proper names in a rather arbitrary and non-traditional manner? My impression is that the analyses of proper names, as done so far by logicians, were in fact concerned either with some proper names only, or, at least partly, with expressions that are not proper names. And it seems that a logical theory of proper names in natural language should cover all proper names and only proper names in that language.

### 3. PROPER NAMES VERSUS EXPRESSIONS USED
### IN SOME RESPECT AS PROPER NAMES

The grammatical point of view is, as is known, formal in the sense of focusing attention on the outward form of the expressions concerned. This applies in particular to the traditional approach to grammar. It is, therefore, to be considered whether in outlining a logical theory of proper names in natural language it would not be advisable to go beyond the grammatical aspect interpreted in this way and to take functional elements into account, thus proceeding in accordance with the trends prevailing in modern linguistics.

I imagine that in this case this would consist in finding out whether other expressions in natural language, which are not commonly believed to be proper names, do not share some semantic properties of proper names as understood in linguistics.

For that purpose we might resort to the well known[13] distinction between an expression itself and its use. According to that distinction, an expression is the class of all tokens of that expression, each token being a real or imagined individual. The use of an expression is a subclass of the former, consisting of those tokens of that expression which semantically each have the property $C$, namely the property of referring to a given object outside that language to which the expression used so and so belongs. Then it is not about an expression that we say that it denotes, designates, identifies or mentions something, or speaks about something or refers to something, but about its given use, as distinct from other uses.

This will help abandon the unfortunate tradition of logical analyses of language, which consists in taking into account the dictionary meaning of an expression, while disregarding its contextual meaning in a given linguistic situation of speaking or writing,[14] on which the linguist correctly focuses his attention.

Now if we assume that the characteristic property of the proper names is that they are mostly used with reference to individuals, it is not difficult to find out, by taking the concept of the use of an

[13]   P. F. Strawson, "On Referring", *Mind*, LIX (1950), 320-44.
[14]   *Cf*. O. Jespersen, *The Philosophy of Grammar*, 8th ed. (London, Allen and Unwin, 1958) (1st ed. 1924), pp. 64-70.

expression as the criterion, that what are called common names often occur in the same rôle. Moreover, proper names are not always used in that way. For instance, the name "John", as long as it occurs in a dictionary, is not characterized by singular use with respect to referring or denoting. And in the preceding sentence it has not been used so as to establish the identity of a definite person; it has occurred there in a metalinguistic supposition, in a general way, which refers it to all inscriptions, or their phonic equivalents, equiform with its part included in the quotation marks. On the other hand, in the sentence "The pen lies on the table", spoken in a given situation or occurring in a given context (and not used by way of example, as in the present case), the given use of the word "the pen" univocally specifies an individual, which is believed to be the characteristic function of proper names.

In this connection we might adopt THE THIRD REQUIREMENT: INSTEAD OF MAKING A DISTINCTION BETWEEN PROPER NAMES AND EXPRESSIONS WHICH ARE NOT PROPER NAMES, WE SHOULD DISTIN-GUISH, in the suggested theory of proper names in natural lan-guage, BETWEEN EXPRESSIONS USED AS PROPER NAMES, for instance as to singularity of denotation, AND EXPRESSIONS USED in that respect NOT AS PROPER NAMES.

## 4. DEGREES OF THE PROPERTY OF BEING A PROPER NAME

Without discussing the correctness of the various opinions, held both by linguists and logicians, we can notice that two things, some-times interconnected, have often been used as the criterion of distinguishing proper names from other expressions; one is whether a given expression means anything, and the other, whether it consists of one word or more.

I am convinced that Searle, quoted above, and probably Xenakis as well, both of them authors of fairly recent papers on proper names, would agree that "Berlin" is a proper name, whereas "Frankfort-on-the-Main" is not. The logician who holds the opinion that proper names have no meanings often refuses to accept as a proper name terms consisting of two words or more, because he sees in them descriptions, that is typical expressions to which a meaning is ascribed, for instance in the sense of Mill's or Frege's connotation. He looks undisturbed when he has to do with a single word, currently treated as a proper name. Yet the property of being a single word is not reliable from that point of view. Yet "Greenwich" means a "green village"; "Newcastle" is written as a single word, but if we disregard the spelling convention, it does not fare better than does "New York".

The problem reduces to historical and present-day meanings of expressions and the issue of their lexicalization. We can easily imagine a person arguing that "Newcastle" is not "new + castle", because Newcastle is not new, but old, and is not a castle, but a city. That is true. But, on the other hand, the lexicalization of words is a slow process, and not a sudden jump from a certain state of things to its negation. The historical meaning can be seen through the present-day lexicalized meaning of a word, or through an alleged lack of meaning. It can be seen if the observer has some linguistic knowledge at his disposal, but it does work even if the language user is a complete layman in linguistic science: in choosing a first name for their child the parents are often inspired by what is termed the etymological meaning of the name.

It seems that this processual nature of linguistic phenomena makes it reasonable, in such cases as making a distinction between a proper name and a description because of lack or presence of meaning and the fact that the given term consists of one or more words, to consider varying degrees of the property of being a proper name, varying degrees of the property of being a description, and varying degrees of the property of being a common name.[15] In this we should be assisted by the analysis of word formation.

This results in the following REQUIREMENT, to be observed together with the preceding one, properly modified: LET US TRY A DISTINCTION BETWEEN EXPRESSIONS USED AS PROPER NAMES IN A GREATER DEGREE, AND THOSE USED AS PROPER NAMES IN A LESSER DEGREE.

[15]   Cf. Jespersen, The Philosophy of Grammar.

## 5.  PROPER NAMES VERSUS SUBJECT AND PREDICATE

Aristotle's[16] formulations yield certain rules concerning the relationship between proper names and the subject and predicate in a proposition. One may predicate about first beings, such as Socrates, but one may not use them as predicates: only second beings, such as man,[17] may serve the latter purpose. Now it seems that this gave rise to misunderstandings about interpretations, misunderstandings that have survived 2300 years. First of all, Aristotle did not have in his terminology any instruments for making a precise distinction between ontological and grammatical categories. His *"kategoroumenon"* is ambiguous: in some cases it occurs as "a word in the grammatical sense", in other cases as "an element of a proposition in the logical sense", in still other cases, as "an attribute" or "property". Hence the identification of a proper name with the subject, made later under Aristotle's influence, is ambiguous too, for it may involve either the grammatical subject of a sentence, or the logical subject of a proposition. And yet Aristotle's remarks are often treated as a veiled syntactic rule.[18] Yet syntax is concerned with relationships between words, and not with relationships between the entities corresponding to those words. Should then syntactic rules really be implied by Aristotle's formulations, then it would follow that the word "John" can only be the grammatical subject of a sentence, but cannot be the grammatical predicate in a sentence. This, I think, is refuted by such examples as "That city is London", where "is London" may be treated as a compound grammatical predicate, where "London" occurs as a grammatical predicate noun, and where I cannot find any violation of the syntactic rules of the English language. It might be said to this that in addition to syntax as part of grammar there is also logical syntax, with the rules of which Aristotle was concerned; or, that the word "London" used in this way ceases to be a proper

---

[16]   Aristotle, *Categories*, 5.
[17]   T. Kotarbiński, *Gnosiology* (Oxford, Pergamon Press, 1966), pp. 7-11 and 389 ff.
[18]   Xenakis, "Logic of Proper Names".

name; or, that in this sentence "London" is the grammatical subject.

But in this paper, conceived as prolegomena, the point is not to solve this or that problem, but to lay foundations for a theory of proper names. Let us, therefore, suppose for the time being, as it were by way of experiment, that Aristotle's intention was to speak about grammar, and hence that a proper name may be only the grammatical subject of a sentence, but never a grammatical predicate. Is this free from ambiguity?

It would be difficult to find a greater divergence of opinions than that which is observed in the case of the linguists who try to define (grammatical) 'subject' and (grammatical) 'predicate'.[19] Here are some examples.

(a) The subject is the word(s) referring to an element that is relatively known, while the predicate is the word(s) referring to the element added as something new.  (b) The predicate determines and specifies that which originally was undetermined; thus the subject is the *determinandum* which owing to the predicate becomes a *determinatum*.  (c) The subject is that which is referred to, and the predicate is that which is stated about the subject.  (d) The subject is the primary element of a sentence, while the predicate is its secondary element; hence the subject is relatively definite and specified, and the predicate is less so, and thus the predicate can be referred to a greater number of things than can the subject.

Even if we pass over in silence all the objections that could be raised against these formulations, which are burdened with obvious and grave errors, we have to say this: IF WE ARE TO DISCUSS THE SUBJECTIVE (IN THE GRAMMATICAL SENSE OF THE TERM) NATURE OF PROPER NAMES, WE HAVE FIRST TO ESTABLISH WHAT A GRAMMATICAL SUBJECT IS. Those logicians who ascribed to proper names the function of the grammatical subject in a sentence, and denied them the function of the predicate — which is a fairly common opinion — were too prone to believe that these concepts are well defined in linguistics. And yet even such a simple and apparently obvious rule that any noun can be the subject of a sentence in any language

[19]  Jespersen, *The Philosophy of Grammar*, Chap. XI, pp. 145 ff.

may not be formulated: as Ryle[20] points out, in English "this dog", "a dog", "the dog", "dogs", "all dogs", "most dogs", "grass", "hydrogen", and "man" can occur in such a function, but *dog* without quotes, cannot.

Now some comments on the predicate. The logicians' liking for a triadic decomposition of a sentence into subject, copula, and predicate does not always find favour with the linguists.[21] Now: (a) in such languages which, like English, have the continuous form "John is walking" is not an equivalent of "John walks"; (b) in tenses other than the present tense there is no equivalent of the logical copula that is a-temporal in nature; (c) many languages lack the copula, which makes it impossible to analyse sentence in accordance with the pattern mentioned above; (d) there is no reason to stress only the copula *is*, since other verbs and even words that do not belong to the class of verbs occur in that function ("he *grows* old", "she *blushed* red", "to take *for* granted", "to look upon somebody *as* a fool"). Hence the conclusion that IF WE DENY THE FUNCTION OF GRAMMATICAL PREDICATE TO PROPER NAMES, AND ASCRIBE IT TO COMMON, WE HAVE TO REVISE THE PRINCIPLE OF THE TRIADIC ANALYSIS OF THE SENTENCE, TO DEFINE WITH PRECISION WHAT A PREDICATE IS, AND TO ABANDON THE HABIT OF RENDERING TWO DIFFERENT TERMS, 'PREDICATE' AND 'PREDICATIVE', BY ONE AND THE SAME TERM 'PREDICATE'.

Assume now that those who in proper names see the subject, but never the predicate, have the logical subject in mind. Situation then is not any better than it was before. Jespersen[22] lists quite a number of the various pairs: logical subject — logical predicate; here as some of them:

(a) Every primary element of a sentence is a subject; in "*Pierre donne un livre à Paul*" there are three subjects: "*Pierre*", "*livre*", and "*Paul*" (Couturat). (b) The logical predicate is identified by stress; it is often the grammatical subject or an adjective belonging to the latter; but in the sentence "The king will NOT come" the

[20] Ryle, "The Theory of Meaning".
[21] Jespersen, *The Philosophy of Grammar*, p. 131.
[22] *Cf.* footnote 19 above.

logical predicate is "not" (Höffding). (c) The phrase *"guter Vater"* has *"Vater"* as its logical subject, and "gut" as predicate; in the phrase *"einen Brief schreiben"* *"schreiben"* is the logical subject (Steinthal). (d) In the sentence "I came home yesterday morning" the grammatical predicate is "came", but the logical predicate is "came home yesterday morning"; in "gold is a metal" "is" is the grammatical predicate, and "metal" is the logical predicate (Sweet). (e) In the case of sentences in the passive voice that part of the sentence is the logical subject which is the grammatical subject of its equivalent in the active voice. (f) In the sentences of the type "It is difficult to find one's way in London" or "it cannot be denied that Newton was a genius" "it" is the formal subject, while the infinitive or the subordinate clause is the logical subject. (g) In what are termed subjectless sentences like *"mich friert"* *"ich"* is the logical subject.

While abstaining from critical remarks, which it would be very easy to make, let us confine ourselves to a practical conclusion. IN THIS CASE, TOO, BEFORE WE PROCEED TO ANALYSE THE PROBLEM WHETHER A PROPER NAME FUNCTIONS AS THE LOGICAL SUBJECT, WE HAVE FIRST TO DEFINE WHAT A LOGICAL SUBJECT IS.

Hence the NEXT REQUIREMENT: THE DEFINITION OF THE CONCEPT OF SUBJECT OUGHT TO BECOME THE STARTING POINT FOR A DISCUSSION OF THE SUBJECTIVE NATURE OF PROPER NAMES. Complying with this requirement should also help to solve another problem, namely the formulation of the practically forgotten issue of the objective nature of proper names. I mean here the grammatical object. Now without engaging in the discussion of whether it would be possible to make a distinction, analogical to the preceding one, between grammatical object and logical object (each of them in the various inter-pretations), I think that the same properties which, in the opinion of many scholars, predestine the proper names to the function of the subject (the individual character of the proper names, their purely denotative, i.e., identifying, functions, etc.) predestine them in the same way to the function of the object in a sentence. Hence the ADDITIONAL REQUIREMENT is: IT IS NECESSARY TO EXAMINE THE OBJECTIVE NATURE OF PROPER NAMES.

## 6. THE MEANING OF PROPER NAMES

The meaning of proper names was that problem in which the scholars concerned with that class of expressions were the most interested.

Mill[23] claimed that proper names denote only, but never connote; hence, if a dog is named "Fido", then that word does not provide any information, be it correct or wrong, about the characteristics of that dog, his life, the place it lives, etc. Hence, as Ryle[24] notes, a proper name cannot be understood correctly, or misunderstood, or uncomprehended; neither can it be translated into another language, correctly or incorrectly. Proper names are conferred in an arbitrary manner, and, contrary to descriptions, they do not convey either truth or falsehood, because they do not inform about anything.

As is known, Frege[25] considered all those expressions in which the extralinguistic referent is a definite object in the broadest sense of the term to be proper names, regardless of whether such expressions consist of one word or more. In his opinion, the sense of a proper name conceived in this way is understood by every person who knows a given language, that is the totality of denoting words, to which that proper name belongs. He added that that comprehension of sense sheds unilateral light on that extralinguistic referent of a proper name, if such a referent exists: we can never achieve this that whenever an arbitrary sense is given, we can immediately tell whether it is an attribute of that extralinguistic referent. He also assumed that an expression has a sense always if its structure is grammatically correct and if that expression replaces a proper name. He compared that sense to the real image in a telescope when we watch the Moon (the analogon of the extralinguistic referent). The image on the retina would, in terms of this metaphor, correspond to the observer's experience. It could be said about the sense (the real image) that it is objective, as it can serve

[23]   Cf. Ryle, "The Theory of Meaning", footnote 5 above.
[24]   Ryle, "The Theory of Meaning".
[25]   Cf. Frege, "Über Sinn und Bedeutung", footnote 6 above.

several observers, and relative, as it depends on the point of view. Frege made the reservation that when it comes to the sense of genuine proper names, such as "Aristotle", opinions may diverge. It might, for instance, be suggested that the sense of the word "Aristotle" is: a disciple of Plato and a teacher of Alexander the Great; but the following suggestion might also be made: a teacher of Alexander the Great, who came from Stagira. According to our choice we shall interpret the statement "Aristotle was born in Stagira" in different ways. As long as the same person or thing is concerned, such fluctuations of the sense are admissible.

Russell[26] ascribed meaning to proper names, which in his terminology appear as 'names'; for instance, he used to say that "Socrates", "Plato" and "Aristotle" have different meanings. A proper name, or a name, is for him a simple symbol, the meaning of which is a certain individual, and hence something that can occur only as subject; a simple symbol is a symbol like "Scott", the parts of which, i.e., letters, are not symbols, whereas in a compound symbol, such as "the author of *Waverley*", its various parts, being words, are symbols. He adds that everything that looks like an individual is in fact subject to further analysis, but we can be satisfied with the concept of 'relative individual', i.e., a term which in a given context occurs only as subject. In this interpretation a proper name directly designates an individual which is the meaning of that proper name; the proper name has that meaning of its own, regardless of the meanings of any other words. Hence, if "Scott" and "Sir Walter" are used as proper names, and not as veiled descriptions, then they are synonymous, like a given English word and its French equivalent. Hence the proposition "Scott is Sir Walter" means the same as "Scott is Scott". Thus, if a given word is a proper name, then it must name something, since otherwise it would be devoid of meaning. Consequently, the question whether Homer existed is meaningful only if the word "Homer" occurs as a veiled description, and not as a proper name.

Jespersen[27] agrees with Mill and his followers that if a proper

[26]   B. Russell, "Descriptions" (*cf.* footnote 7 above).
[27]   *Cf.* Jespersen, *The Philosophy of Grammar*, pp. 64-70.

lgl

name, such as "John", is given in isolation, then we cannot give its meaning. But he also says that the same applies to a large number of common names, and that this kind of analysis is erroneous. Expressions must be examined in definite uses and in definite contexts, and then it will appear that, contrary to Mill, not only do proper names connote, but they even connote a greater number of attributes than does any common name. As in the case of common names, a proper name, when encountered for the first time, is just only, for instance, a surname, and that is all. But as our knowledge of the man who bears that name increases, the connotation of that proper name increases too. For it is absurd to think that the connotation of an expression is something inherent in that expression and independent of our knowledge and of the use of that expression. Transformations of proper names into common names prove that proper names, as they are actually used, do connote. How could a proper name, treated as a non-connoting sequence of sounds, become connotative as soon as it becomes a common name? The process can be explained as follows: out of the set of properties characteristic of the bearer of a given proper name and connoted by that proper name, one property, the best known one, is brought out and used to characterize somebody or something else, endowed with the same property. An analogous process is observed in common names. The transference from "Croesus" to "croesus" differs at the most in degree from the transference from "human" to "humane". Since connotation is not denied to such common names as "Negro", "dog", "Frenchman", or "Londoner", although it is difficult to say what is connoted by each of those terms, then there is no reason to deny connotation to the proper name "Smith": the members of the family using that surname have other characteristics as well. And in the case of the bearers of a proper name such as "Maria", which is conferred arbitrarily, the problem of their common characteristics is not more complicated than in the case of the objects termed 'temple': at least all Marias are women, while "temple" denotes a place of public worship in some cases, and a part of the head in others. Every name in the grammatical sense (*nomen*), whether proper or common, always connotes that property or those properties by which its bearer(s) can be recognized, and thus distinguishes him or them from other things or persons.

Strawson[28] holds that meaning is a function of an expression, and not of its use, and that to give the meaning of an expression (here he resembles Wittgenstein) is to give general directions for its use to refer to or mention particular objects or persons. He also singles out what he terms "descriptive meaning", that is conventional limitation, in application to things of a certain general kind or to things that have certain general characteristics. Now to pure proper names, such as the names of persons, dogs, etc., he denies descriptive meaning, except such which a given proper name may acquire by being used as an appellative of a person, animal, or thing. 'Impure' proper names, that is nominal phrases written with a capital letter, stand midway between the pure proper names and descriptions: the former have a minimum whereas the latter have a maximum of descriptive meaning. In Strawson's opinion, no reference should be made to the meaning of pure proper names, such as "Horace", also because their correct use, as words referring to something, is not ruled by any general conventions that would be contextual or ascriptive in nature; the pure proper name is used only by conventions adjusted *ad hoc* to each particular use. The phrases written with a capital letter in this case too stand midway between pure proper names on the one hand, and pronouns and descriptions on the other. He concludes that the ignorance of the proper name of a person is not the ignorance of the language in question, and this is why we usually do not speak of the meaning of proper names. But it should not be said that proper names are meaningless.

Quine[29] does ascribe meaning to proper names, which can be inferred from his remark that the name "Paul" is a singular, but a very ambiguous term.

Ayer[30] states explicitly that proper names must have meanings,

[28]  *Cf.* Strawson, "On Referring", footnote 13 above.
[29]  *Cf.* Quine, *Word and Object*, footnote 12 above.
[30]  *Cf.* Ayer, "Imiona Wlasne", footnote 9 above.

because if in the sentence "Napoleon died in St. Helena" the words "Napoleon" and "St. Helena" are replaced by "Wellington" and "Elba", respectively, the sentence acquires a new meaning. Hence a proper name, although it does not connote, and hence is not an abbreviation of a description, does help to establish the meanings of those sentences in which it occurs.

Searle[31] gives the following answer to the question whether proper names have a sense: if we ask "whether or not proper names are used to describe or specify characteristics of objects, the answer is 'no'. But if we ask whether or not proper names are logically connected with characteristics of the object to which they refer, the answer is 'yes, in a loose sort of way'." In a determined way this is done by descriptions, while proper names serve as "pegs on which to hang descriptions."

A different stand is held by Xenakis,[32] who denies meaning to proper names. This is not refuted by the fact that we say that "Gugliemo" means "William" or that "Bill" means "William", because one proper name may not be the meaning of another. On the other hand, the sentence "'Peter' means 'rock'" refers not to the meaning of a proper name, but to its origin. And in the case of "'Paris' means a city" we have to do with an answer to a wrongly formulated question "What does 'Paris' mean?" Thus proper names are identifying labels, which are affixed arbitrarily. They are not reducible to descriptions, are not definable, do not occur in dictionaries as words, and they do not give opportunity to make linguistic mistakes consisting in their incorrect use, for there are no rules governing their function of denoting.

This brief review of opinions leads to the conclusion that the authors who analyse the problem of the meaning of proper names refer to different things, and that in a double sense. First, they interpret the concept of 'proper name' in different ways, and, secondly, they interpret the concept of 'meaning' in different ways. No wonder then that their conclusions are widely divergent.

Connotation as interpreted by Mill is not exactly the same as con-

---

[31]   *Cf.* Searle, "Proper Names", footnote 11 above.
[32]   *Cf.* Xenakis, "The Logic of Proper Names", footnote 10 above.

notation as interpreted by Frege, and Jespersen's view differs widely from both. Practically only the shape of the term remains the same; in its content Jespersen's connotation bears some resemblance to the traditional interpretation of the term, and also some resemblance to signification or Lewis's intension.[33]

According to Russell, the meaning of a proper name is logically just the designatum or the denotatum of that simple symbol.

Other groups of opinions are represented by contemporary British (Ayer, Strawson, Ryle) and American (Quine, Searle, Xenakis) researchers. We can notice there influences of Wittgenstein (the sense of an expression is the rules of its use) and logical positivism and empiricism (sense is ascribed to sentences only, and the separate words are syncategorematic with respect to sentences).

But the point here is not to analyse in detail or to criticize the opinions outlined above, but to draw a conclusion in the form of the NEXT REQUIREMENT. THE RESOLUTION OF THE PROBLEM OF THE MEANING OF PROPER NAMES REQUIRES (in addition to determining, in accordance with the first four requirements, the meaning of what is to be examined) THE DECISION IN WHAT SENSE WE ARE TO INTERPRET MEANING. It seems that we may eliminate in advance, as erroneous, the identification of meaning with the object (e.g. the real object) corresponding to a given expression. The other kinds of meaning are useful in varying degrees, according to the interpretation of the concept of proper name. For instance, the concept of connotation is quite a good instrument when it comes to analyse the difference in meanings which occurs between equivalent descriptions. This is why it is worth while referring to that concept in the case of highly descriptive uses of proper names, that is, in the case of compound proper names, and also proper names consisting of one word, but with a word-formative structure that clearly interevenes in actual uses. The concepts of Lewis's intension and signification

---

[33]  C. I. Lewis, "The Modes of Meaning", *Philosophy and Phenomenological Research*, VI, 2 (Buffalo – New York, 1943) 236-49 (A Symposium on Meaning and Truth).

may also prove useful.[34]  Carnap's[35] concept of intension as an individual concept seems to be more suitable in the case of the categories of proper names mentioned above, than in the case of 'pure' proper names.  He admits himself that — except for dependent contexts — his intension coincides with Frege's connotation. On the other hand, when it comes to the analysis of the meanings of one-word proper names and of minimally descriptive uses of proper names that interpretation of meaning which is found, for instance, in Strawson[36] seems more useful.

## 7.  THE SINGULAR CHARACTER OF PROPER NAMES

The issue of the singularity of proper names is complicated by the fact that it arises as it were at crossroads.  It is the meeting point of ontological and metaphysical issues (what is an individual?),[37] semantic issues (singularity with respect to designation, or singular intention with respect to meaning), syntactical issues (the individual nature of an expression as predestination to the function of the grammatical or logical subject only, and other issues as well.  This fact has given rise to numerous misunderstandings.

Some of them can, perhaps, be traced back to the Aristotelian[38] distinction between primary and secondary entities, as mentioned above; others, perhaps, to some remarks by Frege,[39] made partly as a pious wish with reference not to proper names, but to what he terms proper names, that is, almost all expressions.  He says that it is a shortcoming of languages that they admit expressions which, although by their grammatical form intended to denote an object, sometimes do not satisfy that condition, which depends on factual

[34]  Lewis, "The Modes of Meaning".
[35]  R. Carnap, *Meaning and Necessity: A Study in Semantics and Modal Logic* (Chicago, 1947), I, § 9 and III, § 29.
[36]  *Cf.* Strawson, "On Referring", footnote 13 above.
[37]  *Cf.* P. F. Strawson, *Individuals: An Essay in Descriptive Metaphysics* (London, Methuen & Co., Ltd., 1959), p. 255; and Reichenbach, *Elements of Symbolic Logic*, § 48.
[38]  *Cf.* Aristotle, *Categories*, footnote 16 above.
[39]  *Cf.* Frege, "Über Sinn und Bedeutung", footnote 6 above.

circumstances. He adds that we must demand that in a logically perfect language every expression which is constructed as a proper name — in his sense — in a grammatically correct way should in fact designate an object; and that no symbol should be introduced as a proper name if there is no certainty that it has a designatum. Here the comment must be made that that designatum or object in Frege's sense is conceived very broadly, not necessarily as a concrete individual: in one of his examples he refers to the point in the geometrical sense of the term.

Russell[40] made two steps further: from Frege's concept of proper name to his own concept of proper name in the logical sense of the term, and from Frege's pious wish to his own categorical demand that only one concrete object should correspond to a given proper name, since otherwise that proper name becomes meaningless.

The same demand, though without the scare of meaninglessness, is repeated by Reichenbach.[41] When a proper name has no counterpart in a single concrete object, then it ceases to be a proper name. This requirement is extended so as to cover correct, or proper, definite descriptions.

A decline of rigour and radicalism on this issue coincides with a rising tide of Aristotelian tradition, in which the singularity of an expression does not depend on the actual number of extralinguistic counterparts, treated as individuals, which that expression has.

Quine[42] says that a proper name, even though borne by thousands, is not a general, but a singular — though very ambiguous — term. But his arguments are drawn from the field of grammar, and not of extralinguistic facts: that a proper name is not preceded by an article, and that, which is disputable, it does not take on the plural form. Moreover, he makes a clear distinction between typical occurrences of a proper name and that name as a dictionary item.

Ryle[43] remarks that the basic pattern "Fido" — Fido is untenable

[40]　*Cf.* Russell, "Descriptions", footnote 26 above.
[41]　*Cf.* Reichenbach, *Elements of Symbolic Logic*, footnote 8 above.
[42]　*Cf.* Quine, *Word and Object*, footnote 12 above.
[43]　*Cf.* Ryle, "The Theory of Meaning", footnote 5 above.

in face of the relation "Saturday" — Saturday and "Mr. Pickwick" — Mr. Pickwick.

Jespersen[44] is rather liberal in his treatment of the issue of singularity of proper names. It is not by that criterion that he wants to distinguish them from other expressions. He points out that there are five Romes and a great number of Johns. And although he admits that in the strictest sense proper names have no plural, in the same way as the pronoun "I" does not have it, yet in a modified sense they do have it occasionally, namely in such instances as "three Johns", "the Browns", "Judases", "two Rembrandts". He adds that what is designated by a proper name always is an abstraction, because a concrete individual is changing incessantly in time, whereas its name is supposed to cover and to fix permanent elements of its changing outward aspects, that is, to bring them to a common denominator. That is why the more specialized the abstraction to which a given expression refers, the more probable it is that that expression has been selected in an arbitrary manner, and thus comes closer to a proper name.

Echoes of Aristotle's opinions can be found in latest logical theories in emphasizing the demonstrative, or identifying, function of the proper names, as opposed to the predicative, or ascriptive, function of the common names. Thus the centre of gravity of the issue of singularity of proper names has shifted perceptibly. It is stated explicitly[45] that it is a superstition to believe that a proper name is logically attached to a single individual; and that it would be obviously false to assert that a given proper name is used with reference to one thing or person only: many terms that are *par excellence* proper names are correctly referred to great numbers of persons. The point is that the referential, demonstrative, use of a proper name is not determined by its own descriptive sense, and that it is not governed by any general language rule, but by conventions adopted *ad hoc* for each separate set of applications of that proper name to a given person.

When analysing these modified opinions on the singularity of

[44]   *Cf.* Jespersen, *The Philosophy of Grammar.*
[45]   *Cf.* Strawson, "On Referring", footnote 13 above.

proper names we have to realize the following things. That referential, demonstrative, and identifying character is an attribute not only of the typical uses of proper names, but also of all expressions used singularly, and hence demonstrative and personal pronouns, certain descriptive phrases, singular common nouns, and sometimes also adjectives used as substantives. Next, to be used in this way, a given expression need not occur as subject in a sentence; it may be not only an object in a sentence, but may also occur outside any sentence, provided that the extralinguistic situation guarantees its singular use (shop sign, trade mark label, etc.). On the other hand, the fact that a given expression occurs as subject in a sentence does not by itself determine its singular use: consider the case when that sentence is quoted by way of example. It is only the context, taken together with other circumstances, that determines the singular character of a given use. In a word, the individual (i.e., subjective) character of an expression is neither a necessary nor a sufficient condition of the singularity of that use; and it is not only proper names that are individual in that sense.

The foregoing considerations yield the FOLLOWING REQUIREMENT. Before discussing the issue of singularity of proper names we have to DECIDE two things. First, HOW THE SINGULARITY OF AN EXPRESSION IS INTERPRETED. Here it would be advisable to adopt Kotarbiński's[46] distinction as between singular expressions, expressions with singular intention, and individual expressions. Secondly, WHAT IS UNDERSTOOD BY AN INDIVIDUAL. We would also have to take into account the previous requirements, especially those from Chaps. 3 and 4. Further, such distinctions as between designatum, denotation, and extension (cf. Lewis[47]), or more detailed ones, may prove useful.

## 8. PROPER NAMES AND DESCRIPTIONS

The title of this chapter is not conceived as an antithesis. But it occurs as such in the headlines of many papers on logic, for the

---

[46]  Cf. Kotarbiński, *Gnosiology*, footnote 17 above.
[47]  Cf. Lewis, "The Modes of Meaning", footnote 33 above.

opinion is fairly common among the logicians that proper names ought to be opposed to descriptions. In my opinion this calls for a revision. The starting point may be, on the one hand, the fact that many natural language expressions which are universally, and also in the eyes of the linguists, are interpreted as proper names, also share the nature of descriptions. On the other, it might be the critique of logical characteristics and theories of descriptions, a critique that has been often taken up.[48]

One of the earliest and most comprehensive theories of descriptions, which I find difficult to accept — I mean the theory of Bertrand Russell[49] — includes among its valuable observations one that is particularly inspiring, namely that a proper name may sometimes be used as a description.[50] But for Russell it then ceases to be a proper name, and becomes a description, whereas in my opinion it may still remain a proper name, because it is at all impossible to draw a sharp demarcation line between proper names and descriptions.

Now even among those expressions which are believed to be 'pure' proper names we can find such which have some descriptive value or force. That is why it very rarely occurs that a white-haired dog should be named "Blackie". The proper name "Johnson", with its patronymic suffix -son means "John's son", but "John's son" is a description. Common names also may have that descriptive force. If "denial of one's self" can pass for a description, I see no reason why should we deny the nature of a description to such a word as "selfdenial". The same, though less visibly to a layman, applies to such words as "worker", where the suffix plays the rôle analogous to that of independent words in the case of classical description. It would be difficult to accept Russell's view[51] who

[48] *Cf.* Strawson (footnote 13 above); Quine (footnote 12 above), pp. 184ff.; P.T.Geach, *Reference and Generality. An Examination of Some Medieval and Modern Theories* (Ithaca-New York, Cornell University Press, 1962); and by the same author "Russell's Theory of Descriptions", *Analysis*, X, 4 (1950); see also Strawson (*Individuals*, see footnote 37, Chap. V).
[49] *Cf.* Russell, "On Denoting", footnote 7 above.
[50] *Cf.* Russell, "Descriptions", footnote 26 above.
[51] Russell, "Descriptions".

adopts the spelling convention, that is, the fact that the connoting phrase consists of at least two words, to be criterion of the descriptive nature of that phrase. Thus among proper names, not necessarily compound ones, we can find expressions that are descriptive in nature; the same applies to one-word common names.

On the other hand, it seems that a more flexible approach is advisable in the case of descriptions themselves. Their descriptive nature reaches its peak only if they are used as predicates. But if a description occurs in the stylistic function of a periphrase — and when it does so then it usually functions as the subject or the object in the sentence — then its descriptive value becomes minimal, probably not greater than the descriptive value of many a 'pure' proper name. When, to avoid monotony in formulations, in a paper on Byron I write "The author of *Childe Harold's Pilgrimage* died in Greece", then the words "the author of *Childe Harold's Pilgrimage*" perform there principally the referential function and are intended to point to a person, like a gesture or a 'pure' proper name does. Hence what are termed descriptions are not always used as descriptions.

As can be seen, the much emphasized difference between the proper name, as conferred quite arbitrarily, and the description, the use of which is restricted by facts, is a difference of degree only, and moreover depends on actual use: a surname is adopted not quite arbitrarily, although it is a proper name, and certain polite forms of address are sometimes used without any confrontation of their meaning with facts.

Further, it does not seem to be unreservedly correct to say that a proper name carries no information and conveys neither truth nor falsehood.[52] When I hear the word "Boston", I can guess with considerable probability that it is a place name, and when I hear the word "John", that it is a person's name. Thus the difference between proper names and descriptions with respect to their descriptive value, as it occurs in certain uses, is a difference of degree.[53]

[52]  *Cf.* Ryle, "The Theory of Meaning", footnote 5 above.
[53]  *Cf.* Strawson, "On Referring", footnote 13 above.

In this connection, it is only in degree that the dependence of the referential function of proper names on the context in which they occur differs from the dependence of descriptions on the context: 'pure' proper names are often more context-dependent than are 'pure' descriptions.[54]

It could be difficult to agree fully with the assertion that proper names, though not abbreviations of description, depend on the latter in the sense that a necessary condition of using a proper name in a referential way consists in the ability of formulating a description of that individual to which that proper name is to refer.[55] The objection is due to the fact that we can refer to the object in an ostensive manner.[56]

I would be willing to agree with the well known remark that proper names stand midway between 'pure' demonstratives and 'pure' descriptions,[57] but only on the condition that this means that proper names sometimes occur as demonstratives, and sometimes as descriptions. But the same applies to one-word common names, and to descriptions as well.

Thus there is no reason, I think, to treat descriptions and proper names as mutually exclusive classes of expressions. By referring to the remarks made in Chaps. 3 and 4 we might formulate the FOLLOWING REQUIREMENT in connection with a future theory of proper names: AFTER ADOPTING THE SUPPOSED ANTITHESIS BETWEEN PROPER NAMES AND DESCRIPTIONS AS THE STARTING POINT OF STUDY, WE HAVE TO EXAMINE THE DEGREE OF DESCRIPTIVENESS OF THE EXPRESSIONS USED AS PROPER NAMES.

## 9. CONCLUSION

In my opinion a future theory of proper names in natural language should answer the question when a given expression, simple or compound, is used in a given context in what respect, and to what

[54]  Strawson, "On Referring".
[55]  *Cf.* Strawson, footnote 37 above.
[56]  *Cf.* Ayer, "Imiona Własne", footnote 9 above.
[57]  Ayer, "Imiona Własne".

degree, as a proper name. We should not, I think, strive to define proper names as a separate class of expressions. The same could be applied to other categories of words and phrases in natural language, and even — perhaps — to the grammatical classification into what is usually termed parts of speech.

## SUMMARY

1. *Linguistic Characteristics of Proper Names.* — The analysis of proper names has for decades been sponsored in logic by John and Fido, a man and a dog. Yet the category of what are termed proper names in natural language is rich, varied, and not quite strictly defined, and thus certainly goes beyond these two proverbial examples. We have therefore first to establish what is considered a proper name in natural language.

According to Sørensen's *Word Classes in Modern English with Special Reference to Proper Names* (Copenhagen, 1958) the following categories of expressions can be distinguished among proper names:

PERSONAL PROPER NAMES, e.g., "John", "Smith", "John Smith";

TOPOGRAPHICAL PROPER NAMES, e.g., "the Thames", "Newcastle-on-Tyne", "the Atlantic", "the Golden Gate", "the Sudan", "France", "Greenland", "the Hebrides", "Windermere", "Lake Michigan", "Scawfell", "Mount Everest", "the Pyrenees", "London", "the Hague", "Hyde Park", "the Green Park", "Oxford Street", "the Vauxhall Bridge Road";

NAMES OF BUILDINGS AND SHIPS, e.g., "Westminster Abbey", "the Dorchester (Hotel)", "the Hotel Cecil", "St. Paul's Cathedral", "the (cruiser) Kent";

TITLES OF BOOKS AND PERIODICALS, e.g., *"The Dream and the Business"*;

COMPOUND PROPER NAMES, e.g., "Eton College", "the Emperor Alexander";

QUASI PROPER NAMES, e.g., "God", "Satan", "Heaven", "Monday", "Christmas", "September", "summer", "father", "mother", "cook", "nurse", "man", "woman".

On the other hand, according to the same author the following expressions are not proper names: "the Channel" (because it is possible to ask "What channel?" and to reply "That one which separates England from the Continent"); "the United States" (because "the" is here a definite article); "the Alps" (because it is possible to ask "what Alps?"); "the Sun" (because it is possible to ask "What sun?" and to reply "The sun the earth goes round"); "the man"; "a man".

Sørensen gives the following definition: "A proper name" $=_{df}$ "a four-dimensional primary A-nominal junctional which is not compatible with an a-relative clause but is compatible with b-relative clause and which is in all constructions compatible with a verb which contains a perfect-tense flexive, and which contains neither a number flexive nor a determinative flexive."

In the light of that definition the list of the categories of proper names, as given by Sørensen, seems incomplete. We could join to it: names of parts of the world, heavenly bodies, historical periods and epochs, cultural trends and movements, heroes of literary works, the vast category of proprietary terms, etc. This shows that the expressions which are considered proper names do not always semiotically resemble the "John"-"Fido" pattern. Hence the first requirement: the list of examples of those expressions which are commonly believed to be proper names must be made possibly comprehensive.

2. *Logical Characteristics of Proper Names.* — This chapter includes a review of opinions and theories concerned with proper names (Mill, Frege, Russell, Reichenbach, Ayer, Xenakis, Searle, and Quine). Logicians do not agree on which expressions of natural language are proper names. Hence the second requirement: when constructing a theory of proper names we have to decide whether that is to be: a theory of expressions commonly considered to be proper names in natural language; or a theory of proper names in the traditional grammatical interpretation of the term; or a theory of proper names in the interpretation of modern linguistics; or, as it happened in logic, a theory of a category of

expressions, isolated from natural language on the strength of a certain principle and with a certain end in view, and then termed proper names, in some cases contrary to current intuitions and opinions of linguists.

3. *Proper Names versus Expressions Used in some Respect as Proper Names.* — The point of view of traditional grammar is formal in the sense that it focuses attention on the outward form of expressions. It is suggested here to take into consideration functional elements as well, in accordance with the trends prevailing in modern linguistics. For that purpose the distinction can be made between: a token of an expression; the use of an expression; an expression. A token of an expression is a given concrete case of an expression as written out or spoken out; an expression is the class of all its tokens; the use of an expression is a subclass of the latter, consisting of tokens referring, for instance, to the same object. By taking the use of expressions into account we abandon the practice of treating words as isolated dictionary items and take into consideration the context and the extralinguistic situation in which a given expression occurs, that is, its pragmatic aspects. This helps to find out that certain expressions, which neither in current opinion nor in the eyes of the linguists are proper names, share — in some respects and in some uses — those semiotic properties which are ascribed to proper names in the classical sense of the term. Conversely, in some uses and in some respects, pure proper names do not reveal properties ascribed to them as characteristic of proper names. Hence the next requirement: instead of treating proper names and expressions that are not proper names as mutually exclusive classes, we have to make a distinction between expressions used in some respect as proper names and expressions used in the same respect not as proper names.

4. *Degrees of the Property of Being a Proper Name.* — Further analysis, resorting to the concept of the use of an expression, results in the successive requirement: distinction must be made between expressions used as proper names in a greater degree and those used as such in a lesser degree.

5. *Proper Names versus Subject and Predicate.* — The relationship between proper names on the one hand and the subject and the predicate on the other hand — was studied by Aristotle. But to solve that problem we must first — and this is the next requirement — to answer the question whether the terms 'subject' and 'predicate' occur as the grammatical subject and the grammatical predicate of a sentence, or the logical subject and the logical predicate of a proposition; and next, in which sense of those ambiguous terms. The traditional analysis of a sentence into subject, copula, and predicate (the "A is B" pattern), commonly used in logic, also requires a revision. Only then can the problem be investigated, whether proper names can be used only in the rôle of the subject, as distinguished from common names that can also function as predicates. This leads to the next requirement: we have to investigate whether proper names can function as objects in sentences.

6. *The Meaning of Proper Names.* — The focal issue in discussions concerned with proper names was whether they have meanings. Opinions on that issue of Mill, Frege, Russell, Jespersen, Strawson, Quine, Ayer, Searle, and Xenakis are listed. It turns out that those who referred to meaning in those discussions actually meant different things. Hence the consecutive requirement is: in order to answer the question formulated above we must first decide how we interpret meaning. The suggestions made by Lewis, Carnap, and Strawson may prove helpful in that respect. In defining the concept of meaning we must be guided by the consideration in what kinds of analyses that concept is to be used.

7. *The Singular Character of Proper Names.* — The problem of the singular character of proper names occurs at the meeting point of such issues as the ontological and metaphysical concept of an individual; the semantic issue of singularity with respect to designating, as distinct from the singular intention with respect to meaning; the syntactic issue of the individual character of an expression as predestining it only to the rôle of a grammatical or logical subject. Some opinions of Frege, Russell, Reichenbach,

Quine, Ryle, Jespersen, and Strawson are listed in this connection. That listing yields the following requirement concerning a theory of proper names: we have to answer the questions what is understood by an individual and what is understood by the singular character of an expression (Lewis's distinction between designatum, denotation, and extension may be introduced here). Only then can we proceed to examine the problem whether singularity is a property of proper names.

8. *Proper Names and Descriptions.* — The title of this Section is not an antithesis, although it occurs as such in most authors. In accordance with the requirement of analysing proper names by resorting to the concept of the use of an expression we cease to see in proper names and descriptions mutually exclusive classes of expressions. The requirement is formulated that the degree of descriptiveness of proper names and conversely, the degree of the property of being a proper name, of those expressions which are descriptions in the traditional sense of the term be studied; and, obviously, such a study must in each case take into account a given use of the expression studied.

9. *Conclusion.* — A future theory of proper names in natural language ought to answer the question when a given expression is used, in a given context and a given extralinguistic situation, in what respect and in what degree, as a proper name. Such a theory should not aspire to formulate a definition of proper names as a separate class of expressions. The same applies to the theory of other kinds of expressions in natural language, among them a grammatical classification of parts of speech.

# NOMINAL EXPRESSIONS AND LITERARY FICTION

## 1. FICTITIOUS SUBSISTENCE

Literature is sometimes described as the art the works of which are works of fiction. They refer to an imaginary world, and not to a real one. That imaginary world is supposed to consist of FICTITIOUS OBJECTS. But in what does their fictitious nature consist? In what does physical existence differ from fictitious subsistence? Are all fictitious objects alike as to their mode of subsistence, or can they be classified into distinct categories?

Answers to these questions can be found in logical analyses concerned with the problems of existential quantification. Here is one of the various possible examples of the description of the various modes of FICTITIOUS SUBSISTENCE.[1]

The first category of fictitious objects consists of SUBJECTIVE THINGS, which next to the objective, physical ones form the subclass of direct things. Subjective things are those 'seen' in dreams, and also those objects which we treat as objective and real things, although objects different from them are objectively and really given to our observation. Thus, for instance, while watching light and dark points on a screen or a photograph, we 'see' persons, buildings, furniture, etc.

The second category of fictitious objects might include those to which we ascribe LOGICAL SUBSISTENCE. We refer to subsistence of this kind when the assumption of physical existence is not self-

---

[1]  *Cf.* Hans Reichenbach, *Elements of Symbolic Logic* (New York, The Macmillan Company, 1948), § 49.

contradictory. In this sense a unicorn subsists logically, since the existential statement "a unicorn exists" is not self-contradictory. Sometimes another variation of this concept is introduced, when those things and facts that are logically possible are considered to subsist logically. Still another variation of logical subsistence can be found in what are termed judgements about belief:[2] if a person believes that something is so and so, we interpret this so as if he believed in the existence of a fact, which practically means logical subsistence, because that SO AND SO does not exist physically.

The mode of fictitious subsistence of INTENTIONAL OBJECTS comes close to the last-named concept. Every transitive verb has its object(s), that is, grammatical complement(s); likewise, mental acts, e.g., acts of desiring, willing, etc., have their complements, namely those intentional objects. An intentional object is what I desire, what I intend to do, what I try to do, what I expect. That intentional object is similar to a subjective thing in its mode of being, but nevertheless differs from the latter by not being connected with our direct ideas and does not form their subject matter. The goal of our intention is not an idea, but a realization of an idea.

At the moment we are most interested in those fictitious objects to which literary subsistence is ascribed. Literary and art theorists as well as theorists of aesthetics pay much attention to explaining that kind of being. But logical papers also provide some information on the subject, because logicians, though not interested in an analysis of a literary work as the principal subject matter of their research, do find in such an analysis elements that are important to them. It is so because there are certain essential analogies between this or that mode of fictitious subsistence and the being of mathematical objects or the being of abstract equivalents of expressions, such as denotata and extensions.

Literary subsistence may be interpreted by reducing it to the physical existence of corresponding sentences in a given text, or by reducing it to some kind of existence of ideas and emotions in the reader's psyche. In the latter case we have to do with a mode of

[2]  *Cf.* Bertrand Russell, *Inquiry into Meaning and Truth* (New York, Norton, 1940), pp. 22 and 336-42.

being similar to that which is characteristic of subjective objects, "seen" by the reader of a literary work.[3] The first case, on the contrary, might consist in a relativization with respect to the author to whom the sentences occurring in a text owe their physical existence.

There are many various kinds of fictitious subsistence. The foregoing specification does not exhaust them all, and was not meant to do so. The intention is to make the reader watchful when he happens to hear someone say that literature is an art of fiction. The above remarks show that such a statement can be interpreted in many different ways. One of the many sources of such differences is the variety of mode of fictitious subsistence. And it seems that each of those modes may have something to do with literature.


## 2. NOMINAL EXPRESSIONS

It would be interesting and instructive to examine the various modes of fictitious subsistence in literature, without confining oneself to what is termed literary subsistence. But we cannot engage in that all here, since we wish to concentrate upon the relationship between NOMINAL EXPRESSIONS, especially those used as singular, and FICTITIOUS SUBSISTENCE.

The traditional explanation of the problems of literary fiction consists in linking it with the problem of the truth-value of the sentences occurring in a literary work. This is a good method of analysis, but I think that it can be usefully expanded by the study of the function performed by non-sentential expressions in creating fiction; we mean here nominal expressions in the grammatical sense of the term, that is, first of all nouns and adjectives. We are concerned with one-word expressions, such as "John", "Hamlet", "table", "Death" (with a capital $D$, as a personification), "rich", with compound expressions treated so as if they were single words ("John Smith", "New York", "Newcastle-on-Tyne", and perhaps also "Dr. Jekyll"), with expressions consisting of two or more words,

[3]   *Cf.* Reichenbach, *loc. cit.*

such as "My Fair Lady", "he who has climbed Mt. Everest", "the death of a salesman", "captain's daughter", and also such pronouns as "he", "this", etc.

In logic, those expressions are divided into certain subclasses, but the criterion of division varies from case to case.[4]

For instance, we may speak of EMPTY, SINGULAR, and GENERAL expressions, according to the number of the designata they have: an empty expression has none, a singular expression has one, and a general expression, more than one. Moreover, according to definition, by a designatum is meant either the concrete, real, individual object that corresponds to a given expression in its given meaning and in a given language, or an object that need not necessarily be concrete and real, but is interpreted in some other way. The problem of designatum becomes still more complicated when we come to consider what an individual is. At any rate, this classification of expressions depends, as can be seen from the above, on a state of things in extralinguistic reality.

The second classification refers to an immanent, linguistic, criterion to introduce the following subclasses: EXPRESSIONS WITH A SINGULAR INTENTION and EXPRESSIONS WITH A GENERAL INTENTION; here the distinction is based on the way the meaning of a word or phrase determines its extension. For instance, the description "John's only son", as it makes the proviso of uniqueness, has in this sense a singular intention regardless of whether the John in question has only one son, or more than one, or is childless. General intention is ascribed to the expression "red object on my desk",[5] without an article, and that regardless of whether on my desk there are more red objects than one, or just one, or none. It seems that within this classification we might take into account the third subclass, namely EXPRESSIONS WITH AN EMPTY INTENTION. It would consist, according to one of the many possible opinions, of self-contradictory expressions, absurdities like "square circle", because

[4]    Cf. Tadeusz Kotarbiński, Gnosiology, "On the Classification of Names", pp. 389 ff. (Oxford, Pergamon Press, 1966).
[5]    Cf. C.I. Lewis, "The Modes of Meaning", in Philosophy and Phenomenological Research, 4, No. 2 (Buffalo – New York, 1943), pp. 236-49.

their very meanings account for the fact that they cannot be applied to anything that could be conceived in a non-contradictory manner. They would, of course, be empty expressions — also in the sense of the previous classification.

The third classification adopts a syntactic, or rather logical syntactic, criterion, that is one belonging to the field of logical syntax. Following Aristotle,[6] expressions are classified into INDIVIDUAL and GENERAL. Aristotle classified entities — it is not clear whether he meant extralinguistic entities, or linguistic expressions, or logical analogues of linguistic expressions — into those about which we may predicate (Socrates), but by means of which we may not predicate, and those by means of which we may predicate (man). It is difficult to decide whether for Aristotle Socrates, or "Socrates", or "Socrates" but only in the function of the (grammatical? logical?) subject of a sentence, or all three were an individual entity. Similar doubts pertain to man or "man". In any case the interpretation of his views tended to make distinctions between expressions, and not between extralinguistic entities, and thus drifted away from ontology. It also resulted in the following distinction: individual expressions are those which may occur only in the function of the subject, and general expressions are those which may occur in the function of the predicate. It probably remains a mystery whether in this formulation reference is made to subject and predicate in the grammatical or the logical sense of the terms, and to which of the many meanings of those terms. Typical examples of individual expressions would be provided by one-word proper names, were they even empty in the sense of the first classification (e.g., "Aphrodite"). As examples of general expressions we might quote "table", "John's father", "Hercules' father", "Hercules' son", that is, general, singular or empty expressions in the sense of the first classification, and along with them those which are marked by singular intention or by general intention.

In addition to the foregoing classifications, the following distinction will prove useful: A TOKEN OF AN EXPRESSION, THE USE OF AN

Cf. Aristotle, *Categories*, 5.

EXPRESSION, AN EXPRESSION.[7] The word "dog", as written here, is one of the many tokens of that expression; as can be seen, a token of an expression is a concrete thing, located in space and time. The set of all tokens of an expression, conceived as an abstraction, is an expression. And now the use of an expression. I have a dog whose name is "Trot". Now whenever I use a token of the expression "dog" with reference to my Trot, I have to do with the same use of the word "dog". When, on the contrary, I use a token of the word "dog" to refer to Kazan, my dog-friend from Zakopane, this is a different use of the word "dog". Still another use is exemplified by the insertion of a token of the word "dog" in the sentence "the dog is a friend of the man", where not any definite dog is meant, but reference is made either to every dog or to the dog 'in general'. Finally, in all those cases when a token of the word "dog" has occurred in this text, it has not been used with reference to any dog, but has served as an example, which is still another use of that expression.

It must be realized that the semantic properties singled out above: singularity, singular intention, individual character, etc., are associated not with an expression, but with the use of an expression. Hence the same expression may be singular in one use (e.g., the word "chair" in the sentence "Offer me the chair, please") and general in the other (e.g., the word "chair" in the sentence "Not every piece of furniture is a chair"). Likewise, it may have a singular intention in one use, and a general intention in the other; it may be individual in one use, and general in the other. On the other hand, meaning is associated with the expression, and not with its use or its token. The meaning of an expression may be defined as the general rules of such a use of that expression that it should refer to certain things.

By analogy, the distinction may be made between A SENTENCE, THE USE OF A SENTENCE, and A TOKEN OF A SENTENCE. We then shall say about a given use of a sentence, and not about a sentence, that it is true or false, or that the question of its truth-value does not arise at all. To the sentence itself we shall ascribe a meaning,

[7]    *Cf.* P. F. Strawson, "On Referring", *Mind*, LIX (1950), 320-44.

understood as general rules of using that sentence to construct true or false statements.

An isolated expression, which occurs as a dictionary item, is ascribed a DICTIONARY MEANING, distinct from the MEANING SHAPED BY THE LINGUISTIC CONTEXT, in which an expression used so and so occurs, and also by the EXTRALINGUISTIC SITUATION, which accompanies a given use of that expression. Hence the expressions which we encounter in definite acts of speaking and writing have their dictionary meanings modified by the context and factual circumstances. The general rules of the use of a given expression, as mentioned above, become then specialized.

The distinctions listed above will be used in an analysis of the functions of nominal expressions in works of fiction.

### 3. NOMINAL EXPRESSIONS VERSUS REAL USE ($U_R$) AND FICTIVE USE ($U_F$)

A comparison of a literary and a non-literary text helps to grasp the difference between the denoting function of nominal expressions in each of them.

Should we list such expressions, drawn from a literary work, whether poetry or prose, and compare it with a list of items drawn from a scholarly work, it would turn out that it is not the choice of the types of expressions, but the semantic functions of expressions of the same type that decide whether a given work creates fiction or not. The items on the two lists would be much alike. It can be expected that a list of expressions drawn from a Napoleonic epic or a historical novel about the Napoleonic period would resemble much more a list of nominal expressions drawn from a scholarly monograph on Napoleon, than the latter list would resemble a third list, namely that of nominal expressions occurring in a scholarly monograph on Copernican discoveries in astronomy. And yet both a history of the Napoleonic period, and a history of Copernican discoveries refer to real facts, whereas a Napoleonic epic or a historical novel about the Napoleonic period create fiction. It can also be expected that should we draw two lists of nominal expressions, one including the items drawn from all past and present written and spoken literary works, and the other including the items drawn from non-literary texts, then the two lists would not differ essentially from one another. The vocabulary of the artistic language, used in creating fiction, does not differ essentially from the vocabulary of the non-literary language, used in describing reality. This applies, however, at the most to the shape and the dictionary value of expressions.

If the class of the extralinguistic elements corresponding to a language, that is, all that to which all the expressions of that language refer, is termed the MODEL of a language, then the previous observation can be formulated as follows. The fact that the model of a language is fictitious in the sense that it consists of fictitious objects need not affect the lexicon of that language. A REAL MODEL ($M_R$) and a FICTITIOUS MODEL ($M_F$) may both correspond to the same lexicon. On the other hand, it may happen that two different real models correspond to two different lexicons; the same applies to two different fictitious models.

The question arises whether we have to do with the same language if a fictitious model ($M_F$) and a real model ($M_R$) are counterparts of the same lexicon. Hence, is the language $L_R$, which consists of the expressions $E_{R_1}$, $E_{R_2}$, ..., $E_{R_n}$ and has the real model $M_R$, identical with the language $L_F$, if the latter has the same grammar as $L_R$ and consists of all and only those expressions which are equiform with those mentioned above, namely of the expressions $E_{F_1}$, $E_{F_2}$, ..., $E_{F_n}$ such that $E_{F_1}$ is equiform with $E_{R_1}$, $E_{F_2}$ with $E_{R_2}$, etc., and if the language $L_F$ has the fictitious model $M_F$? It seems that the answer should be in the negative. Even if the models $M_R$ and $M_F$ are isomorphic in the sense that each REAL OBJECT $O_R$, which is an element of the model $M_R$, has its counterpart in the FICTITIOUS OBJECT $O_F$, which is an element of the model $M_F$, and conversely, and if every relation between objects $O_R$ in the model $M_R$ has its counterpart in a corresponding relation between objects $O_F$ in the model $M_F$, and conversely, the languages $L_R$ and $L_F$ are not identical. The identity of lexicons, the identity of grammatical structures, and the isomorphism of models are necessary, but not sufficient conditions of the identity of the languages $L_R$ and $L_F$.

Why are $L_R$ and $L_F$ not identical? To answer this question we have to compare a pair of corresponding nominal expressions, $E_{R_1}$ of the language $L_R$ and $E_{F_1}$ of the language $L_F$.

"The horse broke off through the trees dragging him, bumping, face downward, and Robert Jordan stood up holding the pistol now in one hand."[8]

This sentence from *For Whom the Bell Tolls* is an example of the language $L_F$. Its part, "the horse broke off through the trees", might equally well belong to the language $L_R$. The nominal expression "the horse" is equiform in both cases and has the same dictionary meaning. But when it is spoken in CURRENT SPEECH ($L_R$), then the context and/or extralinguistic circumstances of the statement modify the original dictionary meaning of that nominal expression in another way than it happens in the case of a literary statement. Hence in $L_R$ we have to do with a singular use. The word "the horse" ($E_{R_1}$) has its counterpart in one concrete horse, and the word 'the pistol' ($E_{R_2}$), one concrete pistol. In the literary passage, on the contrary, we have to do with an empty use with singular intention. Nothing in the model $M_R$ corresponds to the words "the horse" and "the pistol" ($E_{F_1}$, $E_{F_2}$); hence they are empty in terms of that classification. On the other hand, in the model $M_F$ each of those expressions has its counterpart in a fictitious individual or in an intentional object; this is why we say that they are used with singular intention.

It might be added that in the FICTIONAL LANGUAGE ($L_F$) the rôle of the context as the modifier of the dictionary values of the expressions used is relatively greater than in the language $L_R$. It is so because in the fictional language concrete extralinguistic situations that accompany the utterance of words and/or sentences cannot affect their use in this way as they can in the case of current speech ($L_R$). In $L_R$ the presence of a real object $O_{R_1}$ often settles the fact that a given expression $E_{R_1}$ is used ostensively, i.e., as if the speaker pointed to that object. If a person is in his home and says: "The

---

[8]  Ernest Hemingway, *For Whom the Bell Tolls*, Chap. 21 (Overseas Editions, Inc.), p. 266.

bulb in the bathroom is gone", then the proximity of the bathroom $(O_{R_1})$ and the bulb $(O_{R_2})$ causes it that the general names in the dictionary sense "the bathroom" $(E_{R_1})$ and "the bulb" $(E_{R_2})$ occur here in an ostensive singular use. On the contrary, in the language $L_F$ the context is often the only, and usually the principal, modifier of the dictionary value of expressions: the competition of factual, extralinguistic, circumstances is incomparably weaker.

Let it be agreed that the term FICTIVE USE $(U_F)$ is used in such cases as "the horse" $(E_{F_1})$ and "the pistol" $(E_{F_2})$, where those expressions occur as EMPTY and with SINGULAR INTENTION, and are elements of the fictional language $(L_F)$.

The fictive use understood in this way can sometimes be encountered outside literature as well, and in literary works we also sometimes have to do with uses of other kinds. But anyway that fictive use must be considered characteristic of poetry and artistic prose. By using nominal expressions in such a way we call FICTITIOUS OBJECTS to life. On the other hand, when those expressions occur in REAL USE $(U_R)$, then they serve to point to, or to identify, a given concrete object $O_R$. They do not create fictitious subsistence, but refer to objective existence.

By using the terms 'fictive use' and 'real use' we may say that the languages $L_R$ and $L_F$ are not identical in spite of the identity of the lexicon, the dictionary equisignificance of corresponding expressions, the identity of grammatical structure and the isomorphism of the models $M_R$ and $M_F$; they are not precisely because equiform and lexically equisignificant expressions may occur in different uses: in the real use $(U_R)$ in the language $L_R$, and in the fictive use $(U_F)$ in the language $L_F$.

### 4. NOMINAL EXPRESSIONS IN FICTIVE USE $(U_F)$ VERSUS THE REAL MODEL $(M_R)$ AND THE FICTITIOUS MODEL $(M_F)$

When those nominal expressions which occur in the fictive use $(U_F)$ are defined as empty but having a singular intention, then at least the first part of this characteristic, which refers to emptiness, is formulated with reference to the real model $(M_R)$.

It might be disputed whether it is correct to characterize the word $E_{F_1}$, in its use $U_F$, and belonging to the language $L_F$ which has its model $M_F$, with respect to the model $M_R$ that corresponds to the language $L_R$. Consequently, would it be not correct, instead of claiming that the word "the horse", when used as $E_{R_1}$ in the language $L_R$, is singular, and when used as $E_{F_1}$ in the language $L_F$ — is empty but with a singular intention, to say that it is singular also in the use $U_F$, within the language $L_F$, because in the model $M_F$ it has a counterpart, even though that counterpart is fictitious. Now characterizing the expressions $E_F$ in the language $L_F$ as empty by referring to an alien model $M_R$ — has its traditions and arguments in its favour.

For instance, Russell[9] claims it vigorously, when he says: "The question of 'unreality', which confronts us at this point, is a very important one. Mislead by grammar, the great majority of those logicians who have dealt with this question have dealt with it on mistaken lines. They have regarded grammatical form as a surer guide in analysis than, in fact, it is .... It is argued, e.g. by Meinong,[10] that we can speak about 'the golden mountain', 'the round square', and so on .... In such theories, it seems to me, there is a failure of that feeling for reality which ought to be preserved even in the most abstract studies. Logic, I should maintain, must no more admit a unicorn than zoology can; for logic is concerned with the real world just as truly as zoology, though with its more abstract and general features. To say that unicorns have an existence in heraldry, or in literature, or in imagination, is a most pitiful and paltry evasion. What exists in heraldry is not an animal, made of flesh and blood, moving and breathing of its own initiative. What exists is a picture, or a description in words. Similarly, to maintain that Hamlet, for example, exists in his own world, namely, in the world of Shakespeare's imagination, just as truly as (say) Napoleon existed in the ordinary world, is to say something deliberately confusing, or else confused to a degree which is scarcely credible.

[9]  *Cf.* Bertrand Russell, "Descriptions" (Chap. XVI of *Introduction to Mathematical Philosophy* [London, Allen and Unwin, 1919]).
[10]  A. Meinong, *Untersuchungen zur Gegenstandstheorie und Psychologie* (1904).

There is only one world, the 'real' world: Shakespeare's imagination is part of it, and the thoughts that he had in writing *Hamlet* are real. So are the thoughts that we have in reading the play. But it is of the very essence of fiction that only the thoughts, feelings, etc., in Shakespeare and his readers are real, and that there is not, in addition to them, an objective Hamlet. When you have taken account of all the feelings roused by Napoleon in writers and readers of history, you have not touched the actual man; but in the case of Hamlet you have come to the end of him. If no one thought about Hamlet, there would be nothing left of him; if no one had thought about Napoleon, he would have soon seen to it that some one did."

In addition to more general philosophical considerations, which include the admission of the real world as the only reality, there is also another reason for which we are inclined to compare the language of fiction ($L_F$) with an alien real model ($M_R$). Now the truth-value of propositions is determined in classical two-valued logic by applying the Aristotelian criterion of agreement with reality, precisely that reality to which $M_R$ belongs. A comparison of sentences from the language $L_F$ with the world of fiction that includes the fictitious model $M_F$ would introduce different concepts of truth and falsehood, which would also be based on the agreement of a sentence, or, strictly, a given use of a given sentence, with reality, but with a reality of another kind. Likewise, it would become disputable whether such a sentence is a form of a proposition, since the latter is defined in terms of truth and falsehood but in their previous interpretation.

But the law of the excluded middle and the principles of classical two-valued logic could be renounced, and it could be assumed that there are such uses of sentence that are devoid of the properties of truth and falsehood, although the sentences as such are meaningful, because in other circumstances they could be used to state something true or false.[11] According to that theory, we come across such an alleged, apparent use, a use that might be termed dud, when the subject of a given sentence is a nominal expression that does not

[11]    *Cf.* Strawson, "On Referring".

refer to anything in the real model ($M_R$), and does not identify any real individual ($O_{R_1}$), but — being an expression with a singular intention — refers to a definite single fictitious object ($O_{F_1}$), to a single element of the fictitious model ($M_F$). From that point of view it would be a misunderstanding to compare statements belonging to the language of fiction ($L_F$) and the real model ($M_R$). In particular, it would be a misunderstanding to say, having read in *For Whom the Bell Tolls* about Maria that "Her teeth were white in her brown face and her skin and her eyes were the same tawny brown. She had high cheeckbones, merry eyes and a straight mouth with full lips,"[12] that it is not true. From that point of view it would also be a misunderstanding to say that it is true.[13] Of course, if the terms 'truth' and 'falsehood' are used in the traditional interpretation. For if we take these terms so, the issue of truth and falsehood in such cases does not arise at all.

The advantage of this theory is that it complies with the current intuitions associated with the term 'false'. We are inclined to treat as false those statements in which something is predicated counter-factually about somebody or something existent, but not those in which anything — no matter what — is predicated about something nonexistent.[14] Another advantage is the fact that it grasps a certain peculiarity of our attitude toward literary fiction, namely that to which Ingarden[15] draws attention: fiction is not taken quite seriously, which results in the quasi-truth of the sentences belonging to a literary work, sentences which accordingly are described as quasi-propositions. The disadvantage of the theory in question is that it renounces the law of the excluded middle. The disadvantage, however, can, as it seems, be eliminated while the advantages can partly be saved. For that purpose it suffices to make use of Russell's distinction between the PRIMARY and the SECONDARY use of

---

[12]   Ernest Hemingway, *For Whom the Bell Tolls*, Chap. 2 (Overseas Editions), p. 22.
[13]   *Cf.* Leonard Linsky, "Reference and Referents", *Philosophy and Ordinary Language*, ed. Ch. A. Caton (Urbana, 1963).
[14]   *Cf.* Alfred J. Ayer, "Proper Names and Descriptions" (in Polish), *Studia Filozoficzne*, No. 5,20 (Warszawa, PWN, 1960).
[15]   Roman Ingarden, *The Literary Work* (in Polish) (Warszawa, PWN, 1960).

DESCRIPTIONS.[16] The secondary use of a denoting phrase is defined as such in which the phrase occurs in a proposition ($p$), and the $p$ is an element of the entire proposition. For instance, the denoting phrase "the present king of France" occurs as secondary in the sentence "The present king of France is not bald", if that statement is interpreted according to the formula "it is not true that $p$", in other words, "it is not true that: there exists a person who is now king of France and is bald." On the other hand, we have to do with a primary use in the case of the following interpretation: "There exists a person who is now king of France and is not bald". The first interpretation, which includes a secondary use, yields a true sentence; the second, which includes a primary use, yields a false sentence. As can be seen, the law of the excluded middle has been preserved. But the price to be paid would be the treatment of all empty nominal expressions with a singular intention, and hence nominal expressions in a fictive use ($U_F$), so common in literature, as descriptive expressions in Russell's sense. Moreover, his theory of descriptions would have to be adopted. Finally, which perhaps would arouse the least protest, all independent declarative sentences which occur in a literary text would have to be treated as elements of a larger whole being taken into account. Only such an operation results in the secondary character of a denoting phrase. Thus, for instance, "Her teeth were white ..."[17] would require the following interpretation: "Hemingway, as the author of *For Whom the Bell Tolls*, imagined that the heroine of his novel, whom he gave the name 'Maria', had white teeth ...". In this interpretation the word "Maria" occurs as a latent description, and moreover that description is included in an element of a proposition; we have thus to do with a secondary use, and with a true statement. Not everyone would decide to accept such interpretational complications, and not everyone would be willing to adopt Russell's theory of descriptions.

A simpler solution — also without a renunciation of the law of the excluded middle — would consist in making a distinction be-

---

16  *Cf.* Bertrand Russell, "On Denoting", *Mind*, XIV (1905).
17  *Cf.* footnote 12 above.

tween A WEAK AND A STRONG INTERPRETATION OF GENERAL CATE-
GORICAL SENTENCES, e.g., SaP. In the weak interpretation, such a
sentence merely states the inclusion of the class S in the class P,
without any assumption as to the existence of a real designatum of
the name S. Hence the sentence may be true also if S is empty.
This is, however, not a universal solution, since only general and
singular statements can be presented after the SaP pattern. The
pattern does not apply to particular statements, which are always
subject to the strong interpretation. And literary texts do include
such statements too. In view of the emptiness of S they would be
false. Moreover, that emptiness is established by a comparison of
the nominal expression in question with the real model ($M_R$), which
has been the subject matter of controversy.

It seems, however, that there is no need to settle that controversy
in a decisive way, for neither is the fictitious model ($M_F$), consisting
exclusively of fictitious objects ($O_F$) the proper model of literature;
nor is the real model ($M_R$), consisting exclusively of concrete
objects ($O_R$), a model entirely alien to literature; nor are the fictive
use ($U_F$) and the language of fiction ($L_F$), as consisting solely of
expressions of the type $E_F$ in such a use, the specific use and the
specific language of the verbal art.

## 5. LITERARY USE ($U_L$), LITERARY LANGUAGE ($L_L$), AND LITERARY MODEL ($M_L$)

Literary context modifies the original, dictionary value of the expressions it includes — in a number of ways. True, the modification
which turns an expression that from the dictionary point of view
is general or singular into an expression used as fictive ($U_F$), and
hence into an empty one with a singular intention, is very significant,
yet it certainly is not the only modification. At the most, it strikes
the eye because it differs from that in current speech, where the
context and the extralinguistic situation modify expressions in a
different way, so that, for instance, what by its dictionary value is
a general nominal expression becomes a singular expression in a
given real use ($U_R$).

It suffices to examine a number of sentences drawn from a historical novel, which have as the SUBJECT the PROPER NAME of a historical person. It turns out that even in the same syntactical function we have to do with the real use ($U_R$) on one occasion, and with the fictive use ($U_F$) on the other; thus, on one occasion the expression is used as singular, and on the other, as empty with a singular intention. Some sentences are about the real Napoleon, whereas others are about (in a different sense of the word) an imaginary Napoleon. The same applies by analogy to the expressions occurring as object (i.e., complement) or apposition, and not only to the proper names of persons, but also to the proper names of places and events, and even to common names. The well-known fragment of Stefan Żeromski's novel *The Ashes*,[18] which describes how Napoleon stopped over the wounded Cedro, one of the heroes, reads: "The Emperor stood over him still for a long while. He looked into his face with stony eyes. Finally he raised his hand to his hat and said, '*Soit*'." This sentence creates an imaginary situation, and the term "the Emperor" occurs in a fictive use ($U_F$) as an empty name with a singular intention. But when in the same novel Żeromski refers to Napoleon's stay in Bayonne and writes: "The Emperor lived here in Marrac Castle and kept the Spanish kings, Carlos IV and Fernando VII, with him"[19], the sentence refers to real Napoleon and the term "the Emperor" occurs in a real use ($U_R$) as a singular name. While the adjustment of the former sentence, in the use $U_F$ given in this case, to the real model ($M_R$) would be a misunderstanding, since the result of such an operation is known in advance, the adjustment of the latter sentence to the same model is fully justified.

In addition to this OSCILLATION OF USES ($U_R$ and $U_F$) of the same expression as it occurs in the same syntactic function, we can notice in literary texts a difference between the use of a given nominal expression when it functions as the subject, and its use when it

[19]  *Ad hoc* translation from Stefan Żeromski's *Popioły* [The Ashes], Vol. III, Chap. "Widziadła" [Nightmares].
[13]  *Ad hoc* translation from the same novel as note 18 above, Chap. "Szlak Cesarski" [The Imperial Route].

functions as the predicate. This is connected with the characteristics inherent in the said classification of those expressions into
individual (to be used only as subjects) and general (to be used also
as predicates). The principal semantic function of an individual
expression, such as pure, one-word, non-descriptive proper names,
is to indicate a certain individual, to mention him or to identify him.
A nominal expression which occurs in literary texts in that syntactic
and semantic function very often occurs in a fictive use ($U_F$) and
thus creates a fictitious entity ($O_{F_1}$). When, however, it occurs as
a general name, e.g., in the predicate, if often occurs in a real use
($U_R$). Hence in the former case we have to do with it being used
as an empty expression with a singular intention, and in the latter,
e.g., as a general name. Thus even such a short literary context as
a single sentence may modify the same expression in semantically
different ways in accordance with the syntactic function of the word
in question. Within a given sentence the gap is as it were bridged
between the world of fiction and the real world: the extralinguistic
counterpart of an individual expression (in the sense of the classification referred to above) is among imaginary entities, whereas the
extralinguistic counterpart of the general expression constitutes
part of reality. If we have the sentence in a novel: "John was a
secret emissary",[20] its subject, the proper name "John", occurs in a
fictive use ($U_F$) as an empty expression with a singular intention;
its counterpart is the imaginary hero of the story. But the predicate
"secret emissary" occurs in a real use ($U_R$) as a general name, and
the whole sentence may be interpreted so that it states the inclusion
of the class of the subject in the non-empty and non-singular class
of the predicate. It would be contrary to the intention of the author
to interpret the sentence as stating that fictitious John was a
fictitious secret emissary; no, fictitious John was a "true" secret
emissary. Likewise, if it is said that "Tom was a short, spry man
of seventy, a veteran of the Crimean War",[21] then Tom is an
imaginary person, created by the expression "Tom", empty and

---

[20]   Example invented *ad hoc* by the translator on the analogy of the original
example drawn from Polish literature.
[21]   Same as note 20.

with a singular intention. On the contrary, the properties of being a spry man of seventy and a veteran of the Crimean War are real in the sense that they are ascribed to real individuals as well.

The individual or general use of a given nominal expression need not coincide with the occurrence of that expression as subject or predicate, respectively, although those cases are typical. On the other hand, the coincidence of the individual use with the fictive use ($U_F$), and of the general use with the real use ($U_R$) is notorious. This applies also to pairs of equiform expressions, or, to put it another way, to the different uses of the same expression. Suppose there is a story about Ivan, who was a Cossack, and it is said about him that: "He knew how to be a courtier among courtiers, a Cossack among Cossacks, and a brigand among brigands." [22] Here the word "Cossack" occurs as a general, i.e., predicative, expression, and also as a general name in a real use ($U_R$). If later on we read about Ivan that "... the nobleman was enraged by the fact that the Cossack was so impudent," [23] the same word "Cossack" (if we disregard the use of articles) occurs as an individual expression in a fictive use ($U_F$); it creates a fictitious entity, namely Ivan ($O_{F_1}$) and hence occurs as an empty expression with a singular intention.

Here again we have to do with oscillation, this time between an individual and fictive use, when a given nominal expression occurs as empty with a singular intention, often in the function of subject, and general and real use, when a given nominal expression occurs as general, often in the function of predicate. Thus even within a single sentence such a small literary context as the subject part of that sentence may modify the original, dictionary value of a given nominal expression in a way different from that in which the predicate part would do in the case of the same expression. As a result, in the subject position we may obtain an individual, fictive, and empty use with a singular intention, while in the predicate position we obtain a general and real use. Such sentences are, as it were, BIPOLAR: they have both a fictitious and a real referent. Hence in such cases it is difficult to decide that the model proper for them

[22]   Same as note 20.
[23]   Same as note 20.

is fictitious ($M_F$), while the real model ($M_R$) is to be rejected, or *vice versa*. Both models are, each in a different respect, suitable as the criteria of the truth of such a sentence, interpreted in the classical sense on one occasion, and in the coherential on the other. And both are in some respects useless. Hence neither of them may be either accepted or rejected without reservation.

The fictive use ($U_F$) of a nominal expression is not the only kind of use that may be encountered in a literary work. The real use ($U_R$) occurs there as well. THEY ARE IMPOSED alternately upon one and the same expression and modify its original dictionary value in different ways. How it happens is determined by the literary context, and this is what is characteristic of literature, and not — as it is currently believed — the fictive use only. Let this oscillation between $U_F$ and $U_R$, this SHIFTING of the fictive and the real use, be termed 'LITERARY USE ($U_L$)'. A nominal expression which occurs in the literary use ($U_L$) will, according to the context, be either empty with a singular intention, or singular, or general. On one occasion it will create a fictitious entity, and on another it will mention a real entity or will predicate. On one occasion it will occur as an individual expression, and on another as general.

The language of literary works is not a language of fiction ($L_F$), consisting solely of expressions occurring in a fictive use ($U_F$), and hence of expressions symbolized as $E_{F_1}$, $E_{F_2}$, $E_{F_3}$, etc. It also includes expressions occurring in a real use ($U_R$), and hence expressions symbolized as $E_{R_1}$, $E_{R_2}$, $E_{R_3}$, etc. It is thus a MIXED language. We shall term it 'LITERARY LANGUAGE ($L_L$)', of course in a sense different from that in which a literary language differs from dialects.

The model of the literary language ($L_L$), i.e., of the artistic language of works of literature, is not, as is often believed, the fictitious model ($M_F$), consisting solely of fictitious objects ($O_{F_1}$, $O_{F_2}$, $O_{F_3}$, etc.). It consists of both fictitious and real objects ($O_{R_1}$, $O_{R_2}$, $O_{R_3}$, etc.). In that sense it is HETEROGENEOUS. We adopt for it the term 'LITERARY MODEL ($M_L$)'. In that model we can indicate various relations. Some hold between fictitious objects; others hold between real objects; but there are also such that associate a fictitious object with a real one. The last-named find their formulations in the 'bipolar' sentences of the language $L_L$, mentioned above. Thus the model $M_L$ accommodates both real existence and fictitious subsistence of various kinds: of subjective things, of intentional objects, of entities endowed with logical subsistence, etc.

Literature — poetry and novelistic prose — is referred to as an art of fiction, and it is believed that the world of literary fiction is an imaginary world which — as opposed to reality — consists of unreal entities only. But in fact that world includes concrete objects in addition to imaginary ones. Literary fiction is not pure imagination: it combines that which subsists in fantasy only with what exists objectively. Such at least is the conclusion reached as a result of the foregoing semiotic analysis of nominal expressions occurring in literary use ($U_L$) within the literary language ($L_L$) that has a literary model ($M_L$).

SUMMARY

1. *Fictitious subsistence.* — When it is said that literature is an art of fiction, various things may be meant by that, since there are various modes of fictitious subsistence, e.g. the subsistence of subjective things, 'seen' in dreams; logical subsistence, when the supposition of physical existence is not self-contradictory; the subsistence of intentional objects; the literary subsistence of persons and objects that appear in poetry and prose works, which is reducible to the physical existence of corresponding sentences in the text or to the mental experiences of the author and/or the readers.

2. *Nominal expressions.* — The concept of literary fiction is usually explained by an analysis of the truth-value of sentences occurring in a given literary text. But it may as well be based on an analysis of the semantic function of the nominal expressions occurring in that text. Those nominal expressions include nouns, adjectives, pronouns, and noun and adjectival phrases. They are classified in

several ways: into empty, singular, and general — according to the number of the designata of a given nominal expression in a given language and a given use; into those with a singular, a general, and an empty intention — according to the way the meaning of a given expression determines its denotation; into individual and general — according to whether they can function only as subjects of sentences or as predicates as well. It is also useful to make a distinction between: a token of an expression, a use of an expression, and an expression. The first is a definite thing, the third, the class of all tokens, and the second, a subclass of the latter, consisting of those tokens which in the same way perform the function of referring to their extralinguistic counterparts. Finally, a distinction will be made between the dictionary value of an expression, as isolated from the context and the situation accompanying its use, and the contextual value, modified by the context and the situation.

3. *Nominal expressions versus real use* ($U_R$) *and fictive use* ($U_F$). — When a nominal expression is used to refer to a real object ($O_R$), then that expression occurs in a real use ($U_R$) and is symbolized $E_R$. When it refers to a fictitious object ($O_F$), then it occurs in a fictive use ($U_F$) and is symbolized $E_F$; in such a case it is an empty expression with a singular or general intention. Expressions $E_R$ combine to form the real language ($L_R$), which as its linguistic model has a real model ($M_R$) consisting of real objects ($O_R$). The language of fiction ($L_F$) consists of expressions $E_F$ and has as its counterpart a fictitious model ($M_F$) which is a set of objects $O_F$. $L_R$ and $L_F$ are different languages even if their lexicon is the same, i.e., if their expressions are pairwise equiform, if their expressions are pairwise equisignificant, if the grammatical structure of both languages is the same, and if the models of those languages are isomorphic. This difference is caused by the fact that in the language $L_R$ we have to do with a real use of nominal expressions, whereas in $L_F$ we have to do with a fictive use of those expressions.

4. *Nominal expressions in fictive use* ($U_F$) *versus the real model* ($M_R$) *and the fictitious model* ($M_F$). — If a nominal expression that

occurs in a fictive use ($U_F$) is classified as empty, this is done so with respect to the real model ($M_R$), although that is not the proper model of the language of fiction ($L_F$). We can, however, in this way characterize a sentence drawn from a literary text as to its being true or false in the classical interpretation of those terms. But it is also possible to renounce the law of the excluded middle with reference to the truth-value of such a sentence and to claim that if an expression in the use $U_F$ occurs as a subject of such a sentence, then the sentence is neither true nor false. If the expressions $E_F$ are interpreted in the light of Russell's theory of descriptions, it is possible — unfortunately in a complicated and non-intuitive way — to save the law of the excluded middle. The weak interpretation of universal statements in a literary text yields an analogous result, but is not valid for all occasions.

5. *Literary use* ($U_L$), *literary language* ($L_L$), *and literary model* ($M_L$). — Expressions $E_F$, the use $U_F$, and the language $L_F$, although characteristic of literature, are not specific for it, since they also occur outside literature. Moreover, in a literary text itself we can encounter expressions $E_R$ and the use $U_R$. Frequently the same expression E, in a given place of the text occurs in the use $U_R$, and hence as $E_{R_1}$, and in another place of the same text it occurs in the use $U_F$, and hence as $E_{F_1}$. It is the literary context which in each case modifies in a different way the original dictionary value of a given nominal expression. For instance, it is a typical situation that a given expression occurs in the subject position in the use $U_F$, that is, as $E_{F_1}$, and in the predicate position in the use $U_R$, that is, as $E_{R_1}$. There is a coincidence between the individual nature of an expression and its fictive use, and between its general nature with its real use. This is accompanied by an oscillation, or shifting, of the uses $U_R$ and $U_F$. This alternate imposition of $U_R$ and $U_F$ upon the same expression $E_1$ is termed literary use ($U_L$) and is claimed to be characteristic of literature. The term "literary language ($L_L$)" will be used with reference to the mixed language consisting of both expressions $E_R$ and expressions $E_F$, that is, the language in which nominal expressions occur in the literary use ($U_L$). This is the

language of literary works. Its model is the literary model ($M_L$), which is heterogeneous, as it consists both of objects $O_R$ and objects $O_F$. Various relations hold between objects of a given type, and also between objects of different types. $M_L$ is the model of literature, sometimes also called the world of literary fiction. It combines that which subsists only in imagination with that which exists objectively.

# SEMIOTIC FUNCTIONS AS APPLIED TO
# THE ANALYSIS OF THE CONCEPT OF METAPHOR

## INTRODUCTION

The concept of metaphor is used in two senses, a broader and a narrower one.

The former comes from Aristotle who in his *Poetics*, XXI, writes: "Μεταφωρὰ δ'ἐστιν ὀνώματος ἀλλωτριου ἐπιφωρὰ ἤ ἀπὸ γένους ἔπι ἐῖδος ἤ ἀπὸ ἐίδους ἐπί γένος ἤ ἀπὸ ἐίδους επὶ εῖδος ἤ κατὰ τὸ ἀνάλωγον".

The concept of trope, related to metaphor in that broader sense of the term, has been defined by Quintilianus in his *Institutio oratoria*, L.VIII.6.1: "*Tropus est verbi vel sermonis a propria significatione in aliam cum virtute mutatio.*"

In the narrower sense of the word, metaphor, also called metaphor proper, is, alongside of metonymy, synecdoche, hyperbole, irony, anti-irony, etc., one of the tropes, that is, one of the variations of metaphor in the broader sense of the term. That metaphor proper is being described in various ways, but the oft-recurring opinion is that it is an abbreviated comparison.

In this paper, metaphor in the broader sense of the word will be briefly called 'metaphor', and metaphor in the narrower sense of the term, that is a concept included in the former, will be called 'metaphor proper'.

The analysis which follows will be concentrated on the concept of metaphor — in conformity with the ancient tradition and the practice of linguistic research. The various tropes will be analysed only because of being covered by that concept; consequently, their peculiarities and rhetoric and poetical values, which distinguish one trope from the other and which are so willingly brought out and stressed by literary and poetical stylistics, will not be discussed here.

On the contrary, the analysis which follows will be more general and more theoretical and abstract in nature, since it will be concentrated on the structure and the mechanism of the very CONCEPT of metaphor, i.e., of metaphorical expression. The author's objective is to point out the specific properties of all the expressions of that kind, regardless of the artistic functions which they may perform in literature, and almost regardless of the rhetoric category in which they are classified by traditional stylistics.

This is to be achieved by means of SEMIOTIC analysis. For it is obvious that if the problems of metaphor are connected with certain cases of the appearance of signs as such then the most proper choice is that of a method of research which is specifically adapted to the subject matter of that research, has at its disposal the instruments of modern science and makes it possible to treat the issue in a most general manner.

Thus, the analysis which is to follow now consists in an endeavour to apply the semiotic functions of the sign to the analysis of the concept of metaphor. That analysis will of necessity be an outline rather, and an experimental one at that, since as far as the author knows no such semiotic analyses of tropes have been made so far. No claim is made, either, to offer a complete theory of metaphor, although this paper may be the first step towards building such a theory (first, of course, in the logical, and not historical, sense of the word), for it seems that the laying of logical foundations is the best approach to and preparation for such endeavours.

## I. BASIC CONCEPTS AND THE THEORETICAL FOUNDATIONS OF THE ANALYSIS OF METAPHORS

### 1.  *Basic Concepts*

The following semiotic instruments will be used in the analysis of the concept of metaphor: sign, designation, designatum, denoting, denotation, meaning or sense or connotation, specific property, essential property, peculiar property, expressing, replacement, and language. Here is the most important information about them.

The SIGN is an object which is accompanied by the communicative intention of its author as such or its user as such, on the one hand, and by semiotic interpretation by the person who perceives it, on the other, owing to which it acquires the so-called semiotic 'transparence', or performs certain semiotic functions. The functions now referred to, i.e., designating, denoting, meaning and expressing, are relations between the sign and certain objects or properties that are external with respect to that sign.

Thus the sign sometimes DESIGNATES a certain object or certain objects which belong to extra-linguistic reality and are called DESIGNATA of that sign which is their name in a given language.

The set, in the distributive sense, of all the designata, or the class, in the distributive sense, of the designata of a given sign is its DENOTATION; thus, the sign denotes the class of its designata.

Further, every sign MEANS something, or CONNOTES, or has a SENSE, or, in other words, has a CONNOTATION; that connotation is the set of the ESSENTIAL PROPERTIES jointly connoted by that sign.

Essential properties are some of the SPECIFIC PROPERTIES, i.e., those which are attributes of all the elements of a given class and of them only (thus, in a special case, of all the designata of a given sign and of them only).

The PECULIAR PROPERTY is a property which is an attribute of a certain object in contradistinction to other objects treated as elements of the same class as the former object.

The next semiotic function of the sign — apart from semantic functions: designating with denoting, and meaning or connoting — is EXPRESSING. This is a pragmatic relation between the sign and its author or user as such. Thus it may be said that the sign expresses the experiences among others of its user, and it expresses them if it has been used to inform other persons about the experiences of its user.

REPLACING, or INTERCHANGING, differs from these semiotic functions in being a relation between signs and not, as it the case of the functions described above, between the sign and something outside the linguistic reality. Two signs replace one another, or interchange, if one may appear in place of the other and the TRUTH-VALUE or the SENSE of the statement of which each of them is an element, does not change. In the former case we have to do with the replacement of equivalent signs and that replacement takes place *salva veritate*; in the latter, we have to do with the replacement of signs which are synonymous as well, and then replacement takes place *salva sensu*. These and other cases (such as replacement *salva analycitate*) are covered in linguistics by the term SYNONYMITY, which usually is not defined in any precise manner and consequently refers not only to synonymous, but also to nearly synonymous words, and not only to equivalents but also to signs with similar denotations.

The remaining concept is that of LANGUAGE or SEMANTIC SYSTEM. It is a certain set of signs, determined by syntactic, semantic (e.g., the rule of DENOTING) and other rules.

The preceding remarks are not, and have not been meant to be, a set of definitions of semiotic terms, but have been conceived as concise elementary information about them as instruments in the future analysis of the concept of metaphor. That is why they are confined to pointing, not always in a precise manner, to those issues which are the most important with respect to such analysis.

## 2. *Theoretical Foundations*

Before engaging in the analysis announced before it is worth while paying attention to one point more. Now every sign appears in a certain definite social situation: it is usually produced by some person and is perceived by some person. This means that, except for extraordinary cases, one has to take into account, apart from the really existing object which is the token of the sign in question, also the person of its author as such and the person of its interpretant as such, and also the relations between these three elements. Moreover, there also comes in question the fourth element, namely that fragment of reality to which that sign refers and which is a transcendent object of ideas of the author and of the interpretant of the sign.

This gives a quadrangle *sui generis*, the apices of which are: the author of the sign, the sign, the interpretant of the sign, and that fragment of reality which is the designatum of the sign. The sides and the diagonals of that quadrangle are relations between them. So far only two of them have been mentioned as semiotic functions of the sign, namely the semantic relation of designating, which occurs between the sign and the corresponding fragment of reality, and the pragmatic relation of expressing, which occurs between the sign and its author as such.

The remaining relations are not semantic functions and their nature is rather psychological. They are: the pragmatic relation between the author and the sign, which is included in the genetic process, that is process of producing the sign; and the pragmatic relation between the interpretant and the sign, which is included in the process of perception, of taking cognizance of the sign. The remaining relations are those between the author and reality, and between the interpretant and reality. The former may be included in the process of producing the sign, since the perception of reality by the author often is a preliminary step to his making use of the sign in order to inform others about what he has perceived. The latter may be included in the process of perceiving the sign, since the perception of reality by the interpretant often completes or modifies what has been conveyed to him through the intermediary of the sign.

This shows that one has to distinguish THREE PHASES OF EXISTENCE OF THE SIGN: THE SIGN IN ITS READY-MADE FORM, its ORIGIN, and its INTERPRETATION. Only the last two are — even to a large extent — the domain of psychology. The first one — the proper subject matter of the present analysis — belongs to SEMIOTICS. That is why it would be a psychologistic attitude to treat the sign in its ready-made form (not in the process of being produced or interpreted) as a psychic phenomenon. In particular, this applies to the metaphor as well, since every metaphor is a sign. The choice of the metaphor in its ready-made form, or, in other words, of a metaphorical expression, as the subject matter of this analysis, in contra-distinction to the process of making or interpreting a metaphor, that is in contradistinction to a metaphorizing author as such or a metaphorizing interpretant as such, is explained by the present author's intention to grasp the objective and verifiable aspect of the phenomenon, an aspect which may be subjected to methodologically mature forms of semiotic analysis.

So much for the basic concepts and the theoretical foundations of the analysis of metaphors.

## II.  THE SEMIOTIC ANALYSIS OF STYLISTIC TROPES

### 1.  *The Metaphoric Triangle* $EE_1E_2$

Expressions which are defined as metaphorical by experts on linguistics, stylistics, rhetorics and poetics will now be analysed. In doing so the present author will observe the traditional classifications of tropes without engaging, for the time being, in the discussion whether it is correct or not. Analysis will cover consecutively: metaphor proper, metonymy, synecdoche, periphrase, irony and anti-irony. This will show whether they reveal common traits from the semiotic point of view, traits which would justify the preservation of the general term 'metaphor'; further, what these traits are (if any); and finally, what differences are to be found between the various tropes and whether such differences justify the preservation of the usual boundaries between the various particular concepts that are subordinated to the general concept of metaphor.

The knowledge of existing descriptions of metaphor, even most general and equivocal ones, shows that in the case of all stylistic tropes two expressions are taken into consideration. Terminology varies greatly, according to the standpoint and the theoretical approach of the scholar concerned, e.g., "the real, or prosaic, meaning" and "the way of conveying it", "the original idea" and "the borrowed idea", "that what is really to be said or thought" and "that what is compared with the former", "the basic idea" and "nature imagined", "the basic object" and "that what is similar to it", or "meaning" and "metaphor", or "the idea" and "its image", or "the proper term" and "the metaphorical term", or finally, in Richards's terminology, "tenor" and "vehicle". Thus, "sun rays" would be an example of the first element of each of these pairs, and "the hair of the Sun", an example of the second element of those pairs. In this paper, they will be symbolized $E_2$ and $E$, respectively.

Yet the present analysis will, contrary to existing tradition, be based not on two, but on three terms. This seems to be an essential modification, if the presentation of the complete picture of the structure and the semiotic mechanism of the concept of metaphor is taken as the objective. Let that third term be symbolized $E_1$. In the example used above, it would be "the hair" in the so-called proper sense.

Thus, the analysis of the concept of metaphor will consist in investigating the semiotic relations between the metaphorical expression $E$ and each of the non-metaphorical expressions $E_1$ and $E_2$, as well as between $E_1$ and $E_2$, that is, all the relations within the figure which will be called the METAPHORIC TRIANGLE $EE_1E_2$. $E$, $E_1$ and $E_2$ are expressions belonging to the language L.

## 2. *Metaphor Proper*

The analysis of the concept of metaphor will be based on the following examples of metaphorical expressions: "the roaring of waves", "bull's health", "a torrent of tears", "golden hair", and "the stars of (her) eyes".

Let us first consider THE RELATION $E - E_1$ OR $E_1 - E$, which holds between a certain proper expression, or, as it is sometimes said, an expression understood literally or verbally, and a metaphorical expression, formed from the former, or *vice versa*.

It can easily be seen that (1) $E$ and $E_1$ are equiform; (2) at least one designatum of the expression $E_1$ and every designatum of the expression $E$ share the property $P$ or the properties $P_1$, $P_2$, ... $P_n$.

For instance, the designata of the word "star" as the name of a heavenly body ($E_1$) and the designata of the word "star" as the name of shining eyes are such objects which share the property P, namely that of shining.

In such a case as "the hair" ($E_1$) and "the hair of the Sun" (E), only certain designata of the expression $E_1$ have the properties $P_1$, $P_2$, ..., $P_n$ which are shared by the hair of the Sun, that is sun-rays, namely the properties of being bright, long and straight. No one will say about sun-rays that they are the hair of the Sun having in mind the short, woolly and dark hair of a Negro.

It often happens that the property P, which characterizes all the designata of the expression E, is an attribute of the typical elements of the class $E_1$, i.e., such which have the greatest number of properties characteristic of that class. E.g., the property of being healthy and strong, alluded to by the expression "bull's health", is an attribute not of all but only of some elements of the class of bulls.

(3) The denotations of the expressions E and $E_1$ are either mutually exclusive or overlapping.

For instance, no star is a brightly shining eye, which has metaphorically been called "a star". Likewise, no hair is a sun-ray, which has metaphorically been called "the hair of the Sun".

But there are also such cases as the literal understanding of the word "golden" (colour) and the metaphorical understanding of that word in the expression "golden hair" which denotes bright and shining hair. As is known some object which are of golden colour are bright and shining, but some others, like old florin gold or a reddish gold alloy are either not bright or not shining.

(4) The expressions E and $E_1$ are non-synonymous.

For instance, the word "roaring" in its proper sense which appears, e.g., in the expressions "the roaring of lions", has a different sense, or connotes other essential properties, from the metaphorical sense of the word "roaring" in the expression "the roaring of waves".

But here too one may point to a certain connection between the basically different connotations of E and $E_1$:

(5) The property P (or the properties $P_1$, $P_2$, ..., $P_n$) which is (are) attribute(s) of at least some designata of the expression $E_1$,

is (are) connotative, or essential, property (properties) of the expression E.

For instance, the connotative properties of the metaphorical word "torrent" (E) in the expression "a torrent of tears" is a comparatively large quantity of tears following one another in a rapid succession. Those properties have been taken into consideration which are attributes of at least some torrents $(E_1)$, perhaps even the typical torrents, but probably not all of them, namely the large quantity and the rapid flow of water.

The formulation "the property P which is an attribute of AT LEAST some designata of the expression $E_1$", admits the case in which that property is an attribute of all the designata of the expression $E_1$, and even all of them and only them, that is a case in which it is their specific property. Thus, e.g., all the stars in the astronomical sense of the term, and even in the ordinary use of the word, covering the planets and their satellites, have the property of shining, which is included in the connotation of the word "star" used metaphorically with reference to shining eyes.

The relationships described under (2), (4) and (5) can be completed by reference to the resulting ABSTRACT and PARTICULARIZING nature of the metaphorical expressions. It will be convenient to raise those points in the description of the pragmatic function of expressing, performed by the expressions E and $E_1$.

(6) The expression E expresses (as to content) the experiences of the person (as such) who has made use of a metaphor, and that in the following manner:

(a) That person PERCEIVES the property P or the properties $P_1$, $P_2$, ..., $P_n$ shared by the designata of the expression E and designata of the expression $E_1$ and intends to BRING IT (THEM) OUT; consequently he turns it (them) into connotative property (properties) of the expression E.

(b) That person DISREGARDS CERTAIN, sometimes even specific, PROPERTIES OF THE DESIGNATA OF THE EXPRESSION $E_1$ and constructs the metaphorical expression E in such a way that those disregarded properties should be in that expression neither connotative properties nor properties implied by the former ones.

Thus, the person who speaks metaphorically about the hair of the Sun disregards the fact that the true hair is made of a cornuous substance, and when he speaks of bull's health he abstracts from the fact that bulls are herbivorous animals. Thus, metaphorical expressions are abstract in nature in the described sense of the term.

In this connection:

(c) The person who uses a metaphor has in mind the expression $E_1$ NOT IN ITS WHOLE EXTENSION.

This means that, as has been mentioned above, he has in mind, e.g., not all the bulls when he speaks of bull's health, but only the strong and healthy specimens.

It is in this that the particularizing tendency of the metaphorical expressions consists.

The semiotic relations and properties described above make up what might be called METAPHORIZATION, or SEMIOTIC MODIFICATIONS, which account for the fact that the non-metaphorical expression $E_1$ becomes the metaphorical expression E, in this case a so-called metaphor proper.

The relation $E-E_2$, or $E_2-E$, will be discussed now; it holds between a certain metaphorical expression and the non-metaphorical expression which is replaced by the former.

(1) The expressions E and $E_2$ are non-equiform, e.g., "the hair of the Sun" (E) and "sun-rays" ($E_2$).

(2) The expressions E and $E_2$ are equivalent, i.e., they have the same denotation, or sometimes the denotation of the expression E is subordinate with respect to the denotation of the expression $E_2$, which will be symbolized thus: Den E sub Den $E_2$.

Equivalence, however, must be considered the typical case, for attention should be paid to the fact the expression $E_2$ most often does not appear in the context, but is merely implied. Consequently, a lack of extensional equivalence between E and $E_2$ can be ascribed to an inappropriate choice of the non-metaphorical equivalent of the given metaphorical expression.

An example of equivalent expressions is provided by the pair "the stars of (her) eyes" (E) and "shining eyes" ($E_2$). And an example of subordination of E with respect to $E_2$ is the pair "the hair of the Sun" (E) and "sun-rays" ($E_2$), since the hair of the Sun always is sun rays, but not every sun ray may appropriately be called "the hair of the Sun", even if we abstract from the poetical nature of that expression and have in mind only the properties of the designata of the name "sun-rays".

(3) The expressions E and $E_2$ are synonymous or nearly synonymous.

The typical case is that of synonymity. The case of nearly synonymous expressions often consists, in that the connotation of the expression $E_2$ is poorer than that of the expression E, the difference being the property P or the properties $P_1, P_2, ..., P_n$.

If for instance one points to the expression "copious lacrimation" ($E_2$) as the implied non-metaphorical equivalent of the metaphor proper "a torrent of tears" (E), then after a precise reconstruction of the senses of both expressions one may conclude that among the specific properties connoted by the expression E there is the property of being a torrent, or, *sit venia verbo*, the property of torrentness, which is absent in the connotation of the expression $E_2$. But in most cases such a difference can be ascribed to a not quite appropriate choice of the non-metaphorical equivalent of the metaphor proper, an equivalent which often does not appear in the text, but is implied. A quite appropriate choice would result in the fact that the expressions E and $E_2$ could stand for one another *salva sensu* as well, and not only, as is the case here, *salva denotatione et veritate*.

(4) The expression E expresses (as to content) the experiences of the person who has used it, as such, in a somewhat different manner than does the expression $E_2$. Namely, in the experiences of the person who thinks about any of the common designata of these two expressions or about their common denotation, when that person uses the picturesque, metaphorical name E, the above-mentioned specific property P of those objects comes to the fore. This may also be accompanied by certain emotional experiences. But when that person uses the non-metaphorical equivalent $E_2$, that phenomenon rather does not take place.

The semiotic relations between the expression E and the expression $E_2$, as described above, constitute the base of the relation of REPLACEMENT, which holds between metaphor proper and its non-metaphorical equivalent, which usually remains implied.

Finally, there is the relation $E_1-E_2$, or $E_2-E_1$, in other words, the relation between the non-metaphorical equivalent of metaphor proper ($E_2$) and the non-metaphorical expression ($E_1$) from which that metaphor proper has developed following a semiotic modification (or the reverse relation).

(1) The expressions $E_1$ and $E_2$ are not equiform, e.g., "a star" and "a shining eye".

(2) The designata of the expressions $E_1$ and $E_2$ share the property P or the properties $P_1$, $P_2$, ..., $P_n$, which is (are) the basis of comparison (*tertium comparationis*) "$E_2$ is like $E_1$".

Thus, for instance, in the comparision "an eye like a star" the basis is the property of shining (P), and it can be shown to characterize each of the designata of the expressions $E_2$ ("a shining eye") and $E_1$ ("a star").

(3) The denotations of the expressions $E_1$ and $E_2$ are mutually exclusive or overlapping.

In particular, e.g., no sun ray is a hair; see also the description of the relation $E-E_1$, point (3), the second example.

(4) The expressions $E_1$ and $E_2$ are not synonymous.

For instance, the sense of the word "torrent" differs from that of the expression "copiously flowing tears".

(5) Both the connotative properties of the expression $E_1$ and the connotative properties of the expression $E_2$ imply the same property P (properties $P_1$, $P_2$, ..., $P_n$) shared by the designata of both these expressions and forming a *tertium comparationis* in the comparison built of these expressions, or else P or $P_1$, $P_2$, ..., $P_n$ is (are) connotative property (properties) of one of these expressions and is (are) implied by the connotation of the other and hence predestined to the role of *tertium comparationis* in the comparison "$E_2$ is like $E_1$".

Now, e.g., the properties of brightness ($P_1$) and shining ($P_2$) belong to the connotation of the expression "bright and shining"

($E_2$), and are implied by the sense of the word "golden" ($E_1$), and form the basis of comparing brightness and shining to golden objects.

(6) The expression $E_1$ expresses (as to content) different experiences of the person who has used it (as such) than does the expression $E_2$. Yet in both cases the experiences include the idea of the property P or the properties $P_1$, $P_2$, ..., $P_n$ which always is (are) the attribute of both $E_1$ and $E_2$.

Thus the experiences of the person who has used, as such, the word "hair" ($E_1$) differ from those of the person who has used, as such, the word "rays". Yet in both these cases the experiences include the ideas e.g. of thinness and length ($P_1$, $P_2$) as the properties common to some hair and to some rays.

The semiotic relations, as described above, holding between the expressions $E_1$ and $E_2$, determine the structure of the COMPARISON which is built from them. Elements of that comparison are expressions connected with the origin of metaphor proper, namely $E_1$, of which that metaphor proper develops through a semiotic modification, the form of the expression being preserved, and $E_2$, which, although different in form, is its non-metaphorical equivalent. Just because a comparison rests at the root of the metaphor proper, it is often said that it is as it were an abbreviated or condensed comparison, often consisting of one word only.

But it can be seen that such a characteristic would be incomplete. For the structure and the semiotic mechanism of the metaphor proper are determined not only by the relations holding between $E_1$ and $E_2$, but all the relations between E, $E_1$ and $E_2$, as described above, or the whole of the relationships occurring within the figure which has been called the METAPHORIC TRIANGLE.

## 3.  *Metonymy*

The analysis of the concept of metonymy will be based on expressions given by specialists as examples of its variations, namely "he lives from trade" (cause instead of effect), "to read Shakespeare" (the author instead of the work), "roaring steel" (about guns; substance instead of the objects made of it), "the whole village gathered" (the name of a country, a town or a village instead of the names of its inhabitants), "extinct windows" (concrete objects instead of other concrete objects connected with the former ones by a causal relationship).

The study of the relations occurring within the metaphoric triangle $EE_1E_2$ will not include the repetition of the observations made previously in the analysis of the concept of metaphor proper and retaining their value now, but will be confined to indicating new issues which make it possible to distinguish metonymy from metaphor proper.

First comes the relation $E-E_1$, or the reverse one.

(1) Whereas in the case of metaphor proper the property P or the properties $P_1$, $P_2$, ..., $P_n$ was (were) shared by some designata of the expression $E_1$ ("some" being used in the logical sense of the word as "at least some", and not "only some", as in the ordinary usage), especially by the designata which are typical of $E_1$, and by all the designata of the expression E, in the case of metonymy that property or those properties is (are) specific or essential property (properties) of the designata of the expression $E_1$ and are attributes of all the designata of the expression E, and hence appear in its connotation.

If for instance the word "steel" comes to denote metonymically guns made of steel, then the property of 'steelness' (P) is both an essential property of the non-metonymical word "steel" ($E_1$) and a property which is an attribute of all guns made of steel and which appears in the connotation of the metonymical word "steel" (E).

(2) The denotations of the expressions E and $E_1$ may be mutually exclusive, as in the case of metaphor proper, but sometimes they may be in the relation of subordination, namely the denotation of E is subordinated to that of $E_1$, which is symbolized thus: Den E sub Den $E_1$.

For instance, the word "steel", used metonymically to denote a gun made of steel (E), is extensionally subordinated to the non-metonymical word "steel" as used to denote every object made of steel ($E_1$).

One may also additionally draw the reader's attention to a certain NON-SEMIOTIC RELATION OF THE MATERIAL CONNECTION between the designata of the expression E and those of the expression $E_1$.

Thus, for instance, guns of steel, metonymically called "steel" (E), are made of steel. Peasants form a part, in the material sense, of the village understood non-metonymically as a whole consisting of men, buildings, territory, etc.; hence the metonymy "village" (E) used to denote the inhabitants of (that) village. The works of Shakespeare, at least before they were written down, had been tantamount to the nervous system of their author as such, in a certain period of time, and shaped in a certain definite way; consequently they had been tantamount to a part of their author in the material sense. Thus even in the metonymy "I read Shakespeare" one can find that material connection.

The semiotic relations, as described above, which occur between the expression E and the expression $E_1$, or *vice versa*, and also certain non-semiotic connections between the designata of these expressions, make it possible to conclude:

(a) in what consists the semiotic modification of the expression $E_1$, which results in the metonymy E;

(b) in what respect it differs from the semiotic modifications that are characteristic of metaphor proper; and

(c) to what an extent the semiotic modifications that accompany the origin of each of these tropes are similar to one another.

It can be concluded from their recurring properties that each of them is a variation of the same general phenomenon, namely semiotic modifications appearing in the transformation of an arbitrary non-metaphorical expression into an equiform metaphorical expression, which process is here called metaphorization.

Since the analysis of the relation $E-E_2$ does not provide any observations concerning differences between the relation of metaphor proper (E) to its non-metaphorical equivalent ($E_2$) and the relation of metonymy (E) to its non-metonymical equivalent ($E_2$), one may pass directly to the study of the relation $E_1-E_2$. Here too, as before, the study will be confined to bringing out new issues.

(1) Whereas in the case of metaphor proper the denotations of the expressions $E_1$ and $E_2$ always are mutually exclusive, in the case of metonymy apart from that case it may also happen that the denotation of the expression $E_2$ is subordinated to that of the expression $E_1$, or: Den $E_2$ sub Den $E_1$.

For instance, the concept of a gun made of steel ($E_2$) is extensionally subordinated to the concept of an object made of steel ($E_1$).

(2) Whereas in the case of metaphor proper the connotations of the expressions $E_1$ and $E_2$ imply a certain property P which is a *tertium comparationis* in the comparison "$E_2$ is like $E_1$", or else that property is a connotative property of one of these expressions, implied by the connotation of the other expression, in the case of metonymy the situation is different: the property P or the properties $P_1$, $P_2$, ..., $P_n$ is (are) not a *tertium comparationis*, because the expressions $E_1$ and $E_2$ do not form a comparison; but that property or those properties is (are) connotative in the expression $E_1$ and definition-making in the expression $E_2$.

Thus, for instance, the property of villageness belongs as an essential property to the connotation of the expression "village" ($E_1$) in its literal sense, and at the same time it is a property by means of which one can define the word "villager" ($E_2$); more precisely, it is a property a linguistic equivalent of which can form part of the definiens in the definition of the word "villager".

(3) Whereas in the case of metaphor proper $E_1$ and $E_2$ form a comparison, that phenomenon, as has been mentioned above, does not occur in the case of metonymy. But one may point to the non-semiotic properties, referred to above, of the designata of those expressions, namely to the material connections between a certain designatum of $E_1$ and a certain designatum of $E_2$. Within the non-semiotic relation Des $E_1$ – Des $E_2$ one can distinguish, among other things, the relations: between the agent and his work, between substance and a product made of that substance, between a whole and its material part, between an object and its property, and so on.

What has been said about the relation $E_1$ – $E_2$ characterizes the relations between the non-metonymical expression ($E_1$), from which the metonymy (E) develops as a result of semiotic modifications, and its non-metonymical equivalent ($E_2$), in contradistinction to the relations $E_1-E_2$ occurring in connection with the concept of metaphor proper.

The remarks made above concerning the relations which occur in the metaphoric triangle $EE_1E_2$ determine the semiotically distinct character of the concept of metonymy. But it must be borne in mind that, in conformity with the announcement made above, only new issues have been raised, namely those which distinguish metonymy from metaphor proper. All those issues which occur in both cases have been disregarded, and yet it is they which form the majority. Thus there are more similarities than differences between these two tropes.

This proves that they both belong to one and the same general concept, i.e., metaphor. Moreover, the most important differences between them are not semiotic issues at all. Further, from the purely semiotic point of view the demarcation line passes not so much between metaphor proper and metonymy as between metaphor proper and certain variations of metonymy on the one hand, and the remaining variations of metonymy on the other. For it seems that such metonymy as "I am reading Shakespeare" is not more remote from metaphor proper than from such metonymy as "the roaring steel": the expression "I am reading Shakespeare" shows semiotic relations within the metaphoric triangle $EE_1E_2$ similar to those taking place in the case of a metaphor proper. In particular, e.g., $E-E_1$ are mutually exclusive as to their extensions. On the other hand, the metonymy "the roaring steel" reveals extensional subordination within that relation, namely Den E sub Den $E_1$, which does not occur in the case of metaphor proper.

Should we then take the semiotic properties of tropes, their semiotic structure and the semiotic mechanism of functioning as decisive criteria, we might have to reconsider whether the traditional boundaries between tropes have been drawn in the most fortunate manner.

## 4. *Synecdoche*

The specialists describe synecdoche as a variation of metonymy, consisting, in their opinion, in:

(a) replacement of the name of a thing by the name of a part of that thing, which replacement is called *pars pro toto*, e.g. "pavement" for "paved road", "head" for "man";

(b) replacement of a common name by a proper name, e.g., "such was the death of X, the Hector of Y" (where X stands for the name of a person, and Y for the name of a locality);

(c) replacement of the name of a concrete concept by the name of an abstract concept, e.g. "(he is) kindness itself" for "(he is) an extremely kind man";

(d) replacement of species by genus, and *vice versa*, e.g., "vipers and snakes" for "reptiles", "mortals" for "men";

(e) replacement of the plural by the singular, or *vice versa*, e.g., "the enemy" for "the enemies", "we" for "I";

(f) the use of a definite number instead of an indefinite one, e.g., "hundred" for "many";

(g) the nominal use of an adjective, e.g., "the immortal ones" for "gods".

The semiotic analysis of the concept of synecdoche provides the following new observations.

The relation $E-E_1$ or the reverse one.

(1) The designatum of the expression $E_1$ is

(a) a material part of the designatum of the expression E, or

(b) an element of the set which is a single designatum of E, or

(c) the designata of $E_1$ and E are elements of the comparison "E is like $E_1$", or, as in the case of metonymy,

(d) the designata of E and $E_1$ share a common specific or essential property P (specific or essential properties $P_1$, $P_2$, ..., $P_n$). The last case (d) is the most general one and all the preceding cases (a, b, c,) can be subsumed under it.

Examples: (a) The pavement, i.e., the designatum of the non-synecdochic word "pavement" ($E_1$), is a material part of the designatum of the synecdoche based on the *pars pro toto* principle "pavement" (E) or "paved road".

(b) The enemy, the designatum of the non-synecdochic word "enemy" ($E_1$), is an element of the set which is a single designatum of the synecdochic expression "the enemy" (E), used to denote a group or a detachment of enemies.

(c) The person X, denoted by the synecdochic empty name "the Hector of Y" (E), is compared with Homer's Hector, denoted by the non-synecdochic empty name "Hector" ($E_1$).

(d) Mortality is the common essential property (P) both of the designata of the non-synecdochic name "mortal" ($E_1$) and of the designata of the synecdoche "mortal" (E), used to denote men. There is here the extensional relation Den E sub Den $E_1$, which is characteristic of certain metonymies.

(2) Apart from extensional relations known from the study of metonymy, it sometimes occurs in the case of synecdoche that the denotation of the expression $E_1$ is subordinated to the denotation of the expression E, or Den $E_1$ sub Den E.

For instance, if the word "hundred" (E) is used synecdochically as an equivalent of the word "many" ($E_2$), then the relation of E to its non-synecdochic source, or the word "hundred" ($E_1$), denoting literally 100, is such that every $E_1$ is E, but only some E are $E_1$, so that precisely Den $E_1$ sub Den E.

This shows that the process of synecdochization of a given expression, which process consists in a semantic modification of the expression $E_1$ that appears in its literary meaning, a modification which turns $E_1$ into the synecdoche E, has much in common both with the process of metaphorization proper and with that of metonymization, since all the three are variations of the general process of metaforization. It is in two points only that synecdochization differs from the remaining two.

The relation $E-E_2$, or the reverse one, i.e. the relation of synecdoche to its non-synecdochic equivalent it stands for, or *vice versa*, shows the following difference when compared with that relation as occurring in the case of metonymy:

Apart from the case known in metonymy, where a certain property P or properties $P_1, P_2, ..., P_n$ is (are) connotative property (properties) of both the expression E and the expression $E_2$, it may also occur WITHIN SYNECDOCHE:

THE ANALYSIS OF THE CONCEPT OF METAPHOR 161

(a) that the said properties are connotative properties of the expression E and are attributes of all the designata of the expression $E_2$, or

(b) that they are connotative properties of the expression $E_2$ and are attributes of all the designata of the expression E.

An example of the case (a) is provided by the pair: the synecdoche "the mortal" (E) and its non-synecdochic equivalent "man" $(E_2)$.

With the case (b) we have to do, when we compare the synecdoche "the Hector of Y" (E) with its equivalent "the hero characterized by the properties $P_1$, $P_2$, ..., $P_n$", where $P_1$, $P_2$, ..., $P_n$ are properties ascribed, among others, to Hector from *Iliad*.

But in both cases it is to be borne in mind that the expression $E_2$, which is the non-synecdochic equivalent of synecdoche, is in most cases implied and consequently may be chosen not quite to the point. And only such a choice is a fully appropriate one in which the expressions E and $E_2$ are equivalent.

The relation $E_1-E_2$, or the reverse one.

Here two observations, made in the course of the analysis of the relation $E-E_1$, or the reverse one, may be repeated *mutatis mutandis*:

(1) The designatum of $E_1$ is:

(a) a material part of the designatum of $E_2$, or

(b) an element of the set which is a single designatum of $E_2$, or

(c) the designatum of $E_1$ and that of $E_2$ are elements of the comparison "$E_2$ is like $E_1$", or

(d) these designata share a certain specific or essential property P or certain specific or essential properties $P_1$, $P_2$, ..., $P_n$, which case is the most general one and the preceding ones (a, b, c) can be subsumed under it.

The examples remain the same as under (1) of the analysis of the relation $E-E_1$.

(2) Apart from the extensional relations known from the analysis of metonymy, it happens in the case of synecdoche that Den $E_1$ sub Den $E_2$.

The example of the synecdochic use of the word "hundred" instead of "many", quoted under (2) in the analysis of the relation $E-E_1$, holds in this case as well.

The remarks made with reference to synecdoche concerning the relations occurring within the metaphoric triangle $EE_1E_2$ show that the difference between that trope and metonymy, and consequently in an indirect way between that trope and metaphor proper, consists above all in its non-semiotic properties, namely in the fact that the relations between the designata of the expressions $E_1$ and $E$ and between the designata of the expressions $E_1$ and $E_2$ are such as between a part and a whole or an element and a set (in the collective sense of the term), or the like.

But if all the semiotic relations are taken into account, that is including those which have been disregarded as being repetitions of those known from the analysis of metaphor proper, it is seen that there is a close relationship between all the three tropes, which proves that each of them is a variation of one and the same general concept of metaphor.

Further, one might take into consideration whether from the semiotic point of view one should not shift the traditional, though not very clearly marked, boundaries between synecdoche and metonymy or between synecdoche and metaphor proper.

For there are synecdoches that are more like metonymy than like any other variation of synecdoche. These are those which — like metonymies (or, strictly speaking, that variation of metonymy which differs clearly from metaphor proper) — within the relation $E-E_1$ and $E_1-E_2$ reveal the relation of subordination: Den E sub Den $E_1$ and, correspondingly, Den $E_2$ sub Den $E_1$, and within the relation $E-E_2$, also like the metonymies mentioned above, the community of the property P or the properties $P_1, P_2, ..., P_n$ in the connotations of both expressions. On the other hand there is a distinct group which differs both from metonymies and from synecdoches that are metonymy-like; it consists of those synecdoches in which the relations Den $E_1$ sub Den E and Den $E_1$ sub Den $E_2$, not to be encountered in the case of metonymies, occur; this is accompanied by the fact that the connotative property of one of the expressions, E or $E_2$, is not a connotative and even not a specific property of the other, but is merely an attribute of all its designata.

One might then draw the demarcation line between tropes so that metonymies clearly different from metaphor proper, such as "roaring steel" (about guns), together with such synecdoches as "pavement" (about a paved road) would be on the one side, and such synecdoches as "the mortal one" (about man) would be on the other.

Likewise, such a synecdoche which within the relation $E-E_1$ and $E_2-E_1$ includes a comparison, e.g., such as "the Hector of Y", is related to metaphor proper which is sometimes described as an abbreviated comparison. Thus one might consider whether that relationship is not closer than the relationship between such a synecdoche with other synecdoches.

## 5. *Periphrase*

Periphrase is held by experts in rhetorics to be a kind of metonymy. As such it is considered to be, in their opinion, a variation of metaphor. Yet it can be seen at the first glance that the so-called metaphoric triangle $EE_1E_2$ cannot be applied to such expressions as "The Evening Star" for "Venus", or "the author of *The Tempest*" for "William Shakespeare", for in such expressions there is at all no expression E developed from the expression $E_1$ through a semiotic modification of the latter. But they are characterized by the relation which, to be distinguished from others, will be symbolized $N-D$, where N stands for a non-periphrastical expression, in most cases merely implied but not appearing in the text, and D (from the logical term 'description') stands for periphrase.

The relation $N-D$, or the inverse one, may be characterized as follows:

(1) The expressions N and D are not equiform.

E.g., "Shakespeare" (N) and "the author of *Hamlet*" (D).

(2) The property P or the properties $P_1$, $P_2$, ..., $P_n$ which are attributes of (at least) some designata of the expression N are connotative properties of the expression D.

In this formulation the word "some" is to be interpreted in the logical sense, that is as "at least some" and not "only some". Consequently, the said properties may be attributes of all the designata of N, or of all of them and of them only (specific properties).

For instance, the property of being the author of *Hamlet* is the specific property of the only designatum of the name "William Shakespeare" (N), and at the same time a connotative property of the periphrase "the author of *Hamlet*" (D). On the other hand, the property of being fair or having a fair complexion is an attribute of only some designata of the name "woman" (N) and at the same time is a connotative property of the periphrase "the fair sex" (D).

(3) The expressions N and D are equivalent, or sometimes the non-periphrastical expression is extensionally subordinated to periphrase, which is symbolized Den N sub Den D.

Yet equivalence is the typical case, whereas extensional subordination may be ascribed to a certain lack of precision in periphrase, namely to the error of an incomplete statement, or to the fact that the implied equivalent N is not indicated quite appropriately.

An example of equivalence is offered by the expression "Walter Scott" (N) and "the author of *Waverley*" (D). And we have to do with extensional subordination in the case of "the Sun" (N) and "the fiery star" (D), when the word "the Sun" is interpreted as "the central star of our solar system", and "the fiery star" as "a heavenly body shining with its own light".

(4) The expressions N and D are not synonymous.

Any of the examples given above may be quoted here.

(5) See point (2) above.

(6) The expression D expresses (as to content) the experiences of the person who has used it, as such, in the following manner:

(a) That person notices the property P or the properties $P_1$, $P_2$, ..., $P_n$ as attributes of at least some designata of the expression N and since he wishes to emphasize them he turns them into connotative properties of the periphrase D.

Compare here the examples given under (2) above.

(b) That person disregards certain, sometimes even essential, properties of the designata of the expression N and constructs the periphrase D in such a way that these disregarded properties should neither appear in its connotation nor be implied by that connotation.

For instance, the connotation of the expression "the author of *Waverley*" (D) does not include the essential property of the replaced expression "Walter Scott" (N), namely the property of being Walter Scott; that property is even not implied by the connotation of D.

(c) That person sometimes uses a given periphrase not in its full extension and thus compensates the consequences of the frequent error of an incomplete proposition in the case of a periphrase.

If, for instance, someone uses the periphrase "the bishop of Autun" (D), which is a general name, instead of the individual name "Charles Maurice de Talleyrand" (N), then he uses the expression D not in its full extension, but turns it into an individual name as if he said "such and such bishop of Autun". It is in this process that the particularizing tendency, concealed in certain periphrases, consists.

As can be seen, the relation N–D, or the inverse one, in certain respects reminds us of that or the other fragment of relationships which have been disclosed previously in connection with the tropes which have already been analysed.

Thus, e.g., its point (1) is similar to point (1) of the relation $E-E_2$ known from the analysis of metaphor proper, metonymy and synecdoche, since it refers to the non-equiformity of the trope and its implied equivalent. But it must be borne in mind that in all those cases the trope E was an expression with modified semiotic functions, whereas the periphrase D appears in its literal sense, unless, besides being a periphrase it includes a metaphor, such as "the fair sex".

Further, points (2) and (5) of the relation N–D show similarity with respect to points (2) and (5) of the relation $E-E_1$ in the analysis of metaphor proper. But while the latter relation determines the semiotic modifications of METAPHORIZATION PROPER, the relation N–D is a relation of REPLACEMENT, or INTERCHANGEABILITY, between two expressions, each of which is understood LITERALLY, and not metaphorically.

Then, in point (3) of the relation N–D there sometimes occurs the same extensional subordination of the expression which is not a trope to the expression which is a trope, as in point (2) of the relation $E-E_1$ in the analysis of synecdoche.

Next, point (4) of the relation $N-D$, which refers to the non-equiformity of these expressions, has its counterparts in point (4) of the relation $E-E_1$ and of the relation $E_1-E_2$ in the analysis of metaphor proper, and also in the analogous, and therefore disregarded, points of the same relations in the analysis of metonymy and synecdoche.

Finally, point (6a, b) of the relation $N-D$ bears a resemblance to point (6a, b) of the relation $E-E_1$ in the analysis of metaphor proper and to related, and therefore disregarded, properties of metonymy and synecdoche.

For all these numerous similarities between the various fragments of the relation $N-D$ on the one hand and certain fragments in the analysis of other tropes, fragments usually belonging to the relation $E-E_1$, but sometimes also to the relation $E_1-E_2$, the essential difference between the relation $N-D$ and each of the other relations concerned must strongly be emphasized. Now the relation $E-E_1$ holds between a certain metaphorical expression and an equiform expression proper, from which that metaphorical expression has developed through a semiotic modification. Further, the elements of the relation $E_1-E_2$ are two non-metaphorical expressions, of which $E_1$ is as it were the source of the metaphorical expression concerned, and its formal base, since $E_1$ offers to the metaphor in question its shape, and it is on the semiotic material of $E_1$ that the modifications take place which give as a result the metaphor concerned. And $E_2$ is an implied semiotic equivalent of the metaphorical expression which stands for $E_2$.

But in the relation $N-D$ there is no metaphorical expression, and no equivalent of a metaphorical expression, and no expression the semiotic functions of which would be subject to a modification. That is why this is a distinct relation. That fact should not be veiled by its following properties:

(a) that it is a relation of logical replacement; $E-E_2$ also is a relation of replacement, but E is metaphorical, and D is not;

(b) that in the relation $N-D$ the expression N is the source of periphrase, as $E_1$ is the source of metaphor, and that at the same time N is the equivalent of periphrase which stands for it, as $E_2$ is the equivalent of metaphor which stands for it; but here too E is a metaphorical expression, and D is not.

Thus, the relation N–D is a specific relation which should not be confused with any relation occurring within the metaphoric triangle $EE_1E_2$, in spite of a striking similarity of certain details.

That difference was intuitively grasped by classical rhetorics which treated periphrase as a variation of so-called amplification, and metaphor as so-called *difficultas ornata*. But that pertinent distinction was unfortunately blurred by the fact that periphrase was defined as a kind of metonymy, that is a metaphorical trope. The suggestion of the similarities between them, as mentioned above, must have been very strong. There might also have been the untoward effect of the ambiguity of the expressions "instead of" or "to stand for". For in the relation $E$–$E_1$, and in the relation $E$–$E_2$, and in the relation N–D alike one expression STANDS FOR the other. Nevertheless these are different relations.

One more remark to conclude the characteristic of periphrase. In the analysis of metaphor proper, metonymy, and synecdoche, within the relation $E$–$E_2$ or the inverse one we have to do with the semiotic function of LOGICAL REPLACING, which characterizes the SYNONYMITY of the expressions E and $E_2$. But one of the elements of the relation $E$–$E_2$, namely the expression E, is METAPHORICAL, and consequently these cases can rather easily be distinguished from the case of a different, ordinary synonymity, which connects two non-metaphorical expressions.

On the other hand, in a periphrase the relation N–D also is a relation of LOGICAL REPLACEMENT, or interchangeability, *salva denotatione* or *salva veritate*, and consequently — a relation of EQUIVALENCE, but between NON-METAPHORICAL expressions. And since that relation is by its very nature SYMMETRICAL, how can one know which of its two elements is a periphrase (D), and which is a non-periphrastic expression (N), and consequently, in a given case, whether a certain expression, appearing in the text, is D or N?

The following solution is suggested here: it seems that

(a) The expression D is a periphrase not absolutely, but relatively, that is with respect to a certain expression N, and the relation N–D, or the inverse one, determines the structure and the semiotic mechanism of periphrase.

(b) Periphrase has the nature of a logical description, and as such must be a complex expression, and at that an expression consisting not of proper names alone.

Thus the personal pronoun "he", used with reference to Napoleon the Great, is not a periphrase; but the expression "the victor of Austerlitz", as a complex expression, consisting not of proper names alone, is a periphrase with respect to the name "Napoleon the Great". The expression "the Emperor" (used with reference to Napoleon) also is a periphrase if it appears in a CONTEXT from which it follows that it is an abbreviation of the expression "such and such emperor".

The foregoing analysis of the concept of periphrase leads to the following conclusion:

PERIPHRASE IS NOT A VARIATION OF METAPHOR. Thus it is not one of stylistic tropes in the same sence of the term 'trope' in which it appears in Quintilianus' definition stating: "*Tropus est verbi vel sermonis a propria significatione in aliam cum virtute mutatio*" (*Institutio oratoria*, L.VIII.6.1). For in opposition to metaphor proper, metonymy and synecdoche, which are variations of metaphor and are tropes characterized as such, in the case of periphrase there is no "transformation of the proper meaning into another one".

## 6.   *Irony and Anti-Irony*

Analysis of every stylistic trope is not necessary if we want to obtain a full picture of the structure and the semiotic mechanism of the concept of metaphor. It is so because some of them do not show any important peculiarities, so that their analysis would have to consist in the repetition of the observations already made. That is why we disregard e.g. the concept of hyperbole as a trope in which semiotic relations partly resemble metaphor proper (the comparison "$E_2$ is like $E_1$"), partly metonymy (the common property P in the relations $E-E_1$ and $E-E_2$), and partly synecdoche (Den $E_1$ sub Den E, the common property P in the relations $E-E_1$ and $E_1-E_2$, and the well known feature of exaggeration, which is specific to that trope, is of lesser interest here. In a word, from the purely semiotic point of view, hyperbole is not a distinct trope and its analysis does not enrich the description of the structure and the semiotic mechanism of the concept of metaphor. The same can be said with reference to some other tropes.

On the other hand, it is worth while examining the concepts of irony and anti-irony, by bringing out what is new in them and distinct with respect to the concepts that have already been analysed.

Ironic and anti-ironic expressions are explicit or implicit VALUATIONS. Irony is a criticism concealed by a transparent veil of alleged approval, and anti-irony conversely is an approval which has the appearance of a criticism. For instance, the word "beautiful" is used ironically when, putting it not quite precisely, it *de facto* means "ugly", and the word "heinous" is an anti-irony when it *de facto* means "nice".

Their semiotic properties are the same and can be formulated thus:

The relation $E-E_1$, or the converse one.

(1) All the designata of the expression $E_1$ have as attribute(s) the property P or the properties $P_1, P_2, ..., P_n$, which often are specific or essential properties of that expression, and all the designata of the expression E have as attribute(s) properties which often are connotative and which with respect to the former ones are either (a) contradictory, namely nonP or $nonP_1, nonP_2, ..., nonP_n$, or (b) opposite.

For instance, the connotative property of the word "charming" ($E_1$), in its literal meaning, is the possession of charm (P); and all the designata of the word "charming" (E) used ironically, have as attribute the property of being without charm or, more strictly, of being charmless (nonP).

This is an example of case (a). An example of case (b) is the ironical use of the word "good" in the sense of "bad" (and not in the sense "not good"). In the latter case all the designata of the expression $E_1$ have as an attribute the connotative property of being good, and all the designata of the expression E have as an attribute the opposite connotative property, namely the property of being bad, and also the property of being not good, implied by the former, a property which is contradictory with the essential property of the expression $E_1$.

The case of anti-irony is analogous, the only difference being that then $E_1$ is *de facto* derogatory, and E, pseudo-derogatory.

(2) The denotations of the expression E and $E_1$ are mutually exclusive, the following extensional relationships being observable:

(a) The expression E is equivalent to the expression $nonE_1$, which is symbolized Den E $\equiv$ Den nonE.

Or (b) The denotation of the expression E is subordinated to the denotation of the expression $nonE_1$, which is symbolized Den E sub Den $nonE_1$ or Den $E_1$ sub Den nonE.

An example of case (a) is provided by the word "nice" (E) used ironically in the sense of "not nice".

An example of case (b) is the ironical use of the same word "nice" (E), but this time in the sense of "ugly".

(3) The ironical or anti-ironical expression E expresses (as to content) the experiences of the person who has used it, as such, in the following way:

(a) That person notices the property P or the properties $P_1$, $P_2$, ..., $P_n$ which are attributes of all the designata of the expression $E_1$ and which sometimes are its specific or essential properties.

(b) That person thinks that all the elements $e_1$, $e_2$, ..., $e_n$ of a class C have as attributes the properties that are contradictory with the former, that is the property nonP or the properties $nonP_1$, $nonP_2$, $nonP_n$, or properties that are opposite to the former.

(c) That person wants to bring out the above-mentioned properties of all the elements of the class C and therefore gives them the ironical or anti-ironical name E, developed from $E_1$ through semiotic modifications; that name is such that all the designata of the name E have as attributes the properties which are contradictory with, or opposite to, P or $P_1$, $P_2$, ..., $P_n$, and sometimes are connotative properties of that name.

Examples as under (1) and (2).

The relations described above determine the semiotic modification that is proper to ironization or anti-ironization and bring out the distinct features of irony and anti-irony as separate tropes. The remaining relations within $E-E_1$, which have been disregarded here, are the same as in the case of the other tropes, analysed above, which shows that irony and anti-irony are certain, rather peculiar, variations of the concept of metaphor.

This is confirmed by the analysis of the relations $E-E_2$ and $E_1-E_2$. The former does not require discussion since it is the same as in the case of metonymy, with the only exception that in the case of irony $E_2$ is derogatory and E is pseudo-approbatory, and in the case of anti-irony $E_2$ is approbatory and E is pseudo-derogatory.

Those properties of the relation $E_1-E_2$ which are specific to irony and anti-irony result from the properties of the relation $E-E_1$, described above. Thus:

(1) All the designata of $E_1$ have as attribute(s) the property P or the properties $P_1$, $P_2$, ..., $P_n$, which often are specific or essential properties of that expression, and all the designata of $E_2$ have as attributes properties which are contradictory with, or opposite to, the former and often are connotative properties.

Examples can be provided by the expressions, ordered in pairs and understood literally: "good" ($E_1$) — "not good" ($E_2$) and "good" ($E_1$) — "bad" ($E_2$).

(2) The denotations of $E_1$ and $E_2$ are mutually exclusive, and Den $E_1 \equiv$ Den non$E_2$, i.e., Den $E_2 \equiv$ Den non$E_1$, or Den $E_1$ sub Den non$E_2$, i.e., Den $E_2$ sub Den non$E_1$.

(3) $E_1$ in the case of irony is approbatory, and $E_2$ is derogatory, and in the case of anti-irony $E_1$ is derogatory and $E_2$ approbatory.

E.g., in the case of anti-irony $E_1$ — "heinous", and $E_2$ — "nice".

The relations described above, chosen from among those occurring in the metaphoric triangle $EE_1E_2$, which has been applied here to the analysis of irony and anti-irony, reveal the difference between them on the one hand and other tropes on the other. But the whole of the relations $E-E_1$, $E-E_2$, and $E_1-E_2$, or the converse ones, including those which have been disregarded here as having been characterized before, determines the structure and the semiotic mechanism of each of these two concepts. Their essential semiotic similarities with respect to metaphor proper, metonymy and synecdoche show that IRONY AND ANTI-IRONY ARE VARIATIONS OF METAPHOR.

### III. THE SEMIOTIC NATURE OF THE CONCEPT OF METAPHOR (CONCLUDING REMARKS)

The applications of semiotic functions to the analysis of the concept of stylistic trope, presented above in the analyses of metaphor proper, metonymy, synecdoche, periphrase, irony and anti-irony, make it possible to formulate concluding remarks concerning the semiotic nature and the semiotic mechanism of the concept of metaphor or trope.

### 1. *Examples in the Semiotic Analysis of the Concept of Metaphor*

Comparatively simple examples have been used, for didactic reasons, as illustrations in the analyses made above. Those examples were mainly DENOTING NAMES, to the exclusion of empty names (names without designata) and the so-called onomatoids, i.e. words such as "sadness", "fatigue", "property", "travel", "value" and the like (*nomina abstracta* — to use a grammatical term). Further, the examples were limited to such metaphors which the linguists call METAPHORS BY SIMPLE REPLACEMENT, to the exclusion of more complicated metaphors based on genitival or verb forms.

It must be pointed out that such a choice of examples does not result in any undesirable theoretical simplifications which would distort the picture of the problem; it is merely a technical facilitation. Moreover, because of the use of names with designata the analysis of the relations occurring within the metaphoric triangle can be enriched by the demonstration of the relationships between the designata of the expressions E, $E_1$ and $E_2$. On the contrary, in the case of empty names one can speak only of the relations occurring between the alleged counterparts of language signs. Finally, in the case of the onomatoids, i.e., apparent names, or expressions that have no objective counterparts (whether real or fictitious), but only counterparts in the form of certain sets of properties, analysis must of necessity be reduced to the demonstration of relations between those properties; consequently, it is confined to the study of relations between the connotations of the expressions concerned, and, in the case of a certain interpretation, between their denotations, but does not describe relations between the designata of those expressions. Consequently, it is poorer by the presentation of one semantic function, namely that of designating. That is why NAMES WITH DESIGNATA ARE THE MOST CONVENIENT SOURCE OF EXAMPLES IN SUCH CONSIDERATIONS AND PROVIDE A BASIS FOR THE MOST COMPLETE AND MANY-SIDED ANALYSIS.

Besides, examples of more complicated or stylistically or poetically more ingenious metaphors do not contribute anything theoretically new to semiotic analysis, but just cause technical difficulties. For instance, a genitival metaphor like "the fountain of grace" or a verbal metaphor "the ship was plowing the waves", or even a more complex one, covering a whole sentence or a group of sentences, is reducible to simpler elements between which the relations hold that are known from the metaphoric triangle $EE_1E_2$. The only effect is that analysis becomes longer, because relations between the various elements of a complex expression or a sentence must be discussed, until finally one comes to what is the foundation of the structure and the semiotic mechanism of every metaphorical expression.

## 2.   The Metaphoric Triangle $EE_1E_2$ as the Scheme of the Structure of the Relative Concept of Metaphor

In the analyses made so far more space has been devoted to the description of differences between the various tropes than to presentation of those semiotic properties that are common to all of them. It has been done so not because there are more differences than similarities between them, but in order to avoid repetitions. With that end in view the analysis of the concept of metaphor proper was made *in extenso*, and then only those properties of the other tropes have been taken into account which contributed new semiotic properties, and all that what is common to all those tropes and as such appears in every one of them has been disregarded.

Now these specific or essential properties of metaphor will be discussed jointly.

The concept of metaphor is a RELATIVE one. This means that an expression E is metaphorical always WITH RESPECT TO TWO OTHER DEFINITE NON-METAPHORICAL EXPRESSIONS $E_1$ AND $E_2$. It never happens that an expression should just be metaphorical in an absolute manner. Further, the relativization of the concept of metaphor also pertains to language. An expression is metaphorical not in general but with respect to a definite language L.

These properties of the concept of metaphor have been formulated in a somewhat picturesque way, namely that in the analysis of that phenomenon we have to do with the so-called metaphoric triangle $EE_1E_2$.

In that triangle, the base of which let be $E_1E_2$, the expressions E, $E_1$ and $E_2$ belong to one and the same language L, and only E is a metaphorical expression. $E_1$ is a formal equivalent of E, since it is equiform with the latter, and $E_2$ is a semiotic equivalent of E since, although not being equiform with the latter, it is usually its equivalent and possibly also nearly synonymous or synonymous with the latter, which fact entails the community of the property or properties that is (are) attribute(s) of the typical or all designata of E and $E_2$, and sometimes the community of their specific or essential properties.

It might be said that the expression E appears INSTEAD OF $E_1$ and INSTEAD OF $E_2$, but in each of these two cases the role of E which stands for the other expression consists in something else, and that consequently "instead of" has different meanings in both cases.

### 3.   The Metaphorization Relation $E_1-E$ and Simple Polysemy

a.  *Metaphorization and Simple Polysemy*

The statement that E stands for $E_1$ (appears in the place of $E_1$) means that the non-metaphorical expression $E_1$, while preserving its form, undergoes certain semiotic modifications and consequently becomes a metaphorical expression. This has been called META-PHORIZATION. Usually what has happened to the expression $E_1$ is defined as a change in meaning. In fact, however, what is being changed is not meaning alone, that is one of the semiotic functions of the expression $E_1$, but its other semiotic functions as well.

In any case the expression E designates, denotes, means and expresses something else than does the expression $E_1$, although the two expressions are equiform or, in other words, they are externally the same expression.

WHAT THEN IS THE DIFFERENCE BETWEEN THE METAPHORIZATION RELATION $E-E_1$ AND ORDINARY AMBIGUITY OR POLYSEMY OF AN EXPRESSION? For if a word E' is, let us say, ambiguous, it is also so that, while it retains its form, it sometimes designates, denotes, means and expresses something, and sometimes, something else.

The linguists describe that difference by referring, on the one hand, to the origin of metaphor, namely to the psychological mechanism of its formation, and, on the other hand, to the development of new meanings of a given word through so-called regular, i.e., non-metaphorical, changes in meanings; in the latter case the psychological aspects of the process also come to the fore-front. They say that the necessary condition of the birth of a metaphor is a real transfer of ideas into a different conceptual field, a transfer based on perception of analogies between objects, on comparing impressions supplied by the same sense, and on a transposition and synaesthesia of such impressions (cf. W. Wundt, *Völkerpsychologie*, Vol. II, Chap. VIII, "Der Bedeutungswandel", 2nd ed., [Leipzig, 1912]). On the other hand, a regular change in meaning consists, in their opinion, in the fact that the names of certain states and actions come to cover by their extension new objects and thus, non metaphorically but in a natural way, extend the field of their application. That process is supposed to be based on so strong an association of ideas connected with old and new meanings that the whole seems homogenous to the user of a given word.

Without rejecting that description one may endeavour to complete it and also to modify it so as to avoid a genetic and psychological interpretation. This is to be achieved by means of an analysis from the SEMIOTIC point of view, which best shows the objective differences between metaphorization and simple polysemy.

At the first glance it might seem that the difference is as follows:

When an expression belonging to the language L, which has in that language, to put it colloquially, its definite sense, is used metaphorically, then that new, metaphorical, meaning will not belong to the semantic system of L, will not be a normal meaning with respect to the language L, whereas the proper meaning of that expression is a normal, systematic one. On the contrary, in the case of ordinary polysemy of a word we also have to do with its two or more different meanings, but each of them is a systematic, normal meaning belonging to L.

For instance, the word "pearls" has in a certain language L its established sense, namely it denotes a well-known organic product. The semiotic functions of that word, when understood literally, are normal, systematic functions with respect to L. But when the word "pearls" is used to denote metaphorically beautiful teeth, the semiotic functions of that word in that second meaning, while also performed by that word with respect to the language L to which that word belongs, are not normal, systematic, with respect to that language. Thus a proper use of a word, followed by a metaphorical use of the same word, makes us face its ambiguity, but such that only one meaning, the proper one, is normal in a given language, whereas the other, i.e., metaphorical, is not normal. But in the case of a simple polysemy, e.g. of such a word as "last", each of its non-metaphorical meanings is normal, systematic, with respect to the language L.

But such a characteristic of the difference between ambiguity resulting from metaphorization within the relation $E_1 - E$ and simple polysemy fails if one introduces a non-semantic distinction between a metaphorical expression and a genetically metaphorical expression.

Metaphorical expressions have been discussed above and their semiotic status has been determined by the relations occurring within the metaphoric triangle. Genetically metaphorical expressions are such as "handle" (of an instrument, etc.), "neck" (of a bottle), and the like. Semiotically their structure and mechanism do not differ from the structure and mechanism of ordinary metaphor, which means that in both cases the same relations $E-E_1$, $E-E_2$, $E_1-E_2$ are valid. There is nothing strange in that fact since genetically metaphorical expressions after all are metaphors. The difference consists in that the meaning of a genetically metaphorical expression is normal and systematic with respect to the given language L, like every meaning of a simply polysemic word and unlike the meaning of a metaphorical expression.

Thus, e.g., every meaning of the word "leg": (a) any extremity of an animal, (b) a lower extremity of a human being, (c) a vertical base or support of a piece of furniture, etc., is a normal, systematic, meaning in a given language L, in spite of the fact that the word "leg" in case (c) is a genetically metaphorical expression.

Consequently, one has to distinguish in some other way that kind of ambiguity which is proper to metaphorization within the relation $E_1-E$ from ordinary ambiguity or polysemy with which we have to do when, speaking colloquially, no meaning of a polysemic expression E' is a metaphorical one.

In order to characterize that difference the semiotic relations between two equiform but non-equivalent non-metaphorical expressions $E'_1$ and $E'_2$ will be analysed (e.g., "last" as a shoemaker's device and "last" as a measure of weight), and the results obtained will be compared with the already known results of the semiotic analysis of metaphor.

It can easily be seen that the relation $E'_1-E'_2$, which determines ordinary polysemy, is marked by the following properties:

(1) The expressions $E'_1$ and $E'_2$ are equiform.

(2) None of these expressions is metaphorical.

(3) The designata of these expressions have no such common properties that might be considered important because of the semiotic functions of each of these expressions. (They share properties that are common to all things, e.g., extension in time and space, which may, however, be disregarded.)

(4) There is no material connection between the designata of these expressions.

(5) The denotations of these expressions are mutually exclusive.

(6) These expressions are not synonymous.

(7) The connotations of these expressions share no common properties and do not imply the same property that is important because of the semiotic functions performed by each of these expressions.

(8) As far as expressing (as to content) is concerned, there is no community between $E'_1$ and $E'_2$.

(9) The expressions $E'_1$ and $E'_2$ do not form a comparison.

As can be seen, ordinary polysemy differs from that polysemy which appears in the case of metaphor by the lack of the already demonstrated relationships between the designata, between the denotations and between the connotations of two expressions. These relationships appear in the case of the relation $E_1 - E$, but not in the case of the relation $E'_1 - E'_2$. In other words, this fact can be formulated so that the semiotic functions of the expression $E'_2$ are, in the sense described above, autonomous and independent of the semiotic functions of the expression $E'_1$, that is, of the same word, but used in a different sense.

On the contrary, the semiotic functions of the metaphorical expression E are, in conformity with the results obtained above, relative to the semiotic functions of the expressions $E_1$ and $E_2$, from which it follows that in order fully to understand E one has to know and to understand $E_1$ and $E_2$, and also to notice the semiotic relationships and connections occurring between these three expressions of the metaphoric triangle.

b. *Semiotic Oscillation and the Transparence of Metaphor*

The property, described above, which is an attribute of all metaphorical expressions and which distinguishes them from ordinary polysemic words, might be called SEMIOTIC OSCILLATION OF E with respect to $E_1$ and to $E_2$. That oscillation consists in the fact that through the intermediary of the semiotic functions of the metaphorical expression E one can see the semiotic functions of each of the two non-metaphorical expressions $E_1$ and $E_2$ as well as the relations holding between them. This might also be called the TRANSPARENCE of metaphor.

On the contrary, in the case of ordinary polysemy the expression $E'_2$ is not transparent in this sense. If, e.g., I use the colloquial expression "It costs five bucks", the semiotic functions of the word "buck" as the name of an animal do not interfere with the sense of that word as used in the quoted expression.

Semiotic oscillation, or the transparence of a metaphorical expression is neither exclusively nor even mainly psychological in nature. In this connection it is not confined to the processes of making or interpreting metaphorical expressions, but also appears in the case of so-called ready-made metaphor, that is one which is neither being made nor interpreted at a given moment. It appears as objective relations within the metaphoric triangle, as common properties and mutual relationships: first, of the designata, secondly, of the denotations, thirdly, of the connotations of the expressions E, $E_1$ and $E_2$.

c. *Reducibility of the Psychological Aspects of Metaphor to its Semiotic Properties*

As is known, one of the relations occurring within the metaphoric triangle is the pragmatic relation between the sign and the experiences of the person who has used it, as such, that is, the pragmatic function of expressing. Consequently, we have there to do with a certain reference to psychological processes. Just because of that function a complete elimination of the psychological factor from the analysis of the concept of metaphor would not be justified. That factor however seems to be reducible to non-subjective semantic relations between the expressions E, $E_1$ and $E_2$. Let this be explained by an example.

It is a controversial point whether the sentence, "See how white butterflies are playing", uttered by a Negro child who has seen the snow for the first time in his life, and has never before heard about it, contains a metaphor or not (*cf.* Dessoir, *Aesthetik und allgemeine Kunstwissenschaft in den Grundzügen dargestellt* [Stuttgart, 1906], p. 88, and Ch. Brooke-Rose, *A Grammar of Metaphor* [London, 1958], p. 13). It is obvious that the child in question did not metaphorize, but was just mistaken, and that in spite of it that sentence may be treated as a metaphor by an interpretant. But what is here the objective character of the formulation "white butter-flies", metaphorical or non-metaphorical? It is two different things TO BE A METAPHOR and TO BE TREATED AS A METAPHOR. The solution of the issue should be provided by semiotic analysis.

It seems that there is here no case of an ambiguity of the ex-pression "white butterflies", which is characteristic of the meta-phorization relation $E–E_1$, and consequently there are no reasons to build the metaphoric triangle $EE_1E_2$, the relations within which determine the structure and mechanism of every metaphor. It is so because the expression "white butterflies" appears as a name of butterflies, and not of snowflakes; such is the intention of the speaker, who has been mistaken in his judgement based on percep-tion. Consequently, the sentence "These are white butterflies" is false, whereas metaphor is based on a statement which retains its truth, just because the semiotic function of the predicate is modified. Moreover in the case under discussion the relation of expressing, characteristic of metaphor and known from previous analysis, does not take place. All this leads to the conclusion that the exclamation of the Negro child, referred to above, does not include any meta-phor, which does not mean that a sentence equiform with the former might not be a metaphor, on the condition that it would have a different sense or, more strictly, that the whole of its semiotic functions would be different. For the sign designates a given thing or things just with respect to its such and such sense, and a change in sense involves a change of the designata into some other designata.

All this shows that the expression "white butterflies" in the example under discussion does not reveal semiotic oscillations, i.e., the transparence of metaphor, since in the intention of the author of the sentence quoted above that expression has been used in its — to put it colloquially — literal meaning. And THAT INTENTION, I.E., A PSYCHOLOGICAL FACTOR, as such connected with the process of formation and/or interpretation of expressions, BECOMES AN OBJECTIVE FACTOR, WHEN IT COMES TO THE SO-CALLED READY-MADE SIGN AND TAKES ON THE FORM OF ITS SEMIOTIC FUNCTIONS. This is an important point, since it frees us from delving into subjective and unverifiable matters, and makes it possible fully to analyse the issues involved by means of instruments of semiotic analysis alone.

4. *The Synonymity of the Metaphoric Expression (E) and its Semiotic Equivalent ($E_2$) versus Simple Logical Interchangeability*

In the metaphoric triangle $EE_1E_2$ the metaphorical expression E appears, among other things, instead of its semiotic equivalent, that is the non-metaphorical expression $E_2$. Yet the relation $E-E_2$ differs, as is known, from the metaphorization relation $E_1-E$. Although in the latter relation E too stands for a certain expression, but it stands for $E_1$, that is in a different sense of the expression "instead of" than in the case of the relation $E-E_2$. The latter relation is, from the semiotic point of view, a function of RE-PLACING, or INTERCHANGING, so that the elements of that relation are SYNONYMOUS or NEARLY SYNONYMOUS expressions.

This gives rise to the necessity to distinguish between synonymity of that kind and simple, ordinary synonymity. No new analysis must be made, for it will suffice to refer to the results already obtained.

Let it be pointed out that the synonymity $E-E_2$, characteristic of that relation within the metaphoric triangle, is distinguished by the fact that one of the elements of the relation of replacement, namely E, appears as an expression whose semiotic functions have developed from a modification of the semiotic functions of the expression $E_1$, equiform with E and having with respect to the language L a normal, systematic meaning (in the ordinary sense of the term 'meaning'). To put it briefly, E has developed from $E_1$ through metaphorization. It must be borne in mind that it often happens (except for genetically metaphorical expressions) that E is a synonym of $E_2$ only with respect to a given synthetic definition.

On the other hand, in the case of ordinary synonymity both interchangeable expressions appear in their LITERAL meanings, i.e., with respect to the analytical definition of each of them in the given language L. None of them has developed from any other equiform expression.

In the case of the relation $E-E_2$ the element $E_2$ usually does not appear in the text and remains implied. And the good guess consists in finding such an $E_2$ which is not only equivalent but also synonymous with E.

Sometimes, in a two-element genitival metaphor, such as "the flame of love", both elements of the relation appear. The first element is the metaphorical expression E, and the second is its non-metaphorical semiotic equivalent $E_2$, for which E stands. The comparison of the expressions E and $E_2$ in such cases enables us clearly to see the PARTICULARIZING AND ABSTRACT nature of metaphor, as mentioned before.

It is obvious that not the whole extension of the word "flame" and not the whole extension of the word "love" can be taken into account in this comparison. It implies only a violent, bursting flame, and a strong, passionate love. Secondly, not all the properties of the designata of each of these two words will be included in the picture formed by the metaphor; some of them will be disregarded and consequently eliminated.

Thus, when $E_2$, the non-metaphorical equivalent of the metaphorical expression E, is given in the text, then following its connection with that metaphorical expression, it also undergoes certain semiotic modifications, which consist in the limitation of the extension of $E_2$ by completing that expression with implied attributes. Thus in a genitival metaphor one may see a logical abbreviation or omission, and consider an expression of the type "the flame of such and such love" to be its full form.

5.  *The Relation $E_1$–$E_2$ as the Base of the Metaphoric Triangle*

The last relation which determines the structure and the semiotic mechanism of the concept of metaphor is $E_1$–$E_2$, that is the relation between the formal ($E_1$) and the semiotic ($E_2$) equivalent of the metaphorical expression (E).

That relation in part is a reflexion of the relation E–$E_1$, namely in view of the similarity of such semantic relationships as the mutual exclusion of denotations or non-synonymity, and in part a reflexion of the relation E–$E_2$, namely in view of formal similarity (non-equiformity). Consequently that relation is in a way the base of the other two relations, which has found its counterpart in the fact that $E_1$–$E_2$ has been made the base of the metaphoric triangle. That character of the relation $E_1$–$E_2$ is explained by the fact that its elements are at the same time elements of the remaining two relations, $E_1$–E and $E_2$–E, in which each of them plays with respect to the metaphorical expression E the role as it were of the source: $E_1$ of a formal one, since it lends to the metaphorical expression its form, and $E_2$ of a semiotic one, since it lends to the metaphorical expression its semiotic functions.

6.  *Conclusions*

The essential properties of the concept of metaphor are determined by the whole of the relations occurring within the metaphoric triangle $EE_1E_2$.

In briefly summing up the results of the present study of the application of semiotic functions to the concept of metaphor it may be said:

In the language L the expression E is metaphorical with respect the expressions $E_1$ and $E_2$ if and only if:

1.  The relation E–$E_1$:

(a) E and $E_1$ are equiform.

(b) At least some designata of $E_1$ and all the designata of E share the common property P or the common properties $P_1$, $P_2$, ..., $P_n$, which are important with respect to the sense of each of these two expressions. (The exceptions are irony and anti-irony, where the designata of $E_1$ have P or $P_1$, $P_2$, ..., $P_n$ as attribute[s], and the designata of E have as attributes the properties that are contradictory with, or opposite to, the former.)

(c) The denotations of the expressions E and $E_1$ are mutually exclusive or overlapping, or Den E sub Den $E_1$, or Den $E_1$ sub Den E.

(d) E and $E_1$ are not synonymous.

(e) The property P or the properties $P_1$, $P_2$, ..., $P_n$, which is (are) attribute(s) of at least some $E_1$, are connotative properties of E. (The exceptions are irony and anti-irony, where the expression E has as attributes connotative properties which are contradictory with, or opposite to, the properties which are attributes of $E_1$.)

(f) E expresses (as to content) the experiences of the person who has used that expression, as such, in such a way that certain properties and certain designata of $E_1$ are disregarded, and other properties of $E_1$, namely P or $P_1$, $P_2$, ..., $P_n$, are emphasized and turned into properties that are attributes of all the designata of E, or into connotative properties of the expression E. (The exceptions are irony and anti-irony, where E has as attributes of all its designata or as its own connotative properties, properties that are contradictory with, or opposite to, the above-mentioned properties of $E_1$.)

2. The relation $E-E_2$:

(a) E and $E_2$ are nonequiform.

(b) E and $E_2$ are equivalent.

(c) E and $E_2$ are synonymous or nearly synonymous.

(d) If E and $E_2$ are nearly synonymous, then the property P or the properties $P_1$, $P_2$, ..., $P_n$, being attributes of all the designata of one of these two expressions, are connotative properties of the other.

(e) E and $E_2$ perform the pragmatic function of expressing (as to content) the experiences of the person who has used each of them, as such, in a similar manner, with the proviso that the function of expressing as performed by E emphasizes in the experiences of that person the property P or the properties $P_1$, $P_2$, ..., $P_n$ as the dominant one(s).

3. The relation $E_1 - E_2$:

(a) $E_1$ and $E_2$ are nonequiform.

(b) All the designata of $E_1$ and all the designata of $E_2$ have as attributes the property P or the properties $P_1$, $P_2$, ..., $P_n$, which may be specific or connotative properties of both these expressions, or specific properties of one expression and connotative properties of the other. (The exceptions are irony and anti-irony, where the properties that are attributes of $E_2$ are contradictory with, or opposite to, the properties that are attributes of $E_1$.)

(c) The denotations of $E_1$ and $E_2$ are mutually exclusive or sometimes overlapping, or Den $E_1$ sub Den $E_2$, or Den $E_2$ sub Den $E_1$.

(d) $E_1$ and $E_2$ are not synonymous.

(e) The property P or the properties $P_1$, $P_2$, ..., $P_n$ are connotative in the expressions $E_1$ and $E_2$, or implied by their connotative properties, or are connotative properties of one of these expressions and implied by the connotative properties of the other. (The exceptions are irony and anti-irony, where the connotative properties of $E_2$, or those implied by the connotative properties of that expression, are contradictory with, or opposite to, the connotative properties of $E_1$ or the properties implied by the connotative properties of that expression.)

(f) $E_1$ expresses (as to content) different experiences of the person who has used it, as such, than does $E_2$. Yet both in these and in those experiences there is an idea of the property P or the properties $P_1$, $P_2$, ..., $P_n$ as common to both $E_1$ and $E_2$. (The exceptions are irony and anti-irony, where in the experiences expressed by $E_2$ there is an idea of properties that are contradictory with, or opposite to, those expressed by $E_1$.)

## SUMMARY

*Introduction.* — The concept of metaphor is being used in two senses, a broader and a narrower one. The former comes from

Aristotle who in his *Poetics*, XXI, writes: "Μεταφωρὰ δ'ἐστιν ὀνώματος ἀλλωτριου ἐπιφωρὰ ἤ ἀπὸ γένους ἔπι εῖδος ἤ ἀπὸ ἐίδους ἐπί γένος ἤ ἀπὸ ἐίδους ἐπί εῖδος ἤ κατὰ τὸ ἀνάλωγον". A related definition is given by Quintilianus in *Institutio oratoria*, L.VIII,6,1: "*Tropus est verbi vel sermonis a propria significatione in aliam cum virtute mutatio.*" In the narrower sense of the term, metaphor, also called metaphor proper, is, alongside of metonymy, synecdoche, hyperbole, irony, anti-irony, etc., one of the tropes, i.e., one of the variations of metaphor in the broader sense of the term. In the present paper, metaphor in the broader sense of the term is briefly called 'metaphor', and metaphor in the narrower sense of the term, 'metaphor proper'. The paper is mainly concerned with the concept of metaphor, or, more strictly, with the structure and the functioning of metaphoric expressions. The study resorts to semiotic analysis, namely a tentative application of semiotic functions of signs to an analysis of metaphoric expressions.

I. *Basic Concepts and the Theoretical Foundations of the Analysis of Metaphors.*

1. *Basic Concepts.* — The following semiotic instruments are used in the analysis of the concept of metaphor: sign, designation, designatum, denoting, denotation, meaning (connotation), specific property, essential property, peculiar property, expressing, replacement, and language. These elementary semiotic terms are explained in the full text of the paper.

2. *Theoretical Foundations.* — The analysis starts from what is termed the semiotic quadrangle, the apices of which are: the sign, the author of the sign, the interpretant of the sign, and that fragment of reality which is the designatum of the sign. The sides and the diagonals of that quadrangle are graphic representations of semiotic, namely semantic and pragmatic, relations, and the non-semiotic relation which is perception. The present analysis, being semiotic in nature, is concerned neither with the process of

building me aphors nor with the process of interpreting them which belong to psychology, but with ready-made metaphors, i.e., metaphoric expressions.

## II. *The Semiotic Analysis of Stylistic Tropes.*

1. *The Metaphoric Triangle* $EE_1E_2$. — Most analyses of metaphors consider two expressions: a non-metaphorical one, e.g., "sun rays" ($E_2$), and the corresponding metaphorical one, e.g., "the hair of the Sun" (E). The present analysis, however, is based not on two, but on three terms, the third being, in this case, "the hair" ($E_1$) in its literal sense. This yields the triangle $EE_1E_2$, which is termed the metaphoric triangle; its sides represent the semiotic relations holding between the expressions E, $E_1$, $E_2$, of the language L, those expressions being in turn symbolized by the apices of the triangle.

2. *Metaphor proper.* — The analysis of metaphor proper is based on the following examples of metaphoric expressions: "the roaring of waves", "bull's health", "a torrent of tears", "golden hair", "the stars of (her) eyes".

The relation of metaphorization holds between $E_1$, i.e., the expression interpreted literally, and E, i.e., the metaphorical expression resulting from the former. This relation can be characterized as follows:

    A) E and $E_1$ are equiform.

    B) At least one designatum of the expression $E_1$ and every designatum of the expression E share the property P or the properties $P_1$, $P_2$, ..., $P_n$.

    C) The denotations of E and $E_1$ are either mutually exclusive or overlapping.

    D) The expressions E and $E_1$ are not equisignificant.

    E) The property P (or the properties $P_1$, $P_2$, ..., $P_n$), which is (are) attribute(s) of at least some designata of the expression $E_1$, is (are) connotative property (properties) of the expression E.

F) The expression E expresses the experiences of the metaphor user in the following manner: (a) he perceives the property P (or the properties $P_1$, $P_2$, ..., $P_n$) shared by the designata of the expression E and the designata of the expression $E_1$ and, in order to bring it (them) out turns it (them) into connotative property (properties) of the expression E; (b) he disregards certain, sometimes even specific, properties of the designata of the expression $E_1$ and prevents them from being connotative properties (or properties implied by connotative properties) of the expression E; (c) he has the expression $E_1$ in mind not in its whole extension (this is the particularizing tendency of metaphoric expressions).

Consider now the relation of replacement, which holds between the metaphorical expression E, e.g., "the hair of the Sun", and its non-metaphoric equivalent $E_2$, e.g., "the sun-rays":

A) E and $E_2$ are not equiform.

B) E and $E_2$ are equivalent, or the denotation of E is subordinated to that of $E_2$.

C) E and $E_2$ are equisignificant or nearly so. The latter case often consists in the connotation of $E_2$ being poorer, as compared with the connotation of E, by the said property P (properties $P_1$, $P_2$, ..., $P_n$).

D) The expression E expresses the experiences of the metaphor user so that these experiences always include reference to the property P (properties $P_1$, $P_2$, ..., $P_n$).

Finally consider the relation that holds between the non-metaphoric expression $E_1$, from which the metaphor is formed, and the non-metaphoric expression $E_2$ which is a translation of the metaphor:

A) The expressions $E_1$ and $E_2$ are not equiform.

B) The designata of the expressions $E_1$ and $E_2$ share the property P (properties $P_1$, $P_2$, ..., $P_n$) which is (are) the *tertium comparationis* in the formulation "$E_2$ is like $E_1$".

C) The denotations of $E_1$ and $E_2$ are mutually exclusive or overlapping.

D) The expressions $E_1$ and $E_2$ are not equisignificant.

E) Both the connotative properties of $E_1$ and those of $E_2$ imply the property P (properties $P_1$, $P_2$, ..., $P_n$), i.e., the said *tertium comparationis*; or else P (or $P_1$, $P_2$, ..., $P_n$) is (are) connotative property (properties) of one of these expressions and is implied by the connotation of the other.

F) The expressions $E_1$ and $E_2$ express the experiences of the sign user in different ways, but always so that those experiences include a reference to P (or $P_1$, $P_2$, ..., $P_n$).

3. *Metonymy.* — The following examples, quoted by experts, are used in the analysis of metonymy: "he lives by trade" (cause instead of effect), "to read Shakespeare" (the author instead of the work), "roaring steel" (about guns; substance instead of the objects made of it), "the whole village gathered" (the name of a place instead of its inhabitants), "extinct windows" (objects instead of other objects).

The relation $E-E_1$:

A) The property P (properties $P_1$, $P_2$, ..., $P_n$) is (are) specific or essential in $E_1$, and is (are) attribute(s) of all the designata of E and is (are) connotative property (properties) in it.

B) The denotations of E and $E_1$ are mutually exclusive or the denotation of E is subordinated to that of $E_1$.

C) There is a material bond between the designata of E and those of $E_1$.

The relation $E_1-E_2$:

A) The denotations of $E_1$ and $E_2$ are mutually exclusive, or that of $E_2$ is subordinated to that of $E_1$.

B) The property P (properties $P_1$, $P_2$, ..., $P_n$) is (are) connotative in $E_1$ and definitional in $E_2$.

C) A material bond may hold between the designata of $E_1$ and those of $E_2$; moreover, the relations: actor-work, material-product, whole-part, object-property, etc., may hold between a designatum of $E_1$ and a designatum of $E_2$ (but not conversely).

The remaining relations are common to metaphor proper and metonymy, which shows that both are variations of metaphor. The most important differences between the two are non-semiotic in nature. From the semiotic point of view the demarcation line goes not between metaphor proper and metonymy, but between metaphor proper and certain kinds of metonymy, on the one hand, and the remaining kinds of metonymy, on the other.

4. *Synecdoche.* — The experts characterize synecdoche as a variation of metonymy, consisting in the replacement: (a) of the name of the whole by the name of a part; (b) of a common name by a proper name; (c) of the name of a concrete object by a name of an abstract concept; (d) of species by genus, and conversely; (e) of the plural by the singular; (f) of an indefinite number by a definite one; (g) of a noun by a nominal use of an adjective.

The relation $E-E_1$

    A) The designata of E and those of $E_1$ share the property P (or the properties $P_1$, $P_2$, ..., $P_n$), which is (are) specific or essential.

    B) The relation between the denotations of E and $E_1$ is the same as in the case of metonymy, or the denotation of $E_1$ is subordinated to that of E.

The relation $E-E_2$:

The property P (properties $P_1$, $P_2$, ..., $P_n$) is (are) connotative in both expressions, or is (are) connotative in E and is (are) attribute(s) of all designata of $E_2$, or is (are) connotative in $E_2$ and is (are) attribute(s) of all designata of E.

The distinctive characteristics of synecdoche, as compared with metonymy and metaphor proper, consist above all in its non-semiotic properties. The semiotic relations, on the other hand, indicate that it is a variation of metaphor, and that there are synecdoches which resemble metonymy rather than other kinds of synecdoche. Thus here, too, the traditional demarcation lines between stylistic tropes ought to be revised.

5. *Periphrase.* — Periphrase is believed by experts to be a variation of metonymy, and hence, indirectly, of metaphor. Yet an analysis of semiotic relations holding between periphrase and its non-periphrastic counterpart shows that those relations, despite apparent similarities, are essentially different from those holding in the metaphoric triangle. The semiotic analysis of the concept of periphrase also reveals its relative nature and points to relationships between periphrase and description in the logical sense of the term. Periphrase is not a stylistic trope. It is not obtained from another expression by a modification of its semiotic functions, and such modifications are characteristic of all variations of metaphor. Hence periphrase is not a variation of metaphor.

6. *Irony and Anti-Irony.* — Ironical expressions (blames disguised as praises) and anti-ironical ones (praises disguised as blames) are, explicitly or implicitly, valuations.

The relation $E_1 - E$ (ironization or anti-ironization):

A) All designata of $E_1$ have the property P (properties $P_1$, $P_2$, ..., $P_n$) as specific or essential property (properties), whereas a property that is contrary to, or contradictory with, P is an attribute of all designata of E, often as a connotative property.

B) The denotations of E and $E_1$ are mutually exclusive, and
   a) E is equivalent to non-$E_1$; or
   b) E is subordinated to non-$E_1$.

C) The expression E expresses the experiences of the metaphor user in the following way:
   a) He notices that all designata of $E_1$ have the property P, in some cases as specific or essential property (properties).
   b) He believes that all elements of a class C have a property that is contradictory with, or contrary to, P.
   c) He wishes to bring out that property of all elements of the class C and accordingly terms them E, E being obtained from $E_1$ by semiotic modifications such that all designata of E have as attributes properties

contradictory with, or contrary to, the property P; those properties are in some cases connotative properties of E.

The other semiotic relations show that irony and anti-irony, despite their distinct characteristics as compared with the other tropes, are variations of metaphor.

III. *The Semiotic Nature of the Concept of Metaphor (Concluding Remarks)*.

1. *Examples in the Semiotic Analysis of the Concept of Metaphor.* — The examples used in this paper are confined to denoting names, to the exclusion of empty and abstract names, so that the description can cover not only the relations holding between the denotations of expressions, but also those between the designata of expressions. Further, for technical and didactic reasons, the analysis is confined to fairly simple metaphors, namely those obtained by replacement, to the exclusion of metaphors based on genitival or verb forms.

2. *The Metaphoric Triangle $EE_1E_2$ as the Scheme of the Structure of the Relative Concept of Metaphor.* — The concept of metaphor is relative in the sense that an expression E is metaphoric always with respect to two other non-metaphoric expressions $E_1$ and $E_2$, and also with respect to a given language L.

This situation is reflected in the metaphorical triangle $EE_1E_2$, with the base $E_1E_2$. The expressions E, $E_1$, $E_2$, belong to the same language L, but only E is metaphorical, while $E_1$ is a formal equivalent of E (since the two are equiform), and $E_2$ is a semiotic equivalent of E (since the two are usually equivalent, and also equisignificant or nearly so).

3. *The Metaphorization Relation $E_1-E$ and Simple Polysemy.*

(a) *Metaphorization and Simple Polysemy.* — Metaphorization consists in this that a non-metaphoric expression $E_1$ is subjected to the semiotic modifications, as described above, while its form remains unchanged. The resulting metaphoric expression E, which is equiform with $E_1$, not only means something else, but also designates, denotes, and expresses something else. E and $E_1$ are apparently one and the same, though polysemic, expression. What then is the difference between the relation of metaphorization and ordinary polysemy? The semiotic relations holding between two equiform but not equisignificant non-metaphoric expressions are analysed, and different results of such analyses within the metaphoric triangle provide the answer. This makes it possible to criticize the psychological and linguistic descriptions of that difference, as made so far, as incomplete, especially in the case of genetically metaphorical expressions.

(b) *Semiotic Oscillation and the Transparence of Metaphor.* — The semiotic oscillation of metaphor consists in this that the author and the interpretant of a metaphoric expression E both perceive, through its semiotic functions, the semiotic functions of the expressions $E_1$ and $E_2$ (this exactly is called the transparence of metaphor), and also the semiotic relations holding between E, $E_1$ and $E_2$, which results in a superposition of ideas in the minds of those who communicate by means of a metaphor. No such oscillation (between a literal and a metaphoric interpretation of a given expression) exists in the case of ordinary, non-metaphoric polysemic expressions.

(c) *Reducibility of the Psychological Aspects of Metaphor to its Semiotic Properties.* — In the full text, the expression "See how white butterflies are playing", uttered by a Negro child who first saw snow in his life is discussed as an example of the relationship between the pragmatic and the semantic functions of a metaphoric expression. It is concluded that in dubious cases, when it is not clear whether we have to do with a metaphor or with a mistake or a lie, the set of semiotic relations, and not just the mental attitude of the author or the interpretant of a given expression, proves decisive.

4. *The Synonymity of the Metaphoric Expression (E) and its Semiotic Equivalent ($E_2$) versus Simple Logical Equivalence.* — The relation

$E-E_2$ in the metaphoric triangle $EE_1E_2$ is a relation of replacement such that its elements are equisignificant or nearly so. It differs from ordinary logical replacement by having the metaphoric element E, i.e., such as was obtained from the expression $E_1$ by semiotic modifications discussed above. In the case of ordinary logical replacement both elements occur in what is termed literal sense. The comparison of E and $E_2$ makes it possible to notice the particularizing and abstract nature of metaphor.

5. *The Relation $E_1-E_2$ as the Base of the Metaphoric Triangle.* — The relation $E_1-E_2$ is partly a reflection of the relation $E-E_1$ (because of a similarity of semantic relationships, such as the mutual exclusion of denotations, non-equisignificance, etc.), and partly a reflection of the relation $E-E_2$ (because of formal similarities: non-equiformity). It is the base of the metaphoric triangle also in the sense that $E_1$ is as it were the formal source of metaphor, since it lends its form to the metaphoric expression, and $E_2$ is its semiotic source, since it lends to the metaphoric expression its semiotic functions.

6. *Conclusions.* — The full text sums up the conditions sufficient and necessary for an expression E in a language L to be metaphoric with respect to $E_1$ and $E_2$.

APPENDIX:
A SURVEY OF VIEWS AND THEORIES IN THE
LOGICAL THEORY OF LANGUAGE

FOREWORD

The authors of the articles in this survey are members of a seminar in the logical semiotics of natural language. The seminar, which has been conducted for the past several years in the Department of Logic at Warsaw University, is composed of young scholars: logicians, philosophers, linguists, praxeologists, mathematicians etc. For the past year one of the subjects of this seminar has been a survey of the most important views in the field of logical semiotics in the 19th and 20th century as well as the criticism and discussion which it produced. The authors of the papers read in this seminar agreed to write summaries or abstracts of their efforts, which we present here.

The survey is arranged as follows: two lines of development were singled out — the first initiated by Mill, the other by Peirce. In this way two divisions arose, each with its chronological order. That does not mean, however, that it is to be treated as a historical survey. Nor is it a critical survey.

The whole was conceived as an encyclopedic review with a practical purpose in mind, namely, to remind non-specialists as concisely and in as abbreviated a form as possible of the basic concepts, terms, views and theories in logical semiotics.

The articles make no pretense to being original; they do not contain critical remarks by the authors, nor do they conduct a polemic with the positions presented. They are nothing more than intentionally simplified elementary reports.

The survey is therefore not to be treated as a problematic or theoretical review and thus a basis for discussion with the authors. These papers were not written with the intention of having them read at a symposium.[1] They are a mere technical aid to be used by anyone who feels so inclined.

JERZY PELC

---

[1]  International Conference on Semiotics, Poland — September 1966.

INTRODUCTION

Language is the object of research both for linguists and for logicians. The logical theory of language, also called semiotics, has been divided into three branches, syntactics, semantics and pragmatics (see the section concerning Ch. Morris). Syntactics and semantics are developed either as deductive systems which concern artificially built languages or as empirical science concerning common properties of different natural languages. The former are distinguished by the adjective PURE (e.g. pure semantics), the latter by the term DESCRIPTIVE. As for pragmatics, the almost commonly held opinion is that it may be only a descriptive science. The famous works of Gödel, Tarski and others belong to the field of pure semiotics.

Our concern in the present survey is only in the descriptive theories of language, as they have in common with the theories which are developed under the name of linguistics. Although they have much in common, they are different in some important respects. The peculiarities of descriptive logical semiotics, as opposed to the linguistic research, may be summed up in the three points:

1. The logician is interested in that use of language which would support searching for truth, especially in scientific research; this aim influences all logical rules of correct usage.

2. If necessary, the logician takes advantage of results, notions and

technical devices (symbolism) which are supplied by pure semiotics or formal logic.

3. Logical investigations concerning language are often connected, at least as far as their origin is concerned, with epistemological or ontological problems, especially the problems of the foundations of mathematics (Frege, Russell, Quine, Leśniewski, etc.). The only possible exception are some representatives of the 'functionalistic' movement, who seem to be interested in language for its own sake; in this respect their approach resembles the linguistic approach.

There are many theories which satisfy these conditions and belong by the same to the descriptive logical semiotics. As it is not possible to discuss all of them, only those will be taken into account which seem to be the most influential or the most widely known among students of logic. The same criterion determines the choice of historical period which will be reported.

We have tried to approximate a chronological order and, at the same time, to group together those authors who belong to the same line of development or were influenced by one another.

The first group is composed by J. St. Mill, G. Frege, who continued some of Mill's ideas, and B. Russell, Frege's famous competitor. Then follows the thinker who did not belong to the 'camp' of logicians but strongly influenced the development of logical semantics, E. Husserl, whose philosophical activity coincides in time with that of Russell.

At the same time that the aforementioned European authors were establishing the foundations of semantics, on the other side of the ocean the same task was being undertaken by Ch. S. Peirce. His influence on logicians was relatively smaller and his considerable achievements have only recently been discovered by historians of logic. But there were investigators in America who owed much to his ideas. One of them was Ch. Morris. In a sense, C. I. Lewis, the author of the system of modal logic and of an analysis of knowledge and valuation belongs to the same trend. His main contribution to the theory of language is the article presented in this survey. One of the notions which were fruitfully applied in this work was the notion of possible (consistently thinkable) worlds. It was the idea developed also, in greater detail, by R. Carnap.

Carnap belongs to both continents and may suffice for a whole group of philosophers, so many different ideas did he originate in different periods of his development. In this survey the period chosen is that which produced *Meaning and Necessity* — a work of great significance.

Next we present the views of K. Ajdukiewicz, whose theory of meaning resembles that of Carnap, though it was developed quite independently. Ajdukiewicz also contributed to the theory of semantical categories which originated with Leśniewski.

The last paragraph has to perform a double role. It conveys further information about outstanding investigators and, at the same time, it gives an outline of the controversy concerning the very aim of the analysis of ordinary language. According to 'classical' — as it were — logical semantics, in order for ordinary language to become more precise it has to be translated into an ideal artificial language or, at least, modelled on such a language. Because of this programme of reconstruction the term RECONSTRUCTIONISM is often applied. According to an alternative view, everyday language is as precise as is necessary for the needs of everyday life and even for philosophical discourse. It must not be improved upon but carefully investigated and described. Hence the name DESCRIPTIONISM.

WITOLD MARCISZEWSKI

### JOHN STUART MILL

There were many interesting remarks and theories concerning language in ancient, medieval and modern logic, but the first to succeed in initiating the continuous development of certain ideas was John Stuart Mill (1806-1873) in his work *System of Logic Rationative and Inductive* (1843).

Mill distinguished names from so called syncategorematic terms, such as adverbs, prepositions, etc. There are in Mill's writings two different concepts of what is a name. Sometimes he says that for an expression to be a name it must be able to be used as the subject or the predicate of a subject-predicate sentence; it lets in e.g. adjectives as names. Sometimes he confines the class of names to those expressions only which occur in the sentences as their grammatical subjects; it excludes adjectives and leaves only nouns, pronouns and substantival phrases (Cf. G. Ryle "The Theory of Meaning" in *British Philosophy in the Mid-Century* [1957]).

The most important divisions of names are the following:

1. general names which may be affirmed of many objects, as opposed to individual names which may be affirmed of one only;
2. concrete names (e.g., human, coloured), as opposed to abstract names (e.g., humanity, colour);
3. names which are connotative, as opposed to non-connotative names.

The last distinction which, according to Mill himself, most deeply penetrates the nature of language, needs an explanation. We read in the text of Mill: "A non-connotative term is one which signifies a subject only or an attribute only. A connotative term is which denotes a subject and implies an attribute. By a subject is here meant anything which possesses attributes." (Book I, ch. 2). In this text we meet Mill's famous distinction between connotation and denotation; the term "white", for instance, connotes the property of whiteness and denotes all things which are white. Proper names, e.g., "John", "London", are not connotative because they do not convey any information as to the properties of the things named by them.

The distinction between connotative and non-connotative names is related to the preceeding distinctions in the following way. All names which are both general and concrete are connotative. The individual concrete names divide into non-connotative, as proper names, and connotative, i.e. conveying information of attributes, as "the sun", "the first king of England", etc. As for abstract names, they are in a sense non-connotative because the subject denoted is identical with the attribute, but in another sense they may be meant as connotative.

The connotation of names has been identified with their meaning. Mill writes: "The meaning resides not in what [names] denote but in what they connote. The names which connote nothing ... have, strictly speaking, no signification" (*ibid.*). The meaning of compound expressions, including sentences, derives from meaning of their constituents, the most basic of which are the connotative names.

WITOLD MARCISZEWSKI

GOTTLOB FREGE

The next author who made an important use of the notions similar to that of connotation and denotation was Gottlob Frege, a German logician, one of the founders of mathematical logic (1848-1925). The views in question were expounded by Frege in his article "Über Sinn und Bedeutung" (1892).

Frege distinguishes for any name between its nominatum (*Bedeutung*), i.e. the object named, and its sense (*Sinn*), i.e. the way in which the object is given by it. The nominatum corresponds, in Mill's terminology, to the totality of the objects denoted, and the sense corresponds to connotation. The phrase "the way in which the object is given" may be interpreted as: the properties of the object by which we recognize it as the nominatum of the name.

This is illustrated by the following example. The two expressions "the Morning Star" and "the Evening Star" have the same nominatum, because both are names of the same thing, a certain planet. They have not, however, the same sense, because they refer to their common nominatum, that planet, in different ways: by the property of appearing in morning or by the property of appearing in evening.

Thus, two expressions having the same nominatum may have different senses. But two expressions having the same sense must have the same nominatum. When a constituent part of an expressions is replaced by another having the same sense, the sense of the whole is not altered. When a constituent part of an expression is replaced by another having the same nominatum, the nominatum of the whole is not altered, but the sense may be. In other words: The nominatum of the whole expression is a function of the nominata of the names occurring in it; the sense of the whole expression is a function of the senses of the names occurring in it.

In the example quoted above the nominatum is a material object. But it may be also an abstract object as for instance a natural number or a class of things; e.g., the nominatum of the name "philosopher" is the class of all philosophers.

Sentences are treated by Frege as if they were names. They have also their sense and their nominatum which are correspondingly, the proposition expressed and the truth-value (truth or falsehood) of the sentence. This rule, however, holds only for the sentences in ordinary contexts (i.e. *oratio recta*). In the oblique contexts (*oratio obliqua*) the nominatum of the sentence is not its truth-value but the proposition (expressed by it) which is its ordinary sense. The following example may it explain: (A) *Homer believed that Greeks fought the Trojans.* The whole sentence (*oratio recta*) reports a fact concerning Homer; hence it is true as it conforms to this fact. On the other hand, the sentence after "that" (*oratio obliqua*) does not refer to a historical fact but to the thought of the fact. So the reference or nominatum of this sentence is not a truth but the thought expressed in the sentence.

The distinction between ordinary and oblique nominatum proves useful for the solution of a paradox. The paradox arises when a part of an oblique context is replaced by the expression having the same ordinary nominatum; e.g. in (A) we replace the word "Greeks" by the phrase "the compatriots of Plato". What results in this way from the true sentence (A) — proves to be false, as Homer could not think of Plato. Thus the nominatum (truth-value) of the whole context (A) — would change though the nominata of its constituent parts would remain unchanged. This result is clearly inconsistent with the principle mentioned that the nominatum of whole expression is the function of the nominata of its constituent parts. The difficulty, however, disappears if one introduces the notion of oblique nominatum: the oblique nominata of the phrases in question are not the same, as the thought of Greeks is not identical with the thought of compatriots of Plato. Thus there is no reason to expect that after substituting one by another the nominatum of the whole sentence will remain the same.

We cannot go into the further details and consequences of the Frege's theory, which is very ingenious though not always intuitive. What is essential here, it is Frege's treatment of all expressions (with the exception of connectives, prepositions, etc.) as the names referring to singular objects (their nominata) and having by the same an independent meaning.

Frege's way of analysis is continued by A. Church, contemporary American logician; in the terminology of Church and some other authors the word "nominatum" is replaced by "denotation", in the sense however different from that of Mill.

WITOLD MARCISZEWSKI

BERTRAND RUSSELL

The very different line of analysis has been presented by Bertrand Russell (1872-1970) in the book *The Principles of Mathematics* (1903), in the article "On Denoting" (1905) and in the introduction to the famous work *Principia Mathematica* (1913). In later years Russell continued his semantical analysis in the book *Inquiry into Meaning and Truth* (1940).

The expressions such as names of classes or descriptions of individuals have been called by Russell "denoting phrases". The class of denoting phrases of any language includes the expressions which were called names by G. Frege, and connotative names by Mill. But unlike Mill and Frege, Russell treats these phrases as expressions devoid of independent meaning; so, they resemble in this respect the connectives, prepositions, etc. (Mill's *syncate-goremata*). Hence the meaning of a sentence is by no means a function of the meanings of the names occurring in it but, on the contrary, the meaning of constituent names depends on the meaning of the whole sentence. They contribute in a way to the meaning of the sentence in which they occur but "they have no meaning in isolation", "no significance on their own account" (Russell's own words).

There is an important syntactical rule derived from this idea: the rule which demands that in well constructed language the denoting phrases cannot be used as grammatical subjects but only as predicates; in the place of grammatical subject always appears an individual variable. So, instead of saying "The President of France is a general" one ought to say: "There is an x such that x is the President of France and x is a general".

In Russell's theory of denoting the special interest is devoted to individual descriptions, as "the present president of France", "the author of the *Iliad*", etc. They are opposed to what Russell calls proper names but what is very different from proper names in ordinary grammatical sense; let us call them, correspondingly, logical and grammatical proper names. The logical proper names refer to the things which have been known by direct acquaintance (seeing, touching, etc.) and not by description in some terms. So, if a grammatical proper name, e.g. "Homer" has been introduced to the language by verbal explanation (as: "Homer was the blind Greek who wrote the *Iliad*") it is not a logical proper name but the abbreviation of the description "the blind Greek ... etc.". In fact, this name is a concealed description.

This analysis has proved fruitful in consequences and applications but, again, we must dispense us with going into more detailed account. Let it suffice to say that on these ideas the construction of the symbolic language of *Principia Mathematica* has been founded and, besides, the solution of some problems of ordinary language has been suggested.

WITOLD MARCISZEWSKI

### CHARLES SANDERS PEIRCE

Charles Sanders Peirce (1839-1914) was the originator of many
basic assumptions, conceptions and methods of the modern
theory of signs and meaning. He was the first philosopher who
introduced in a determined manner the problem of meaning as a
separate, fundamental philosophical issue, which has to be analyzed
and explored in itself and not only in connection with the problems
of truth. Peirce understood very clearly that before one can verify
a given statement, hypothesis, theory, one has to grasp and clarify
their meaning. He was aware of the great role played by signs and
language in the acquirement and communication of knowledge or
in any kind of human activity, but he also considered signs and
languages as means only. He saw clearly that there is no such thing
as absolute meaning and that all endeavors to establish some general
criterion of meaning are a hopeless enterprise.

Already in 1867 Peirce presented a very original conception of
signs which he developed later into a very intricate and often
obscure theory. Similar to John Locke and to the Stoics Peirce
identified logic with semiotics which he described as the "doctrine
of the essential nature and fundamental varieties of possible
semiosis". (5.488)

Peirce's general understanding of semiotics was very close to that
of our days, especially as represented by Charles Morris. There is
no doubt that the division of semiotics into: syntax, semantics and
pragmatics was inspired by Peirce's division of this discipline into
speculative grammar, critical logic and speculative rhetoric.

A sign was for Peirce "something which stands to somebody for
something in some respect or capacity" (2.228). A sign is always
the subject of a triadic relation involving the sign itself, its object
and its interpretant which is an equivalent sign created in the mind
of the interpreter by the first sign. The triadic character of every
sign-situation led Peirce to distinguish three divisions of signs: the
sign in itself, in relation to its object, and to its interpretant.

Peirce divided further this trichotomy into three trichotomies and
ten classes of signs, later into ten trichotomies and sixty-six classes

and came finally to the conclusion that a theoretical total of 59.049 classes of signs is possible.

Peirce attached the biggest importance to the division of signs into: ICONS, INDICES and SYMBOLS.

Symbols are for Peirce the highest and most perfect forms of signs. The possibility to use and create symbols distinguishes human beings from other animal species, enables them to think in general terms and makes science, culture and art possible.

Peirce considered that signs can function only in sign-situations, that they are functions or relations in concrete processes of semiosis and not "things in themselves".

Peirce's reflections on the nature and functions of signs, his logical studies and discoveries and especially the logic of relatives led him to a new approach towards the problem of meaning and to the formulation of his pragmatic maxim. The pragmatic maxim is also logically and historically a consequence of Peirce's theory of doubt and belief, his criticism of the Cartesian philosophical tradition, his preoccupation with the methods of natural sciences.

He rejects the traditional subjective and formal criteria advanced by Descartes, Leibniz and others and comes to the conclusion that meaning is not some kind of an ideal entity, some kind of essence, substance, structure, image, quality or relation but only the function of specific signs involved in concrete triadic relations characteristic for all processes of semiosis.

The question which Peirce tried to answer through his pragmatic maxim might be formulated like this: What kind of criteria should be applied in order to achieve a full clearness, a full understanding of general conceptions, so as to be able to apply and use these notions in scientific or philosophical propositions, hypotheses and theories?

"Consider what effects, that might conceivably have practical bearings, we conceive the object of our conception to have. Then, our conception of these effects is the whole of our conception of the object." (5.402). This original formulation of the pragmatic principle in *How to Make our Ideas Clear* is very unclear and led many people among others W.James to misinterpretations and vulgarisations of Peirce's thought.

Peirce thought that his pragmatic maxim was applicable only for the clarification of the rational meaning of general conceptions. He did not exclude the possibility of other kinds of meaning besides the rational. Neither did he conceive his pragmatic maxim as a universal criterion for meaningfulness.

The pragmatic maxim was intended to be above all a DIRECTIVE for the establishment of the rational meaning of notions, propositions, theories, a postulate, whose fullfilment would lead to a concrete definition of a given general notion. It was meant as a CRITERION of rational meaning, but one which presupposed a determined THEORY of meaning.

Peirce considered his pragmatic maxim as a method of logic but not as a principle of speculative philosophy. His theory of meaning is an attempt to demonstrate the unity of rational thinking and rational action, of theory and practice. Knowledge is for him not something individual, subjective, isolated, achieved through one single act. It is and should be social, intersubjective, verifiable, developing through a public process.

MARIAN DOBROSIELSKI


CHARLES W. MORRIS

Charles W.Morris continued the tradition of pragmatism, connecting it with the behaviouristic psychology. At the same time he participated in the movement of logical empiricism (Neopositivism). The last point is essential for understanding the views of Morris, since between the wars logical empiricists fought for what they called the unity of science; Morris intended his theory of signs to be a useful instrument for this purpose. The unity of science was to be achieved by establishing a universal language; e.g., the language based on physics, as Carnap formerly suggested, or on the theory of signs, which was Morris's original proposal. Morris believed that the most general theory of signs would make possible the unification of all sciences, not only in the field of social research but formal and natural research as well. Such a theory has been published under the title "Foundations of the Theory of Signs" in the periodical *International Encyclopaedia of Unified Science*, I (1938).

According to Morris, the most effective characterization of what a sign is is as follows: S IS A SIGN OF A DESIGNATUM D FOR A PERSON P TO THE DEGREE THAT P TAKES ACCOUNT OF D IN VIRTUE OF THE PRESENCE OF S. Signs which refer to the same object need not have the same designata, since that which is taken account of in the object may differ for various interpreters (note that what is meant here by "designatum" resembles Mill's connotation or Frege's sense, while the very word "object" corresponds to nominatum).

In the process of communication three kinds of relations are distinguished: semantical relations — relations of signs to the objects to which the signs are applicable; pragmatical relations — relations of signs to their interpreters; syntactical relations — relations of signs to one another. Accordingly, there are three branches of the general theory of signs or semiotics: semantics, pragmatics and syntax (this tripartition has been widely accepted among students of language).

At many points in Morris's work the basic role of pragmatics is stressed. Thus, for instance, the pragmatical relation of applying a sign is used to define a syntactical relation in the following way: if there are two signs, say "animal" and "man", where the former is applied to every object to which the latter is applied, but not conversely, these terms gain relations between themselves (e.g., the relation of inclusion). The syntactical structure of a language reflects the interrelationship of the responses.

In respect to the different semantical functions three kinds of signs are distinguished:
1. INDEXICAL SIGNS which denote only a single object and do not characterize what they denote (such a sign is a particular act of pointing);
2. CHARACTERIZING SIGNS which can denote the plurality of things and characterize what they denote;

3. UNIVERSAL SIGNS, such as the term "something", which denote everything.

The characterizing signs divide into icons and symbols. The former characterize the object denoted by exhibiting the properties of this object as does a photograph, a map, a chemical diagram; the latter do not resemble the physical shape of the object denoted. So called "concepts" may be regarded as semantical rules determining the use of characterizing signs.

Morris makes no use of the term "meaning" which is so frequent in different theories of language. This term may have an explication in some terms of his theory but has in it no explanatory function by itself.

There are many other syntactical, semantical and pragmatical rules which are largely discussed by Morris. As one of the results of this discussion the definition of language is formulated as follows: A language in the full semiotical sense of the term is any intersubjective set of signs whose usage is determined by syntactical, semantical and pragmatical rules.

Morris's views on the importance and applications of semiotics were enthusiastic. According to his own words "Logic, mathematics and linguistics can be absorbed in their entirety within semiotics". This was but a programme. Morris tried to elaborate a more precise theory of signs based on the concepts of stimulus and response in his later work *Signs, Language and Behaviour* (New York, 1946). Of these two works, however, the former has proved to be more influential and stimulating.

WITOLD MARCISZEWSKI

C. I. LEWIS

As Charles Peirce pointed out, the essentials of the meaning-situation are found wherever there is anything which, for some mind, stands as sign of something else. Here, our discussion will be confined to meanings as conveyed by words; by series of ink marks or of sounds. But in discussing verbal meanings exclusively, we do not omit any kind of meanings, but merely limit our consideration to meanings as conveyed by a particular type of vehicle.

LINGUISTIC SIGNS are verbal symbols. A VERBAL SYMBOL is a recognizable pattern of marks or of sounds used for purposes of expression. The connection between a linguistic sign and its meaning is determined by convention. Two marks or two sounds, having the same recognizable pattern, are two INSTANCES of the same symbol.

A LINGUISTIC EXPRESSION is constituted by the association of a verbal symbol and a fixed meaning; but the linguistic expression cannot be identified with the symbol alone nor with the meaning alone. If in two cases, the meaning expressed is the same but the symbols are different or the symbol is the same but the meanings are different, there are two expressions. And if in two cases, the meaning is the same and the symbol is the same, then there are two instances of the expression but only one expression. An expression, as well as a symbol, is an abstract entity.

A TERM is an expression CAPABLE of naming or applying to a thing or things, of some kind, actual or thought of. A linguistic expression may be a term or a proposition or a propositional function. Propositions and propositional functions are terms; but some terms only are propositions, and some only are propositional functions.

All terms have meaning in the sense or mode of denotation or extension; and of connotation or intension.

The DENOTATION of a term is the class of all actual or existent things to which that term correctly applies. A term which names nothing actual, e.g. "Apollo", has ZERO-DENOTATION.

The COMPREHENSION of a term is the CLASSIFICATION of all consistently thinkable things to which the term would correctly apply — where anything is consistently thinkable if the assertion of its existence would not, explicitly or implicitly, involve a contradiction. E.g., the comprehension of "square" includes all imaginable as well as actual squares but does not include round squares.

The CONNOTATION or INTENSION of a term is delimited by any

correct definition of it. If nothing would be correctly namable by
"T" unless it should also be namable by "$A_1$", by "$A_2$" ... and by
"$A_n$", and if anything namable by the compound term "$A_1$ and
$A_2$ ... and $A_n$" would also be namable by "T", then this compound
term, or any which is synonymous with it, specifies the connotation
of "T" and may be said to have the same connotation as "T".

The SIGNIFICATION of a term is its comprehensive essential
character. A term SIGNIFIES the comprehensive character such that
everything having this character is correctly namable by the term,
and whatever lacks this character, or anything included in it, is not
so namable. Thus we have some manner of marking the distinction
between characters of an object which are essential to its being
named by a term in question, and other characters of the object
which are not thus essential.

The modes of meaning mentioned above for terms — denotation
or extension, connotation or intension, comprehension, and
signification — are likewise the modes of meaning of propositions
and of propositional functions.

A PROPOSITION is a term capable of signifying a state of affairs.
One should not confuse a proposition with the STATEMENT or
ASSERTION of it. The element of assertion in a statement is extra-
neous to the proposition asserted. The proposition is the assertable
content; and this same content can also be questioned, denied, or
merely supposed, etc. We find the assertable content, here identified
with the proposition itself, as some participial term, signifying a
state of affairs, actual or thinkable.

The state of affairs, mentioned above, is the signification of the
proposition; not its denotation. When any term denotes a thing,
it names that thing as a whole, not merely the character or attribute
signified. And that thing is, by the law of Excluded Middle, also
denoted by one or the other of every pair of mutually negative terms
which could meaningfully be applied to it. Thus if we should
regard propositions as denoting the state of affairs they refer to,
their denotation would not be subject to the law of Excluded
Middle.

The DENOTATION or EXTENSION of a proposition must be —

according to the law — something which is denoted by one or other of every pair of mutually contradictory propositions. And this thing denoted is the kind of TOTAL state of affairs we call a world. And the denotation of a proposition — since denotation is in all cases confined to what exists — is either the actual world or it is empty. All TRUE propositions have the same denotation or extension, namely, this actual world; and all FALSE propositions have the same extension, namely, zero-extension. As we see, the limited state of affairs signified is merely the ESSENTIAL ATTRIBUTE which any world must possess in order that the proposition in question should denote or apply to it. A statement asserting a proposition ATTRIBUTES the state of affairs signified to the actual world.

A proposition COMPREHENDS any consistently thinkable world which would incorporate the state of affairs it signifies.

The INTENSION of a proposition includes whatever the proposition entails; it comprises whatever must be true of any possible world in order that the proposition should apply to or be true of it.

A PROPOSITIONAL FUNCTION is essentially a kind of predicate or predication; a characterization meaningfully applicable to the kind of entities names of which are values of the variables. E.g. for "x is A", it is "being A" which is this predicate or characterization. Propositional functions are participial terms, as propositions are. But whereas the propositional characterization ("John being now angry") could only characterize reality or some thinkable world, the propositional-function characterization ("being angry") could not be a characterization of a world, but only of a thing, or a pair of things, etc.

The denotation or EXTENSION of a propositional function is the class of existent things for which this predication holds true.

The COMPREHENSION of a function is the classification of things consistently thinkable as being characterized by this predication.

The CONNOTATION of a function comprises all that the attribution of this predicate to anything entails as also attributable to that thing.

If one should wish to speak of THE meaning of a term or propo-

sition or propositional function, it will be evident that MEANING IN
THE MODE OF INTENSION would be the best candidate for this
preferred status. Expressions having the same connotation or
intension must also have the same denotation or extension, the
same signification, and the same comprehension. They would be
called SYNONYMOUS, only on condition that THEIR INTENSION IS
NEITHER ZERO NOR UNIVERSAL, or that — their intension being
either zero or universal — they are EQUIVALENT IN ANALYTIC
MEANING. Two expressions are equivalent in analytic meaning, (1)
if at least one is ELEMENTARY (i.e. it has no symbolized constituent,
the intension of which is a constituent of the intension of the
expression in question itself) and they have the same intension; or
(2) if, both being COMPLEX (i.e. non-elementary), they can be so
analyzed into constituents that (a) for every constituent distinguished in either, there is a corresponding constituent in the other
which has the same intension, (b) no constituent distinguished in
either has zero-intension or universal intension, and (c) the order
of corresponding constituents is the same in both, or can be made
the same without alteration of the intension of either whole
expression.

Intension or connotation may be thought of in either of two
ways, which we shall call respectively linguistic meaning and sense
meaning.

LINGUISTIC MEANING is intension as constituted by the pattern of
definitive and other analytic (or syntactic) relationships of the
expression in question to other expressions.

SENSE MEANING is intension in the mode of a criterion in mind
by which one is able to apply or refuse to apply the expression in
question in the case of presented things or situations.

These two modes of intensional meaning are supplementary, not
alternative.[1]

JERZY PELC

---

[1] C.I.Lewis. "The Modes of Meaning", *Philosophy and Phenomenological
Research*, IV, No. 2 (1943), 236-250.

EDMUND HUSSERL

*Husserl's theory of meaning — from his*
*Logische Untersuchungen period*

*The basic assumptions.* — Besides objects of the real world (as well
as attributes, states of affairs and processes) there are ideal objects.
Ideal objects are accessible cognitively by insight into the essence of
things (*Wesenschau*). Mental phenomena, unlike physical phenomena, are intentional, that is directed at or concerning something
(F. Brentano).

*Concepts, distinctions and assertions.* — In the expression one
should distinguish between its verbal sound, i.e. the concrete
physical phenomenon or the expression itself, and the meaning at
which the act of understanding is directed. Directing is the
significational intention.
    The object of the act of understanding is fully determined by the
significational intention. Such an object is called intentional. It is
an ideal object.
    The act of bestowing meaning creates within the act of under-
standing the reference of the expression to its object. Whether the
corresponding object exists or not in the real world is not essential
for the meaning of an expression. Only in some cases does the
relation to the object in the real world — actually come into play.
In such a case we say that the sense-fulfilling act, i.e. the intuitional
conviction of the real existence of the object, is added to preceding
act. Then the significational intention 'shoots over' the intentional
object and reaches the real one.
    The above mentioned sense-bestowing and sense-fulfilling acts
do not succeed each other but constitute a whole; it is a unique act
of understanding in which various intuitive aspects can appear.
    Because of the variety of intentional counterparts the linguistic
expressions are classified into different semantic categories. The
intentional objects correspond to the names, the intentional states
of affairs correspond to the propositions. To establish termino-

logical distinction we say that words have meaning, and sentences have sense.

The meaning of a name, or the corresponding intentional object, is the ideal object, although not every ideal object is intentional. The ideal object which is the meaning of a word is actualized in each case by a separate act of understanding the word. But not all ideal objects are actualized in this way.

The understanding of a sentence consists in grasping the intentional state of affairs, i.e. the relationships between the intentional objects. These relationships between ideas are independent of the person who understands the sentence and of the time at which the understanding takes place. The sense of a sentence is something objective as opposed to the subjectiveness of the process of understanding. Therefore the truth of a sentence is independent of the circumstances under which it is understood.

There are in language occasional expressions which make it necessary to somehow modify the previous statement. These expressions change their meaning depending on the context but that changeability is systematic and is regulated by definite rules.

In mathematical reasoning there also appear expressions which in principle are meaningless in the sense defined above; they are said to possess only an operational meaning (*Operationsbedeutung*).

KAZIMIERZ CZARNOTA

RUDOLF CARNAP

Carnap (born 1891) has developed his theory of semantical functions of linguistic expressions in *Meaning and Necessity*[1] and several other later works. He is to some extent the continuator of the ideas initiated by Frege, but his conceptual constructions in the theory of meaning are free from the defects and limitations of the view of his predecessor. Especially, the semantical concepts elaborated by Carnap are introduced by precise definitions — in

---

[1] First edition, Chicago, 1947; second edition (enlarged), Chicago, 1956.

contrast with the only intuitive way of introducing of such concepts by Frege.

He defines two equivalence relations which arise between expressions; the first corresponds to the material equivalence, the second — to the logical equivalence of expressions. Two expressions have the same EXTENSION if and only if they are materially equivalent; two expressions have the same INTENSION if and only if they are logically equivalent.[2] The concept of extension is conceived of as the explicatum of the traditional concept of denotation (nominatum), and the concept of intension — as the explicatum of the traditional concept of connotation (sense).

Two expressions having the same extension can be mutually replaced (*salva veritate*) in all extensional contexts. Two expressions having the same intension can be mutually replaced in intensional (modal) contexts.

In the informal explanations Carnap says that the extension of a sentence is its truth-value, the intension of a sentence is the proposition expressed by that sentence. The extension of a (one-place) predicate is a class of suitable objects, its intension — a corresponding attribute. The extension of an individual expression is object named, its intension — a corresponding individual concept. These explanations, however, are not of essential importance. Entities representing the extensions or intensions of expressions may be chosen arbitrarily; they need only satisfy the definitions of the sameness of extensions or intensions.

In addition to the concept of intension Carnap introduces the concept of INTENSIONAL STRUCTURE. This concept is conceived of as the explicatum of the stronger concept of meaning (and the corresponding relation — called the INTENSIONAL ISOMORPHISM of expressions — as the explicatum of the stronger concept of synonymity). Roughly speaking, two expressions have the same intensional structure (are intensionally isomorphic) if and only if they are built in the same way of primitive expressions which have respectively the same intension. Carnap hoped that this concept of

---

[2] These definitions must, of course, include the relativization to the given semantical system.

synonymity would guarantee that synonymical expressions might be mutually replaced in so-called belief-sentences. It seems, however, that none of the concepts of synonymity can play such a role.

The concept of intensional isomorphism has been criticized by many authors as being too weak or — conversely — as being to strong a concept of synonymity.[3] In "Reply to Leonard Linsky"[4] Carnap points out that there exists the possibility of formulating as many different concepts of synonymity as desired, by the gradual addition of different logical transformations to the definition of intensional isomorphism (or to the strongest concept of synonymity which is the concept of equiformity).

BARBARA STANOSZ

[3] L. Linsky, "Some Notes ...", *Phil. of Science*, 16, No. 4 (1949); A. Church, "Intensional Isomorphism ...", *Phil. Studies*, V, No. 5 (1954); A. Pap, "Belief and Proposition", *Phil. of Science*, 24, No. 2 (1957).
[4] *Philosophy of Science*, 16, No. 4 (1949).

## KAZIMIERZ AJDUKIEWICZ

The earliest work of Ajdukiewicz (1890-1963), a Polish logician, devoted to the problems of the theory of language contains a deep analysis and very convincing criticism of the associacionists' theory of meaning and of Mill's theory of connotation.[1] In this article we also find the first sketch of his own semantical theory which was developed in later works.[2]

Ajdukiewicz was interested in the theory of language for philosophical reasons; he was convinced that language plays a very important role in the cognitive process and hoped that the analysis of semantical functions of linguistic expressions might give an

[1] "O znaczeniu wyrażeń", *Księga Pamiątkowa Polskiego Towarzystwa Filozoficznego we Lwowie* (Lwów, 1931).
[2] "Sprache und Sinn", *Erkenntnis*, IV (1934); "Das Weltbild und die Begriffsapparatur", *Erkenntnis*, IV (1934); "Naukowa perspektywa świata", *Przegląd Filozoficzny*, XXXVII (1934).

insight in to the nature of human knowledge. In fact, the theory of language developed by him between the wars is closely connected with his epistemological theory called radical conventionalism.

In that theory the construction of the concept of MEANING plays a fundamental role. It is defined by the concept of MEANING RULES, that is, the rules which establish the motives of acceptance for each sentence of a given language (in the sense that if in language L there is a rule which requires the acceptance of sentence Z in situation S, then everyone who does not accept Z in S, does not speak language L). Roughly speaking, two expressions of a given language are said to be SYNONYMOUS (to have the same meaning) if and only if they are treated in the same way by the meaning rules of that language. From the definition of the sameness of meaning we may receive the definition of the meaning by abstraction: the meaning of expression E in language L is the common attribute of all expressions which are synonymous in L with E.

The class of all meanings of the expressions of a given language was called the CONCEPTUAL APPARATUS of this language. The class of all theses, i.e. of sentences which must be accepted by everyone who speak a given language, was called the LINGUAL VIEW OF THE WORLD. According to radical conventionalism, a view of the world depends upon the choice of a conceptual apparatus.

Then, in these works of Ajdukiewicz language is a subject of analysis with respect to its epistemological function. In another work Ajdukiewicz stated the programme of the semantical theory of knowledge; the subject of a theory of knowledge thus conceived should be the expressions of the defined language.[3]

The concept of language used in these works differs, of course, from the meaning of the word 'language' which we have in mind when we are speaking e.g. about the English language; English, Polish etc. are — from the point of view represented here — the sets of many different languages.

After the Second World War Ajdukiewicz changed his philo-

---

[3] "Problemat transcendentalnego idealizmu w sformułowaniu semantycznym", *Przegląd Filozoficzny*, XL (1937).

sophical point of view to some extent, but he was still interested in the theory of language. He elaborated several semantical concepts as the explicata of some vague concepts of the ordinary language, e.g. the concept of STATE OF AFFAIRS which is the objective correlate of a sentence. Ajdukiewicz hoped that these concepts might help in the solution of certain logical troubles (e.g. in the search for the criterion of interchangeability of expressions in modal- and belief-sentences). Some of these concepts he presented in his lectures and some of them has appeared in print. Especially, he formulated a concept which is similar to Carnap's concept of intensional iso-morphism, and can be called extensional isomorphism: two expressions are EXTENSIONALLY ISOMORPHIC if and only if they are constructed in the same way of primitive expressions which have respectively the same extension (denotation).[4] Two sentences which are extensionally isomorphic are said to express the same state of affairs. According to the above definition the state of affairs expressed by a given sentence may be identified with the arrangement of the denotations of the primitive components of this sentence. In general, Ajdukiewicz proposed calling such arrange-ments of the denotations of the primitive components of expressions the CONNOTATIONS or the CODENOTATIONS of these expressions. Later he modified this concept and defined the connotation of an expression as a certain function, namely, that function which assigns a suitable denotation to the "syntactical position" of each primitive expression.[5] This version was prepared for print, but unfortunately, the author did not complete it.

BARBARA STANOSZ

---

[4] A lecture presented at a session of the Polish Philosophical Society, June 1958.
[5] "Intensional Expressions" and "Proposition as the Connotation of Sentence", *Studia Logica*, XX (1967).

DESCRIPTIONISM VERSUS RECONSTRUCTIONISM

The picture of logical semiotics presented above is rather static. Some connections and influences are pointed out but, in principle, each section is a separate report on a particular author or theory. Now, let us try to grasp them as a whole and transform this series of separate photographs into a moving picture of historical development.

*Reconstructionism.* — In its first stage this development was animated by the idea of rational linguistic reconstruction. One of its sources was the endeavour to find remedies for the antinomies which had been discovered in the language of mathematics. This problem has been met in two different ways, one called axiomatic and the other syntactical. The latter, originated by Russell, is more relevant for this story. It was an attempt to reformulate language formation rules in such a way that all expressions resulting in antinomies would be ruled out as nonsensical. But the rules prohibited by Russell are ordinary language formation rules; hence the conclusion that there must be something wrong with this language. This opinion has been strengthened by Tarski's well-known statement that "it is presumably ... the universality of everyday language which is the primary source of all semantical antinomies."[1] The language of Russell's *Principia Mathematica*, originally intended as a contribution to the philosophy of mathematics, acquired a broader philosophical meaning and is sometimes regarded as the ideal language, mirroring, in a way, the structure of reality; Ludwig Wittgenstein also held this view in his *Tractatus Logico-Philosophicus* period (1922). If this were the case, the syntactical scheme of *Principia* would be a model for any language.

Other sources of reconstructionism, independent of the foundational problem, are: the anti-metaphysical attitude of Positivism and the Nominalist's struggle against Platonic fictions. The former inspired Carnap (in pre-war period) in his efforts to establish rules of meaning which would eliminate all metaphysical "nonsense". Russell and Tarski accused everyday language of generating inconsistencies, while Carnap and other Neopositivists accused it of the admission of nonsense. But again the conclusion was the same:

---

[1] A. Tarski, "The Concept of Truth in Formalized Languages" (Chapt. 1) in *Logic, Semantics, Metamathematics* (Oxford, 1956), p. 164.

everyday language should be guided by an ideal language, artificially constructed by logicians.

The same conclusion has been reached by Nominalists on the grounds of their own assumptions: as everyday language induces a false belief in the existence of abstract entities (as properties, classes, numbers etc.), it should be properly modified. According to the rule recommended by the Polish Nominalists, Stanisław Leśniewski and Tadeusz Kotarbiński, only concrete names (in Mill's sense) may be used as grammatical subjects of sentences; other syntactical rules should provide the means whereby to translate sentences containing abstract terms into expressions free of them. Leśniewski, who developed Husserl's idea of syntactical categories, constructed a calculus of names, which he called Ontology, with only one name category instead of two or more categories of everyday language. Leśniewski's nominalistic ideas have been systematized and continued by Kotarbiński, who stressed their philosophical and methodological value. Another version of nominalism has been originated by Quine and Goodman in United States. Quine's important contributions, connected with his nominalistic attitude, concern the notion of existence and the problem of intensionality.

To summarize, the Reconstructionist demands that ordinary language be reformed on the lines of formal languages of logic, to free it of vagueness, inconsistencies, hyposthases, nonsense and other fallacies which make it an inconvenient tool of scientific or philosophical discourse.

*Descriptionism.* — An opposing trend has been originated by the so-called Oxford Philosophy. The authors who are regarded as representatives of this trend differ one from another in many points, but what is common to all of them is their interest in the problems of ordinary language (resembling in a way Moore's linguistic investigations) and the negative attitude towards reconstructionism. They agree with Russell and Neopositivists that the main object of philosophy is the clarification of concepts but they believe that many concepts are obscure and misleading, not because of the lack of logic in ordinary language, but because of systematic deviation from the ordinary logic of those concepts.

To avoid this deviation the Oxford authors investigate the everyday use of philosophically crucial words, such as "true", "probable" (Strawson, Toulmin), "to know", "to see" (Ryle) etc. It is argued that e.g. the word "true", when used correctly (it means: in accordance with ordinary usage) does not involve any antinomies. In ordinary language this word is not a metalinguistic predicate (i.e. the predicate which is asserted about expressions) but a performative expression (Austin's term). It is not easy to explain what this performatory use is. Let it suffice to define it as that use which consists not in describing facts but in creating certain facts by verbal utterances, as happens when somebody says: "I promise" or "I open the discussion".

Another point which is strongly stressed is a new conception of meaning, following Wittgenstein's last ideas. Ryle and others oppose to Russell's conception of meaning as an extralinguistic entity (a kind of designatum). Meaning is conceived of as the use or the role the expression is employed to perform, not any thing or event for which it might be suggested to stand. As a result, the meaning is to be attributed not only to names, which have their designata, but to the all expressions of language. This conception determines also the methods of investigating meanings; no precise analysis of meaning is hoped for, as the use of expressions undergoes continuous change. Besides, not single uses but collections of uses, differing slightly one from another (the so-called meaning families) are coordinated to many expressions; the word "play" is often given as an example.

The most vital point, perhaps, is the notion of referring. According to classical reconstructionist semiotics, the reference of an expression is established once and for all by the rules of a given language. In the approach proposed by Oxford two more variables are introduced, namely those speaking a language and the time in which they speak. The personal factor was rather neglected in the classical semiotic investigations (with the possible exception of Peirce and Morris, but that is another story). It could not be completely dispensed of, as it is involved in so-called egocentric (indexical) expressions, such as "I", "now", "here" etc., but attempts have been made to get rid of them. What is essential for such expressions is that their reference cannot be established once and for all, but depends on the situation in which they are used. The reference of the word "here", when used in London, is different from the reference of the same word when used in Paris. This property of indexical expressions has been acknowledged by Oxford authors not as regrettable exception but as a normal characteristic of many other expressions too, among which are descriptions, predicates and so on. Consequently the time in which expressions are used is also taken into account. As the actual FUNCTIONING of language is taken into consideration, the trend in question is also called FUNCTIONALISM. Besides the Oxford authors there are other logicians who develop the functionalistic approach, for instance Bar-Hillel. The remaining articles of this collection are also examples of a functionalistic attitude (though some elements of Prof. Kotarbiński's views are also assimilated). Owing to this they may be consulted for other points of the controversy which has been sketched here only in very rough outline.

WITOLD MARCISZEWSKI

# INDEX

# 226

INDEX

ellipticity, 43

entail, entailment, 57, 80, 211

Epicureans, 61

Epicurus, 61, 82

equiform, equiformity, 126-128, 136, 139, 148, 156, 166, 174, 175, 177, 180-183, 187, 192, 193, 216; concept of equiformity, 216; non-equiform, 151, 153, 163, 165, 166, 184, 185, 188, 194; *see also* homomorphous, isomorphism

equisignificance, equisignificant, 128, 139, 188, 192-194; non-equisignificant, 187, 189, 194; *see also* sameness (identity) of intension (meaning), synonymous, synonymy

equivalence, equivalent, 50, 71, 83, 106, 145, 151, 160, 161, 164, 167, 170, 174, 182, 184, 188, 191-194, 204, 212, 215; equivalent in analytic meaning, 212; logical equivalence, 215; material equivalence, 215; non-equivalent, 177; *see also* sameness (identity) of denotation (extension)

equivocality, 29, 43

error of an incomplete proposition (sentence), 42, 47, 164, 165

existence, existent, 209, 211, 213, 220; existential quantification, 119; notion of existence, 220; objective (physical, real) existence, 119-121, 128, 129, 133, 138, 140, 213, *see also* object (concrete, real) (objective, physical thing), subsistence

explicate, *explicatum*, 215, 218

express, 24, 61, 66, 67, 144, 146, 150-152, 154, 164, 170, 175, 178-180, 184-186, 188, 189, 191, 193, 201, 209, 215, 218; *see also* pragmatic function

expression, 21-53, 55, 58-61, 64, 67, 68, 71, 72, 74-78, 80, 82, 84, 85, 90, 93-96, 101, 103, 104, 107-110, 113-118, 120-129, 132-140, 147, 160, 163-171, 173-175, 180, 181, 187, 191-194, 199-202, 209, 212-216, 218, 219, 221, 222; complex (compound), 76, 95, 168, 200, 212; elementary, 212; expression-type, 29; fictional expression, 126-129, 133, 137, 139, 140; genetically metaphorical, 177, 182, 193; individual, 215; intensional, 76, 218; linguistic, 209, 214, 216; metaphorical, 143, 146-152, 156, 163, 166, 173-175, 177-179, 181-184, 186-188, 192-194; non-metaphorical equivalent of metaphorical expression, 148, 151, 165, 166, 173, 174, 177-179, 181-185, 187, 192-194; non-periphrastical expression, 163-168, 191; occasional (egocentric, indexical), 42, 214, 222; ostensive, 92; performative, 221; polysemic, 23, 43, 175-179, 192, 193; primitive, 215, 218; proper (understood literally or verbally), 148-151, 153-163, 166, 169-185, 187-194; simple (one-word), 95, 121; syncategorematic, 35, 59, 61, 71, 106, 198, 202; token (instance) of expression, 22, 25, 29, 94, 116, 123, 124, 139, 145, 209, 213; *see also* appellation, appellative, denominator, description, designator, name, object, phrase, predicate, proper name, sentence, statement, subject, term

extension, extensional, 50, 58, 62, 80, 91, 110, 118, 120, 122, 151, 155, 158, 160, 165, 170, 175, 182, 188, 209-212, 215, 218; extensional context, 215; extensional isomorphism, 218; mutually exclusive extensions, 158; sameness (identity) of extensions (equivalence), 215; subordinate extension, 158, 164, 165; zero-extension, 211; *see also* comprehension, denotation, reference

extralinguistic reality *see* reference

INDEX 227

extralinguistic situation (situational context), 22, 23, 27, 28, 31, 32, 34, 37, 38, 40, 43, 46, 47, 51-53, 60, 72, 73, 81, 82, 95, 110, 116, 118, 125, 127, 128, 133, 139, 145, 217, 221, 222

false, 41, 42, 44, 72, 131-133, 140, 180, 201, 211, 220; falsehood, 75, 79, 101, 112, 130, 131, 201, *see also* truth-value; false proposition, 211; false sentence, 72, 201; falsifiability, 66, 82; falsifiability theory of meaning, 66, 82; falsify, 82

fiction, 119, 121, 125, 130, 138, 140, 219; fictional expression, 126-129, 133, 137, 139, 140; fictional language (language of fiction), 126-131, 133, 137, 139, 140; fictitious model, 126, 128-133, 137, 139, 140; fictitious object, 92, 119, 120, 126-129, 131, 133, 135-140; fictitious subsistence, 119-121, 128, 138, 140; fictive use, 125-137, 139, 140; literary fiction, 119-141; oscillation (shifting) of real use and fictive use, 134, 136, 137, 140

Flew, A., 22, 41, 42

force (*vis*), 55; *see also* meaning, use

formal, formalization, formalize, 49; formal (symbolic) language, 18, 197, 203, 219, 220; formal (symbolic) logic, 49, 50; formula, 49, 50

Frankena, W. K., 48, 67

Frege, G., 18, 34, 39, 52, 53, 58, 61, 62, 65, 71-76, 78, 79, 81, 83, 90, 96, 101, 102, 106-108, 115, 117, 197, 200-202, 207, 214, 215

functional, functionalism, 17, 18, 20-22, 25-27, 30-32, 34, 39, 44-53, 55, 94, 116, 197, 222; *see also* semiotics (functional)

functor, 26

Geach, P. T., 65, 71-76, 111

Geyer, B., 62

Gödel, K., 196

Goodman, N., 220

Halle, M., 17

Hamilton, W., 62

Henle, P., 48, 50, 67

heteromorphous, 43

Hobbes, T., 62, 82

Höffding, H., 100

homomorphous, 42; *see also* equiform, isomorphism

Humboldt, W. von, 59, 81

Husserl, E., 58, 62, 81, 197, 213, 214, 220

hyperbole, 142, 168, 169, 186; *see also* metaphor, trope

hypostasis, 25, 64, 82, 220

*hypotetagmenon*, 61; *protos*, 62; *see also* referent

idea, 59, 61, 62, 67, 72, 73, 120, 146-148, 154, 175, 176, 185, 193, 205, 214; ideal language, 219, 220; ideal object (general entity, *universale*), 62, 72, 205, 213, 214; ideational theory of meaning, 60-63, 72, 73, 81-83; pure idea (*Vorstellung*), 79

*kategoroumenon,* 97
Kotarbiński, T., 18, 30, 32, 97, 110, 122, 220, 222
Kretzmann, N., 59, 65, 74, 75

Lambert of Auxerre, 55
language, 82, 122, 133, 139, 144, 145, 176, 177, 181-183, 186, 187, 192, 194-199, 202-204, 207, 208, 214, 217, 219, 221, 222; artificial, 18, 40, 46-48, 50, 65, 71, 80, 196, 198, 219, 220; artistic, 126; concept of, 217; definition of, 208; fictional (language of fiction), 126-131, 133, 137, 139, 140; functional semiotics of natural language, 17-53, 55, 80; ideal language, 219, 220; instrumental semiotics of natural language, 54-83; language game, 60, 65, 68, 70; lingual view of the world, 217; linguistic expression, 209, 214, 216; linguistic meaning, 212; linguistic reconstruction, 219; linguistic sign, 209; literary language, 133-138, 140, 141; logical theory of artificial language (analysis, descriptive semiotics of artificial language, pure semantics, pure semiotics), 40, 46-48, 80, 196-198; (logical) theory of language ((logical) semiotics, (semiotic) analysis of language), 56, 65, 70, 72, 83, 143, 195-222; (logical) theory of natural language ((descriptive logical) semiotics of natural language, philosophy of natural language, (semiotic) analysis of natural language), 17, 18, 20-22, 25, 30, 39, 40, 44-51, 53, 66, 80, 90, 138, 143, 195-198; model of language, 41, 50, 126, 128-141, 198, 219; natural language, 17-19, 26-28, 31, 39, 40, 42-47, 49-51, 53, 55, 59, 60, 64, 66-69, 76, 80, 84-118, 126, 144, 148, 174, 196; ordinary (colloquial, conversational, everyday, real) language, 18, 19, 49, 50, 126-129, 39, 198, 203, 217-222, *see also* speech (current); (ordinary) language (formation) rule, 69, 70, 109, 219, 221; Oxford linguistic philosophy, 82, 220-222; private language, 59, 63, 82; symbolic (formal) language, 18, 197, 203, 219, 220; universal language, 206; *see also* context, extralinguistic reality, extralinguistic situation, metalanguage, semantic system, sign system
Leibniz, G. W., 205
*lekton,* 55, 61, 62; *see also* meaning
Leśniewski, S., 197, 198, 220
Lewis, C. I., 31, 106, 107, 110, 117, 118, 122, 197, 208-212
lexicalization, 96
Linsky, L., 131, 216
listener, 66; *see also* interpretant, interpreter, reader, sign-perceiver (-user)
literary context, 133, 136, 137, 140; literary fiction, 119-141; literary language, 133-138, 140, 141; literary model, 133-138, 140, 141; literary subsistence, 120, 121, 138, 140; literary use, 133-138, 140, 141
Locke, J., 25, 59, 61-63, 72, 73, 82, 204
locutionary act, 64, 65, 82; *see also* uttering

Mace, C. A., 90, 101, 108, 109, 112
Malcolm, N., 68-70
Mauthner, F., 55, 59, 81
meaning, 22-24, 27, 29-31, 33, 38, 40, 43-47, 51, 53-84, 90, 93, 107, 121, 123, 124, 139, 144, 147, 148, 165, 169, 170, 174-177, 181, 186, 193, 198, 200, 202-206, 208-214, 216, 217, 221; analytic, 212; associationists' theory of

# 236

nificational intention, 213; signification *per aliud* (indirectly), 74; signification *per se* (directly), 74; signify, 62, 74, 210, 211; *see also* codenotation,
connotation, content, intension, meaning, sense, usage
situational context *see* extralinguistic situation
Sophists, 58
Sørensen, H.S., 84-89, 114, 115
speak about (of), 42, 44, 49, 67, 94, 211; *see also* say about, talk about
speaker, 61, 63, 64, 66, 180, 221; *see also* author, sign-producer
speech, 55, 60, 61, 67, 69, 127, *see also* utterance; current speech, 127, *see also*
language (ordinary)
stand for *see* interchange, replace
state, 78, 135; concept of state of things (affairs), 218; general statement, 133;
intentional state of things (affairs), 213, 214; particular statement, 133;
singular statement, 133; statement, 41, 44, 49, 50, 60, 79, 125, 127, 131,
132, 145, 180, 204, 210, 211, *see also* assertion, proposition, sentence;
state of things (affairs), 68, 210, 211, 218; total state of things (affairs),
211, *see also* world; universal statement, 140
Steinthal, H., 100
Stevenson, C.L., 66, 82
stimulus, 60, 63, 64, 67, 81, 82, 208; stimulus-response theory of meaning, 60,
63, 64, 81, 82
Stoics, 55, 58, 59, 61, 62, 81, 82. 204
Strawson, P.F., 22, 41, 42, 66, 94, 104, 106, 107, 109, 111-113, 117, 118, 124,
125, 130, 221
subject, subjective, 32-34, 52, 84, 90, 97-100, 102, 112, 117, 199; grammatical,
97-100, 107, 110, 112, 117, 123, 134-136, 139, 140, 199, 203, 220, *see also*
appellation, appellative, demonstrate, denominator, description, designator, identify, indicate, mention, name, ostensive, phrase, proper name,
refer, term; logical, 97, 99, 100, 107, 117, 123; subject (in Mill's terminology = object), 199, 200, *see also* object; subjective thing, 119, 120, 128, 138,
*see also* object (subjective); subject-predicate sentence, 199, *see also* copula
subsistence: fictitious, 119-121, 128, 138, 140; literary, 120, 121, 138, 140;
logical, 119, 120, 138; *see also* existence
supposition, 55, 65; metalinguistic, 95
Sweet, H., 100
symbol (symbolic sign), 20, 63, 102, 106, 205, 208, 209; instance (token) of,
209; primary (secondary) conceptual content symbolized, i.e., presented
and evoked, 48; simple symbol, 102, 106; symbolic (formal) language, 18,
197, 203, 219, 220; symbolic (formal) logic, 49, 50; verbal symbol, 209;
*see also* sign (conventional)
symmetrical relation, 167
syncategorematic, 35, 59, 61, 71, 106, 198, 202; *see also* expression (syncategorematic)
synecdoche (synecdochic expression), 142, 147, 159-163, 165-169, 172, 186, 190,
191; material connection between the designata of synecdoche and the
designata of the expression understood literally, 159, 161; non-synecdochic
equivalent of synecdoche, 160-163, 165-167, 169, 190; replacement of

usage, 21-27, 29-31, 33, 40, 43-46, 51, 53, 60, 81, 196, 208, 221; rule of, 196; *see also* codenotation, connotation, content, intension, meaning, sense, significance, signification
use, 21-53, 55, 60, 61, 64, 65, 69, 70, 73, 74, 81, 82, 94, 95, 103-105, 110, 112, 113, 116, 118, 123-141, 146, 155, 160, 164, 165, 169, 170, 176, 179, 184-186, 188-192, 196, 203, 205, 207, 208, 211, 212, 220-222; demonstrative, 109; descriptive, 106, 107, 111; empty, 127, 136; fictive, 125-137, 139, 140; general, 95, 124, 136, 140; individual, 136, 140; literary, 133-138, 140, 141; metaphoric, 142-194, *see also* trope; oscillation (shifting) of real use and fictive use, 134, 136, 137, 140; ostensive use, 113, 128, *see also* demonstrate, identify, indicate, mention, refer; performatory use, 221; primary (secondary) use of description, 131, 132; real use, 125-128, 133-137, 139, 140; referential use, 109; rule of use, 106, 124, 125; sign-user (-perceiver), 20, 144, 176, 214, *see also* interpretant, interpreter, listener, reader; singular use, 95, 124, 127, 128; singular use (character) of proper name (singularity of proper name), 107-110, 117, 118, 124; *vis* (force), 55
utterance, 63-65, 221; uttering (locutionary act), 64, 65, 72, 82

vagueness, 220
valuation, 169, 191, 197
variable, 203, 211, 221; individual, 203; value of, 211
vehicle, 148, 209; *see also* metaphor, trope
verifiability, 66, 206; replacement *salva veritate*, 65, 145, 152, 167, 215; verifiability theory of meaning, 66, 82; verify, 82, 204; *see also* true
Vienna Circle, 59, 81, 82
*vis* (force), 55; *see also* meaning, use

William of Sherwood, 55
Wittgenstein, L.J., 54, 58, 59, 64, 66, 68-70, 73, 76, 81, 82, 104, 106, 219, 221
word, 21-24, 26-28, 33, 34, 36, 38, 40, 42, 43, 46, 52, 55, 56, 58, 59, 61, 62, 64-66, 68. 71-74, 76-78, 80, 81, 90, 92, 97, 106, 107, 111, 113, 114, 116, 121, 123, 128, 135, 145, 154, 155, 160, 169, 170, 172, 176, 178, 179, 182, 208, 214, 217, 221, 222; quantifying, 71; word-type, 29
world, 211; actual (real), 211, 213; lingual view of the world, 217; notion of possible (consistently thinkable) worlds, 198, 211; total state of affairs (world), 211
Wundt, W., 175

Xenakis, J., 92, 95, 97, 105, 106, 115, 117

Zawadowski, L., 17

# JANUA LINGUARUM

## STUDIA MEMORIAE NICOLAI VAN WIJK DEDICATA

*Edited by C. H. van Schooneveld*

### SERIES MINOR

*Prices are subject to change*
*Titles without prices are in preparation*

## MOUTON · PUBLISHERS · THE HAGUE